D1483752

Hudson Valley
Tales and Trails

Hudson Valley

Tales and Trails

PATRICIA EDWARDS CLYNE

THE OVERLOOK PRESS · WOODSTOCK · NEW YORK

First published in paperback in 1997 by
The Overlook Press
Lewis Hollow Road
Woodstock, New York 12498

Library of Congress Cataloging-in-Publication Data

Clyne, Patricia Edwards
Hudson valley tales and trails / by Patricia Edwards Clyne
Includes bibliographical references.
Hudson River Valley (N.Y. and N.J.)—History. 1. Title.
F127.HB C57 1990 974.7'3—dc20 89-97017
Book design by Bernard Schleifer

Manufactured in the United States of America

ISBN: 0-87951-760-3

9 8 7 6 5 4 3 2 1

Title page: the shore of Barhyte's Trout Pond in Saratoga Springs where
Edgar Allen Poe is said to have composed "The Raven" one of many
artists who found inspiration at the pine-shaded retreat now called
Yaddo. *(From an 1830 engraving by W.H. Barlett.)*

Dedicated to
SUE,
The Great Guru

CONTENTS

IV. CURIOUS CHARACTERS

V. THE LITERATI

VI. LEGENDS AND SUPERNATURAL LORE

INTRODUCTION

> I thank God that I was born on the banks of
> the Hudson. I fancy I can trace much of
> what is good and pleasant in my own hetero-
> geneous compound to my early compan-
> ionship with this river.

It was with those words that in 1849 Washington Irving introduced his readers to *A Book of the Hudson*, and I cannot think of a better way to begin my own look at this legendary river and its environs. For like Irving, I was born on Manhattan Island within sight of the mighty waterway the Indians called *Muhheakantuck*, and except for brief periods, my life has been spent in the Hudson River Valley. With such childhood heroes as Irving and Carl Carmer to serve as my literary guides, I developed a deep love of the region—a love that has resulted in a lifetime of exploring the Hudson's rich heritage and a concomitant desire to share this experience with others.

As its name implies, *Hudson Valley Tales and Trails* is not a formal history but a miscellany of some of the most interesting aspects of the region, ranging from prehistoric times to the present, and covering the eleven counties bordering the river, from Westchester and Rockland on the south to Saratoga and Rensselaer on the north. While the focus is on little-known places and people, familiar names and events have not been ignored where fresh insights can be supplied. Chapters, therefore, vary in subject matter from light-houses, iron mines, and mysterious stone ruins to Edgar Allan Poe, lost treasures, and unique public parks. There is folklore as well as fact, with a clear distinction drawn between the two.

Although this book is intended for readers of all ages, whether armchair adventurers or outdoor enthusiasts, no matter where they may live, it is especially aimed at the region's present and future residents. For at the time I write this, my beloved valley has become one of the fastest-growing areas in the country—a "boom" that can be a blessing or a curse, depending on how it is handled. The more people learn about and love the place where they live, the more apt they are to protect both its legends and its physical features—perhaps even to feel, as did the Indians, that no one ever really owns the land. Instead, we can see ourselves as mere caretakers whose present actions will affect the lives of future guardians of the land. *Hudson Valley Tales and Trails* is meant to entertain, enlighten, and help to foster such feelings of regional responsibility and pride.

PATRICIA EDWARDS CLYNE

Aiséirí, 1989

I

GENERALLY SPEAKING

1 THE RIDDLE OF THE STONE RUINS

UNUSUAL ROCK FORMATIONS certainly are no surprise in a region noted for its magnificent mountain scenery, but numerous Hudson Valley stones also figure in a long-standing archeological controversy concerning an apparently man-made network of lithic structures that extends down the northeastern coast of the United States and stretches inland along major river valleys.

Some authorities insist that whatever sites are not the result of natural geological processes are the work of native Americans or Colonial settlers. Other researchers disagree, saying that these cryptic relics are proof that long before Columbus sailed west from Europe, North America was explored and perhaps briefly settled by transatlantic voyagers. Various candidates have been proposed—from tenth-century Vikings and sixth-century Celts to the even earlier Phoenicians, Egyptians, and Iberians—but so far no conclusive evidence has been presented for the sites in New York State.

Many a Hudson Valley dweller doubtless has passed by some of the structures in question, since several parks in the area boast at least one such site, and others are visible from public roads. An example of the latter is the "Great Boulder" or "Balanced Rock" that stands beside Route 121 in the Westchester County community of North Salem.

This 60-ton chunk of pink granite, perfectly balanced atop seven cone-shaped limestone "legs," was long believed to be the result of glacial action and/or erosion—a claim that was challenged when investigators realized this rock closely resembles the huge prehistoric stone monuments known as dolmens, which are found throughout Europe. What's more, the boulder's seven support stones form an isosceles triangle, the legs of which are in units of a measurement known as the megalithic yard (2.72 feet). The megalithic yard has been cited by various researchers—including Alexander Thom, who studied structures in the British Isles—as the basic measurement used in laying out dolmens and other Old World megaliths.

In Europe, as at North Salem, dolmens were generally built on an earthen base, since they were often used as tombs, with the capstone covering and marking a grave beneath it. But there is no evidence to suggest such a prehistoric interment at North Salem.

Other, smaller perched rocks (including ones found atop Circle Mountain near Ladentown in Rockland County, at Sam's Point in Ulster, and another at the northern end of Greenwood Lake in Orange) occur on bedrock and, if set there by man, obviously served a different purpose from that of the dolmens.

The smaller perched rocks generally occur high on hilltops and at strategic geographical points, such as mountain passes. Their position indicates they could have been used as landmarks for travelers, or as calendar stones for marking seasonal events like the winter and summer solstices, or the spring and autumn equinoxes. By checking to find out if, for instance, the winter sun on December 22 rises directly over these perched rocks, researchers have established such an astronomical relationship for many of the sites.

Not all perched or balanced rocks appear to have been set up by men. Even the most stalwart supporters of the theory about a pre-Columbian presence in the Hudson Valley concede that glacial action was responsible for many "erratics" left behind by the successive sheets of ice that covered the Northeast millions of years ago. But the traditional teaching that all such balancing acts were performed by Mother Nature no longer seems totally reliable either.

Perched rocks appear to be more prevalent on the west side of the Hudson. But an even more intriguing type of structure—and one unquestionably man-made—abounds to the east. From the Croton River in Westchester, north to Pawling in Dutchess, the land is dotted by dozens of small, one-room stone houses built without mortar and often covered by a layer of dirt.

Bearing a marked resemblance to ancient European dwellings, these structures have been called by many speculative names: Irish churches, witch hovels, Indian sweat lodges, Colonial root cellars, animal pens, icehouses, powder magazines, and hunter's huts. But the simple descriptive term "slab-roof chamber" is perhaps best. For despite the various theories that have been advanced concerning why they were built and by whom, no single answer seems to fit all the many slab-roof chambers still in existence. In Putnam County alone there are at least forty such structures, several of which are located in Clarence Fahnestock State Park.

One type of slab-roof chamber is constructed to admit only snatches of early morning light, and then only during the colder seasons. Some investigators speculate that such chill quarters might have been used as burial vaults by prehistoric explorers, an idea further fostered by the fact that several of these chambers have inscriptions that suggest the presence of early Celts, a wide-ranging people of central and western Europe who, like the Phoenicians, were skilled sailors capable of crossing the Atlantic.

A representative inscription is found a couple of miles northeast of the Balanced Rock in North Salem. The stone on which it was etched is now part of a property-dividing wall, probably placed there by some long-ago farmer clearing a field. The inscription, only one of several in the area, is thought to be in two different ancient scripts, Ogam and Iberian Punic, each of which refers to the sun god.

An easy-to-reach example of still another type of mysterious stone, called a standing stone, is located in the Dutchess County town of Wappingers Falls. It is a slim spear of limestone about a foot wide and almost six feet long, but it is believed to extend for at least another twelve feet below the ground. The stone tilts toward the southwest, as if pointing the way to where Wappingers Creek empties into the nearby Hudson. But whether this standing stone was placed there as a directional marker has not been determined. It and others like it in North America may well have had some religious

significance in ancient times, for they very much resemble the
ritualistic "menhirs" of Europe. Interestingly enough, early settlers in
the Ulster County hamlet of Hurley used similar stone spears as
grave markers, and there is also a local legend that an Indian chief
was interred under the one at Wappingers Falls. The stone is located
at the base of Mt. Alvernia Seminary, near the corner of Oakwood
Drive, amid a group of trees in a front yard. It is on private property,
and hence should be viewed only from the road.

While that standing stone is a solitary structure, other lithic ruins
in the region occur in clusters, or feature more than one kind of
stone. Typical of these are the "Prehistoric Walls" located near the
southwestern edge of Harriman State Park in Ramapo. The site
covers 200 acres overlooking the Ramapo Pass and contains a series
of low walls and piles of rock, some of the latter containing circular
depressions or pits. Obviously, its hilltop location was a factor in
constructing the complex, but though some investigators believe it to
be a Revolutionary War fortification, questions about its origin still
arise.

Mysterious mounds of stones like the ones at Ramapo are common on both sides of the Hudson—from Glens Falls to Croton-on-
Hudson, and from Phoenicia to Nyack. And while many of these piles
may be the result of farmers' clearing of the rocky land (or even due
to an Indian method of trail marking, with stones added by later
travelers), there is evidence that suggests some were built as fire
beacons. Others have niches in their bases, suggesting small ovens or
incense burners.

One of the most interesting accumulations is near Spring Glen,
on the border of Ulster and Sullivan counties, where dozens of stone
piles can be seen on the mountainside west of Aldrich Road.

Although stone piles frequently occur in association with certain
very old mines, most have too careful a construction, too patterned a
placement, to be considered mere tailings (rubble from mine excavations). The old mines themselves are an enigma, in that they were
excavated entirely by hand tools such as the pick and wedge, rather
than with the aid of gunpowder, which Dutch settlers in the region
supposedly were using as early as the mid-1600s.

It has been pointed out that prospecting for minerals—especially for the copper needed to make bronze—would be a most practical reason for the merchant-mariner Phoenicians to have braved the Atlantic Ocean a thousand years before Christ was born, when bronze was still in great demand. And copper ore, though of poor grade, is present at most of the hand-tooled mines that occur along the Old Mine Road running from the Delaware Water Gap to Kingston. But here again, there is no irrefutable evidence that pre-Christian miners ever came to the area.

Not far from the Old Mine Road (Route 209), in the town of Ellenville, the legend-laden "Spanish Mine" lies at the western foot of Shawangunk Mountain. Depending on which storyteller you listen to, the mine's 500-foot tunnel was excavated by sixteenth-century explorers in search of the Fountain of Youth or by local Indians prior to the time the Dutch settlers arrived in the Rondout Valley. At least one researcher, however, thinks it is possible that some non-native group of miners prospected there even earlier than that.

Sporadic activity in succeeding centuries has altered the "Spanish Mine" considerably. However, anyone who climbs the slope above the water-filled tunnel at ground level can find two other untouched openings in the mountain face, one of which seems to have been chiseled out by the primitive pick-and-wedge method.

Equally intriguing are such one-of-a-kind structures as a strange stone floor unearthed during archeological excavations at Fishkill's Van Wyck Homestead (open to the public) and the so-called "Indian Dam" at Plattekill. Said to have been discovered by the first white settlers arriving in the area during historic times, the "dam" is a thick stone wall averaging 10 feet in height and stretching 150 yards along the edge of a swamp, yet it does not seem to have been built to impound water. Nor is it likely that Indians constructed it. Adding to the mystery is a series of rectangular pits, large enough for a man to sit in, set in the top of the "dam." The pits are similar to ones seen at the "Prehistoric Walls" complex in Ramapo, but their purpose is unknown.

The foregoing sites are only a sampling of the many structures in the Hudson Valley that make up the riddle of the stone ruins, a riddle further complicated by modern man's interest in the past. For facsimiles of ancient structures were quite popular in the preceding century, and one wealthy landowner reportedly went so far as to construct a replica of the Roman Appian Way on his east-shore estate. Such counterfeits can easily be mistaken for much older relics, especially those that were left to deteriorate when the land changed ownership.

As for the question of whether the Hudson Valley hosted visitors from across the Atlantic during pre-Columbian times, that may never be answered to everyone's full satisfaction. And maybe that is as it should be, since a dash of mystery adds spice to life.

2 THE IRON HEART OF THE HUDSON VALLEY

THE OVERGROWTH OF decades may mask them, the successive seasons of desuetude may have crumbled their walls, but the many iron mines and furnaces of the Hudson Valley still testify to what was once a major industry in the region—an industry that forged the backbone of a budding nation.

From the Taconics in Columbia to the Ramapos of Orange, and from Putnam's hills to Rockland's heights—anywhere the earth has been turned rust-colored by the rich ore within—the ancient pits and pillars of this early industry offer an enlightening walk into history for anyone willing to brave a few brambles.

Actually, it is possible to learn quite a bit without ever venturing into the forest. Many of the furnaces (and, of course, the museums housing memorabilia of the area's Iron Age) are just a few steps from paved roads. But it is only at the old mines that the great iron heart of the Hudson Valley is seen in its primitive form. There one can best appreciate the indomitable human will that caused great caverns to be carved out of the earth at a time when mining methods were crude and sophisticated explosives were unknown. So it is there such a journey into the past should start, but first a word of caution: the mines described in this chapter are all very old and could be dangerous. They are best viewed from the outside only.

Some of the mines easiest to reach are located in Putnam County's Clarence Fahnestock State Park. On the western side of Pelton Pond, only a few yards from Route 301 (the Carmel–Cold Spring Road), a boulder-strewn, horizontal tunnel roughly 100 feet long has been hacked through the hill. The tunnel is open at either end and drops off into a water-filled pit at its northern terminus, showing how the miners followed the ore vein as it dipped farther belowground. Smaller diggings can be found at the northern end of Pelton Pond at the base of the ridge where the comfort stations are located.

All of these mines were begun sometime after 1756, when Colonel Beverly Robinson (better known for the part he played in the treason of Benedict Arnold during the Revolutionary War) gave two men permission to explore his land for minerals. Subsequently, a rich vein of magnetite (magnetic iron ore) was discovered, and mines opened up all along its 8-mile length. To see a few of these, take Route 301 southwest from the Pelton Pond area of Fahnestock Park to the Dennytown Road (about 3 miles). Turn south on the Dennytown Road to Sunk Mine Road, which runs to the east. Evidence of the mining operations that went on here can easily be spotted on either side of the road.

Much of the iron from these mines was shipped to the West Point Foundry in Cold Spring, where the famous Parrott gun of the Civil War was manufactured. This rifled cannon, named for its inventor, Robert Parker Parrott (who was also the foundry's superintendent), is credited with giving the Union Army superior accuracy and firepower. In fact, the Parrott gun was considered so vital to the victory, one wag suggested that instead of an eagle, the national emblem should be a parrot.

The suggestion was never acted upon, although Robert Parrott and his invention are given due honors at the Foundry School Museum (headquarters of the Putnam County Historical Society) in Cold Spring. The museum is well worth a visit after a trip to the nearby Fahnestock mines, for it offers an informative collection of articles pertaining to the iron industry. In addition, from time to time, the society conducts guided tours to the now defunct West Point Foundry just south of Cold Spring near Constitution Island.

Constitution Island also is associated with another famous weapon forged of Hudson Valley iron. But unlike the nineteenth-century Parrott gun, this was a defensive device, and it was used in an earlier war—the American Revolution. The weapon was a massive chain which in 1778–79 was stretched across the Hudson from West Point to Constitution Island to prevent the British from sailing upriver and capturing the then unfinished military bastion on the western shore. Most links in the chain, made of iron bars 2½ inches thick and over 2 feet long, weighed about 140 pounds each, with some heavier links, 3½ inches thick and 3½ feet long, used at points of extra stress. Under the direction of Captain Thomas Machin, these links were then fastened to floating logs and the chain was stretched across the river for a distance of about 1,700 feet. (An earlier chain, spanning the river between Fort Montgomery and Anthony's Nose, had been removed by the British after their victory at Forts Montgomery and Clinton in October 1777.) Today, representative links of the 1778–79 chain—the total weight of which has been estimated at 150 tons—are displayed on the grounds of the United States Military Academy at West Point, and at Washington's Headquarters State Historic Site in Newburgh. The latter site is particularly apt, since soldiers of the Continental Army jokingly referred to the river barrier as "George Washington's watch chain."

Much of the iron for the West Point chain came from Orange County, where dozens of mines operated in the Ramapo Mountains during the century spanning the 1750s to the 1850s. Chief among them were the Sterling and Lake Mines, the latter extending for thousands of feet beneath the bed of Sterling Lake.

A drive southwest on Long Meadow Road from its junction with Route 210 in Tuxedo will reveal some of the numerous mining operations, including the remains of the Sterling Ironworks at the southern tip of Sterling Lake. Although it is on private property, the old furnace has been restored (with Greek columns surrounding it!) and may be seen from the road. It was here that ore from the Sterling and Long Mines was smelted for the chain across the Hudson. The Long Mine also produced the ore that went into the first blistered steel ever manufactured in New York State, as well as the first cannon.

From the southern tip of Sterling lake, mine seekers can travel south along Sterling Mine Road, where other excavations may be glimpsed through the trees, or they may head north on West Lake Road, passing the Lake Mine and some of its remaining buildings.

For many viewers, even more impressive than the column-fringed Sterling Furnace is the abandoned ironworks at Southfields, on the Orange Turnpike about a mile northwest of its junction with Route 17 in Tuxedo. The huge brick blast furnace, built in 1804 by the Townsend family, who also owned the Sterling works, boasts a double-arched ore bridge. It can best be seen from the road in the colder seasons, when the foliage is sparse. The Southfield Ironworks has been idle since 1887. At one time it was a complex community of a blacksmith shop, a casting house, a stamping mill, and a manor house, among many other buildings. Today it lies in ruins, a relic of a bygone age.

It is possible that someday this rich iron source will once more be called upon, for few of the mines in the region were ever exhausted—they simply couldn't compete with the cheaper Lake Superior ores that became available in the 1880s. When they closed down, they left behind great mounds of rubble (or tailings) that are still fun to pick through for samples of ore.

Souvenir specimens can readily be obtained at such places as the O'Neill Mine and the adjacent Forshee Mine, about 3 miles south of Monroe, on the west side of the Orange Turnpike between Route 17 and the fork of East Mombasha Road. A trail leads from a small parking area southwest into the woods to a huge open pit a tenth of a mile long. Massive boulders that once formed the roof of the mine lie in jumbled disarray around the sides, and offer risky footing to the unwary hiker. But there is no need to go boulder-hopping in order to find an ore sample. The well-defined paths that lead to the mine are full of small pieces easily identifiable by their weight. Iron ore is not always rust-colored, but is generally heavier than other types of rock of comparable size. Magnetite, as its name implies, will also respond to a magnet.

Less accessible than the O'Neill or Forshee, the Bull Mine can be reached only by a rough woods trail that curves up Peddler's Hill from Bull Mine Road near Oxford Depot. The mine can still be entered, though it slopes sharply downward and can be icy even in the summertime. These conditions have resulted in many an accident, and even some deaths, so it is advisable to examine Bull Mine only from the outside. Meanwhile, visitors can enjoy the magnificent view from the crest of the hill, where abundant tailings of magnetite ore assure success for even a first-time mineral collector. Special care should be taken to stay on the existing pathways, as summer foliage tends to camouflage vertical air shafts and pits that pockmark Peddler's Hill.

Mineral collecting is not allowed on state park lands, where still other Hudson Valley mines are located. Therefore, travelers in Harriman State Park must take only photographs of the picturesque Bradley Mine, southeast of the Cohasset Lakes just off New Arden Road. Seeing other mine sites in Harriman Park involves hiking along trails that are as scenic as they are historic. The section of the white-marked Appalachian Trail south of the Cohasset Lakes offers views of the Surebridge Mine, while the Red Cross Trail can be taken to the Hassenclever Mine near Lake Tiorati. In addition, the Orange (or Queensboro) Furnace once operated near the junction of that trail and Tiorati Brook Road.

Perhaps the most evocative hike is along the yellow-blazed Dunning Trail, where one can find not only the flooded Boston Mine but also the Pine Swamp and Hogencamp mines. Near the latter are the scattered remains of mining operations—steel spikes, a concrete machinery base, drainage pipes, and part of a narrow-gauge railway track—as well as the foundations of the mining camp itself. Twenty buildings once stood here, including a saloon and a schoolhouse.

Modern-day strollers through the now quiet forest may find it difficult to imagine the hustle and bustle that went on at the Hogencamp Mine from the mid-1860s to its demise in 1885. What can be readily appreciated, however, are the dangers and difficulties that faced the men who worked there. Shifts were long, the labor was backbreaking, the air was often foul, and the mine was always damp, if not knee-deep in water. Electricity was not yet available, so candles and later carbide lamps were the chief means of illumination.

Yet none of these problems could compare with the ever-present threat of a cave-in. For this very reason, rats were considered the miners' friends. It was believed that the rodents could sense impending danger and would give the men warning by racing out of the mine just before a cave-in occurred. Therefore, to ensure a continuing rat population, at the end of their shifts the miners usually left behind their candle stubs for the rats to eat. Unfortunately, the rodent alarm did not always work, and many miners were killed or maimed as the shafts grew deeper and more dangerous.

Such disasters could prompt the closing of a mine, as did the rockslides that killed nearly fifty miners in a two-year period (1895–97) at the Tilly Foster Mine in Putnam County. This mine, still visible as a water-filled crater off Route 6 near Brewster, was at one time the largest open-pit mine in the world and was unique in other ways, too. It contained a surprising number of minerals—over a hundred—other than the magnetite for which it was mined. Some of these minerals were outstanding examples of their kind, and specimens from the Tilly Foster grace collections in most major museums, as well as the nearby Southeast Museum on Main Street in Brewster.

No discussion of the Hudson Valley's earliest industry would be complete without mentioning the fuel it took to turn raw ore into iron. Mountains of charcoal were required by the ever-hungry forges and furnaces, and without its dense forests to supply that fuel, the Hudson Valley never could have enjoyed the early Iron Age boom that it did.

One method of making charcoal was to burn logs in open pits, and the blackened vestiges of these can be found beside old mine roads throughout the region. Another method was to use beehive-shaped kilns, two of which are still in existence in northern Dutchess County on the site of the Noah Gridley & Son Iron Works (Route 22 and Deep Hollow Road in Amenia). Also to be seen in that vicinity is the stack of the Clove Spring Iron Works on Furnace Road in Beekman, plus the Maltby Furnace stack on Shargroy Road in Northeast.

A short distance west of the Maltby stack, the hamlet of Irondale recalls—if only in name—the industry that was enabled by the Mt. Riga mines just over the border in Salisbury, Connecticut. During Colonial days, ore from these deposits was transported by oxcart west over the Taconic Mountains to Ancram, where the Livingston family built a forge along the Roeliff Jansen Kill in 1740—reputedly the only one of its kind in New York at that time.

Fortunately for the Livingstons, as well as the American cause they supported, by the time the Revolution broke out, closer and larger deposits of ore had been discovered. These included the Weed Orebed at the Ancram-Copake town line and the Morgan Mine, a couple of miles east of Ancramdale. Ancramdale, it is interesting to note, used to be called the Hot Ground, in keeping with an early belief that subterranean mineral deposits generated heat that could be felt on the surface.

The Continental Army was supplied with cannonballs and other war matériel made at Ancram, and it is said that the forge also manufactured some of the links used in the chain the Americans stretched across the Hudson near West Point. Then after the war, its production was devoted to the domestic needs of the fast-developing region, and the Ancram Forge continued to flourish until 1839, when it was washed away by a flood. Six years later, the rebuilt forge was subject to a foreclosure sale, and in 1854 it was converted to a paper mill.

In the following year, the Reynolds Mine was discovered near Boston Corner, and with the coming of the railroad and the Civil War, iron remained an important industry in Ancram, as well as in the neighboring towns of Livingston, Copake, Taghkanic, and Gallatin. At Copake Falls, for instance, the furnace built by Lemuel Pomeroy in 1845 was soon turning out 2,500 tons of iron each year.

However, as happened elsewhere in the Hudson Valley, the end was near. The Reynolds Mine closed down in 1875, followed by the Morgan Mine, though the Weed Orebed lasted until the turn of the century. Milk tanks took the place of ore cars on the railroad, and in time only old ruins remained to testify to the once-vital iron industry in this vicinity—along with place names such as Weed Mines (on Route 22, south of Copake Falls), New Forge (on New Forge Road in the town of Taghkanic), and Spaulding Furnace (on County Road 7, southwest of the village of Ancram).

That the list of sites seems unending only underscores the importance of Hudson Valley iron in the development of our country— an importance that has been given fresh emphasis in the 1980s

reconstruction of the Greenwood Furnace, just east of Route 17 in
the Orange County hamlet of Arden. This massive, four-hearthed,
stone-and-brick structure is part of the Clove Furnace Historic Site,
which is owned and operated by the Orange County Historical
Society, and offers what is perhaps the most comprehensive view of a
nineteenth-century regional ironworks—complete with museum open
year-round.

But whether it be the view of a carefully researched restoration, a
crumbled ruin amid scenic wilderness, or a deep cavern carved out
of rust-colored rock, few folk fail to be impressed by the great iron
heart of the Hudson Valley.

3 DRUMS ALONG THE HUDSON

THE NATIVE AMERICAN drums that once sounded in the Hudson Valley have long since stopped, but silent echoes still remain of a culture that was doomed the day the first European sailed up the river. The white settlers' hunger for land sealed that fate, if not the newly introduced diseases for which the indigenous population had no immunity. So it was that most of the post-contact Indians who did not die eventually withdrew to other areas, leaving behind a heritage now dating back more than 12,000 years.

The earliest known native inhabitants, called Paleo Indians, were nomadic hunters who roamed the region in small bands after the last great glacier of the Ice Age retreated. They were cotemporaneous with the mastodon and possibly hunted those huge herbivores, along with the caribou that then ranged this far south. Caribou bone, as well as that of elk, has been recovered from Orange County's Dutchess Quarry Cave, one of the oldest Paleo Indian sites in the Northeast.

Gradually, nomadic existence gave way to more localized living at seasonal camps, and during the Archaic Period (from around 8000 B.C. to 1500 B.C.) the Indians concentrated more on smaller game and plant gathering for their food. They utilized stone, bone, shell, and wood for tools, with quartz and flint favored for projectile points on weapons such as spears propelled by means of a throwing stick called an atlatl. Bows and arrows were not yet in use; hence, none of the projectile points from the Archaic Period can rightly be termed "arrowheads."

Fish was another mainstay of their diet, and the remains of weirs—stones arranged in a long V-shape to catch eels and other fish—can still be seen in some streams. Armonk, by the way, gets its name from an Indian fishing weir on the nearby Byram River.

All kinds of shellfish also were eaten, and the shores of the Hudson are dotted by middens (refuse deposits) containing the remains of oysters, clams, and mussels. One of the first of these accumulations ever uncovered by modern-day archeologists occurs at Croton Point and is at least 9,000 years old. Supposedly the Indian name for this spot was Laaphawachking, or the "place of stringing," which is possibly a reference to their method of preserving fish by drying or smoking it over a fire. Farther north, at Rocky Point near Saugerties, shell accumulations nine inches thick bear witness to the Indians' long use of this location; the same is true of the Shagabak cove near Hyde Park, Fourmile Point above Athens, and Barren Island off Coeymans—to name only a few.

Around 1000 B.C., soapstone cooking pots began replacing the bark baskets in which the Indians had put hot stones to heat food. Pottery making was also developed during this Woodland Period, along with agriculture. Before this, the Indians had not cultivated crops but depended on whatever plants nature provided, including jack-in-the-pulpit root, the Indian name of which is the origin of "Tuckahoe." By this time, their homes were semipermanent and villages were established, while trade was conducted with other Indians in outlying areas.

That far-ranging trade existed has been determined, in part, by the discovery of artifacts made from materials not available in the Hudson Valley, such as copper from the shores of Lake Superior. Styles or stones distinct to the Hudson region have also been unearthed at ancient sites elsewhere in the country. Flint was a doubly valuable commodity, for not only could it be knapped into razor-sharp tools, but it also produced sparks when struck against iron. And the Hudson Valley Indians had access to a massive deposit of this hard silica stone not far from the river's west shore in Greene County. For many millennia, Flint Mine Hill in Coxsackie was a literal manufactory of implements, and even today visitors (with the permission of the New York State Archaeological Association chapter that owns the site) can find excellent examples of the flint knapper's art.

Indians could easily reach Flint Mine Hill by river travel or by using one of the many trails that crossed the region. For instance, Route 23A in Greene County follows an old Indian path, while Kings Highway in Orange County is part of a long-used north-south route. The latter, by the way, passes along the base of Sugar Loaf Mountain, said to be sacred to the Indians, who buried some of their chiefs on its flank. This same trail, a few miles to the north, skirts Schunemunk Mountain (whose Algonkian name means "excellent fireplace" or "extending upward"—translators differ on this), which once boasted a palisaded Indian village on its north slope.

The Woodland Period continued until the sixteenth century, when Europeans began coming to the New World on a regular basis. Although there is the possibility of much earlier contact, and it is believed that Spanish and Portuguese explorers made brief visits during the fifteenth century, the first fully documented contact came in 1524, when Giovanni da Verrazano sailed into New York Bay. Verrazano, however, did not continue upriver. That remained for Henry Hudson to accomplish in 1609, when he sailed as far north as present-day Albany, leaving in his wake a pattern that would predominate for years to come: sometimes friendly encounters between natives and whites, but more often misunderstanding that led to slaughter.

During this time that archeologists term the Contact Period (from around A.D. 1500 to 1700), the Hudson Valley was home to a complexity of Indian populations. These can be divided into four major groups: west of the Hudson, the Delawares (also called the Lenni-Lenape or Munsee) extended north to the land of the Mohawks, while east of the Hudson the Wappingers occupied the region roughly from Manhattan Island into Dutchess, and north of them were the Mohicans (also spelled Mahicans or Mohegans). Except for the Mohawks, who belonged to the Iroquois Confederacy, their speech was of the Algonkian family of languages, and some authorities believe the Wappingers were a subdivision of the Mohicans.

These four groups were further broken down into "chieftaincies" too numerous to mention, except for some of the ones that are recalled in present-day place names: the Tappans, the Esopus, the Manhattes (Manhattan), the Munsee (Monsey), the Sint-Sincks (Ossining and Sing-Sing), and the Canopus Indians, for whom a lake, stream, and hollow in Putnam County are named.

Just as often, it was the chiefs or sachems whose names were attached to places, especially if they were the ones signing land sales to the white men. For instance, Mamaroneck is named after a Kitchawan sachem, Nanuet after Nanawitt, Katonah after Ketatonah (reputedly buried in Bedford's Katonah Woods), the Mianus River after Meyanos, and Rockland County's Clausland Mountain after Towachack, who adopted the Dutch name of Jan Claus and was among those Indians who signed away the vast acreage known as the Wawayanda and Cheesecock Patents.

The trouble with such land transfers was that few of the Indians who signed them were fully aware of what these deals entailed, for their idea of stewardship was totally different than the European perception of permanent dominion. (The expression "Indian giver" derives from these divergent views.) But even those Indians who might possibly have known, and even those whose minds had not been befuddled beforehand by the white man's rum and brandy, still stood the chance of being cheated by unscrupulous land grabbers.

A case in point is the Rombout Patent in the east Hudson Highlands. During preliminary talks in August 1683, some Wappinger leaders agreed to sell to Francis Rombout (along with his partners, Jacobus Kipp and Guilian Ver Planck) all the land that Rombout could see. Of course, the Wappingers were literally speaking at ground level, but the scheming Rombout led them to the top of South Beacon Mountain (1,600 feet high), and from there pointed out all the land he could see to the north and east—about 85,000 acres in all! Many years later, the Wappingers tried to regain their land legally—even sending envoys to England—but in vain.

Clashes between the two cultures commenced early and continued late, ranging from isolated raids and small skirmishes to the bloody Esopus Indian Wars of the mid-1600s. Early settlers shuddered at such stories as the 1643 slaughter of Anne Hutchinson, the burning of Hurley twenty years later, and the Indian practice of enslaving captives.

The dawn of the eighteenth century did not bring relief, for this was the time of the French Colonial Wars, and it was during one of them (Queen Anne's War) that the infamous Kittle Massacre of 1711 took place at Schaghticoke, in Rensselaer County. (Schaghticoke got its name from a tribe made up of Pequots and other remnants of eastern chieftaincies who were settled there in the 1670s by Governor Edmund Andros. It is said to be an Algonkian word meaning "landslide.")

Although the massacre at the Daniel Kittle homestead did not differ markedly from many others that occurred in the Hudson Valley—eight people killed and three captives taken to Canada by the Indians—it is singular in that it gave rise to one of America's first Gothic novels. Its author was Anna Eliza Bleecker, who herself was forced to flee Tomhannock (Schaghticoke) during the Revolutionary War, and she combined her own experiences with the earlier massacre to write *The History of Maria Kittle,* first published in 1797.

Anna Bleecker did not live to see her novel published. The hardship of twice being forced from her home (once in 1777, then again in 1779), as well as the loss of loved ones and the capture of her husband, destroyed her health. She died at the age of thirty-one in the last year of the Revolution, as much a casualty of the war as any soldier.

And there are many other horror stories from both the French and Indian War and the Revolution; tales that evoked fear in every settler's heart, such as Mohawk Chief Joseph Brant's Minisink Raid of 1779, the Fantinekill Massacre of the same year at present-day Ellenville, and the burning of Wawarsing in 1781.

Places were even named for individual atrocities. There are three Murderer's Creeks that empty into the Hudson. The one in Greene County joins the river just north of Athens, while that in Orange County empties at New Windsor, and has been rechristened the Moodna (thanks to nineteenth-century author Nathaniel Parker Willis, who lived by the waterway and didn't appreciate its gory title). The other Murderer's Creek, located north and east of Castleton-on-Hudson in Rensselaer County, is better known by its Dutch equivalent, Moordener Kill. According to local tradition, it was dubbed that because Indians once tethered a girl to a horse that dragged her to her death along the banks of the stream.

But it must be remembered that atrocity was a two-way street—Indians were also killed or carried off. Henry Hudson once captured a couple of Wickquaskeeks near Spuyten Duyvil, sparking an arrows-against-cannon incident that left many Indians dead. As for the slaughter of Anne Hutchinson, that was avenged in 1644 by a man named John Underhill. Marching into Westchester County with 130 men, Underhill attacked and burned the Indian village of Nanichi-estawack. Some historians say this village was at the south end of Indian Hill in Bedford, while others think it was located in Somers, but most agree that between 500 and 700 native men, women, and children were murdered.

There was a similar follow-up to the burning of Hurley, when in July 1663 a band of Dutchmen led by Martin Cregier surrounded a large Indian village near the junction of the Rondout Creek and Vernooy Kill. The village was empty, so no Indians were killed that day. But the avengers burned down all the dwellings, plus 200 acres of standing corn, then set fire to all the pits in which the Indians had stored food supplies against the coming winter—and starvation can be crueler than any bullet.

The picture was not one of total hostility, however. There were some sincere attempts to live in peace with the Indians and to integrate them into the culture that was taking over their ancestral lands. One memorable try was made by the Moravians, who in 1742 established a mission in the northeast corner of Dutchess County called Shekomeko (and remembered today in a creek and hamlet of the same name). It reportedly was the first Christian congregation of Indians in this country, and for a brief time it flourished.

Distrust of the Moravians' motives caused Governor George Clinton to summon the missionaries to appear before his council in July 1744. They were found innocent of any nefarious acts, but a couple of months later, when the Provincial Assembly passed a law requiring persons living among the Indians to take a loyalty oath, the

Moravians were in deep trouble. Since their religion forbade oath taking, they could not obey the new law, and before the year ended they were ordered to disband the mission. The Moravians sought legal redress, and Shekomeko survived for a while longer, but eventually it became only a memory.

Another worthy and longer-lived effort was made a short distance northeast of Shekomeko, just over the New York border in Stockbridge, Massachusetts. Although Stockbridge was originally intended to serve as a home and mission for Indians of the Houstaonic Valley, displaced members of other tribes (including the Wappingers) were also welcome there, with the divers groups collectively called the Stockbridge Indians.

The valor of Chief Nimham's Stockbridge warriors during the Revolution is detailed elsewhere in this book, so mention here will be of another native American of that group—one whose pursuits were more peaceful and whose presence is felt throughout the Hudson Valley every summer when tall stands of lavender-flowered Joe Pye weed bloom in profusion. The plant is named for an eighteenth-century Indian herbalist who gained fame as a healer by using Joe Pye weed and other botanicals to cure both newcomers and native Americans.

But whatever appreciation there might have been of beneficial contributions by the Stockbridge Indians did not last long. Within five years after George Washington ordered a great feast held for them in honor of the decimating losses they had suffered during the Revolution, the Stockbridge Indians were relocated on a parcel of land in western New York. From there, they were later pushed farther west to Wisconsin, eventually winding up on a reservation in Minnesota, more than a thousand miles from their homeland.

Similar stories can be told about most of the other native American groups that once inhabited the Hudson Valley. Yet even though they no longer roam the region, they are memorialized in the hundreds of place names they left behind. Here are only a dozen, along with their English equivalents: Chappaqua (a separate place), Cohoes (canoe falling), Hoosic (place of stones), Mahopac (where snakes are abundant), Nappanoch (land overflowed by water), Nyack (point of land), Onteora (land of the sky), Ramapo (slanting rock),

Saratoga (place of salt springs), Taghkanick (water enough), Tuxedo (crooked river), and Wawarsing (blackbird's nest).

There are also many other names that, while not derived from any Indian dialect, reflect the native American presence. Pound Ridge, for example, is said to have been called that for an enclosure the Indians built to corral game animals. Ward Pound Ridge Reservation, it should be added, boasts Bear Rock—one of the few regional Indian petroglyphs still extant. And nearby North Castle supposedly was called that for an Indian fort (or castle) on the hill where IBM is now headquartered.

Then there's Accord, which used to be called Mombaccus, a colloquial Dutch term for "place of the mask," because the first white settlers reportedly found an Indian face carved into a tree. The Delawares carved faces into living trees in the belief that the tree's vitality would be imparted to the carving, which was later removed and used as a ceremonial mask. Indeed, they believed that everything in nature was imbued with a spirit, or "manitou"—a word that gives us the Catskills' Great Wall of Manitou, as well as the mountain, road, and hamlet by that name in Putnam County.

Numerous prominences were named for individual Indians as well, including Mount Nimham near Carmel, Tom's Hill in Copake, and Jo-Gee Hill in Wawayanda, while Signal Rock in the Columbia County town of Gallatin recalls the native American method of communicating across distances by bonfire. As for the Indian who gave his name to the rocky promontory where Catskill Creek flows into the Hudson, no one knows much about him except that his name was Hopp and that he had a big nose. Hence, the hill is known as Hop-O-Nose—or so local legend has it.

Speaking of local legend, not all of the Indian place names in the Hudson Valley are "pure." Aside from vagaries of spelling and facts that may have been innocently embroidered with fancy through the years, some resort owners were not averse to dubbing nearby sites with native names merely to attract more trade. Minnehaha Springs in Woodstock is one example, having been accorded that appellation (as Alf Evers points out in his marvelous *Woodstock: History of an American Town*) by one of the owners of the famous Overlook Mountain House. Minnehaha, of course, was the lover of the legendary Mohawk Chief Hiawatha—hero of Henry Wadsworth Longfellow's once immensely popular poem, first printed in 1855. That popularity may also have been responsible for a local Albany legend that tells of Hiawatha living for a time in the Normanskill Ravine—also known as the Vale of Ta-Wa-Sentha, or "place of many dead"—at the southern edge of the city.

In other cases, Indian names are genuine enough, though totally out of place. Lewisboro's Pequot Mills, for example, refers to a series of natural stone basins in which Indians really did grind corn—but not the Pequots, who lived far to the east. And many of the lovely lake names found in Harriman State Park (like Tiorati and Kanawaukee) are not derived from the dialect of the Delawares, who once lived there. But at least they are genuine Indian words and thus serve as reminders of the original inhabitants of the region.

Perhaps the best reminder of all can be found in an old legend that describes how the Indian weather goddess hung a new moon in the heavens each month, after cutting up the old moon and scattering the pieces in the sky. On a clear Hudson Valley night, glance upward at her stellar handiwork—who knows, you might even hear the throb of distant drums.

4 ILLUMINATING THE RIVER

THERE IS SOMETHING alluring about old lighthouses—those solitary sentinels of the night that were once so common along the shores of every important waterway in this country. But the march of modern technology has rendered such manned beacons obsolete, and with each succeeding year, fewer and fewer lighthouses remain to lend their romance to the landscape.

Fortunately, folks in the Hudson Valley literally have seen the light when it comes to preserving these old structures, and the river still hosts a handful of distinctive lighthouses that illuminate the past as they are put to new uses.

As might be imagined, it requires enormous effort to rescue these weatherbeaten relics. However, when enough people care, it can be done—something that was shown decades ago when the tiny beacon tucked under the east end of the George Washington Bridge was threatened with demolition. A storm of public protest convinced New York City Parks Commissioner Robert Moses to step in, and the Jeffrey's Hook Lighthouse was preserved. And while it is pretty much hidden from view except to river travelers and strollers along that section of the Hudson's shore, this 1899 structure has been seen by millions through the pages of Hildegarde Hoyt Swift's best-selling children's book *The Little Red Lighthouse and the Great Grey Bridge.*

That book—which reportedly sold over 2 million copies—probably makes Jeffrey's Hook the best-known of the Hudson's existing lighthouses, though not necessarily the most historic. For each of the old beacons upriver from the "Little Red Lighthouse" has its own tradition-steeped past, including the one at Tarrytown's Kingsland Point.

A familiar sight to drivers crossing the Tappan Zee Bridge, the handsome triple-decked white cylinder known as the Tarrytown Lighthouse has been part of the river scene since 1883. At that time, the lighthouse stood almost a quarter-mile offshore, whereas today a mere 50 feet of water separate it from the east bank. This odd bit of news once prompted a young visitor to ask in awe if the lighthouse had drifted shoreward during the past century. No, the child was assured, lighthouses were built on especially strong foundations to withstand the crush of winter ice and an occasional ramming by river craft. It was the shoreline that had gradually moved west, the result of landfill to accommodate the east-shore railroad and the expansion needs of the nearby automotive plant.

Because the Tarrytown Lighthouse looks as if it is located on that plant's property, some Hudson Valley dwellers may think it is off-limits to the public. But a walkway connects the beacon with Kingsland Point Park, and both are maintained by Westchester County. Guided tours are available during the various Open House Sundays held from spring through autumn.

Only by seeing the inside of such a structure can the unique and ofttimes lonely life of the lighthouse keeper be appreciated. At Tarrytown, all the rooms are round (no corners to dust!), with one room per floor, and a narrow winding stairway connecting each level. The first floor, 18 feet in diameter, served as a combination parlor, kitchen, and dining room, with bedrooms above, and the fifth floor (called the "oil room") was used to house the bell mechanism. Above that was the kerosene-powered light, its beam enhanced by an intricately cut lens that was kept spotless by daily polishing.

Lighthouses like this were called "family stations," since they afforded enough room for the keeper's spouse and children. (The word "spouse" is used purposely, since lighthouse keepers—even in the preceding century—were often women.) But such structures were not the safest place for smallfry, and after two different Tarrytown keepers lost toddlers to drowning, a rule was made prohibiting the presence of very young children at family stations.

There was no rule, however, against the humanitarian efforts of the lighthouse keepers, who frequently risked life and limb to rescue swimmers and sailors, not only at Kingsland Point but at every other lighthouse along the Hudson as well.

No adequate records remain to document all these beyond-the-call-of-duty deeds, but they probably number in the thousands, dating back to 1789 when the U.S. Lighthouse Establishment (later the U.S. Lighthouse Service) was formed. Before that time, there was no overall system of navigational aids to protect river craft from the Hudson's many hazards. Poles might be used to mark a sandbar, echoes listened for on foggy nights to determine the proximity of a promontory, or a bonfire lit to reveal a particularly dangerous point. But it was a hit-or-miss affair, and most ship captains preferred to drop anchor for the night rather than run the risk of wrecking their vessels.

The U.S. Lighthouse Establishment changed all that. The initial step was to form a cadre of lamplighters charged with the nightly responsibility of hanging lanterns at perilous spots along the shore. Later came the lighthouses.

The first government-built structure was completed at Rockland County's Stony Point in 1826. Towering 179 feet above sea level, the stark white hexagonal lighthouse reputedly was built of rock taken from the nearby ruins of a fort that figured in the 1779 Battle of Stony Point. Today, the entire peninsula where the battle took place has been preserved as a State Historic Site, and recent renovations included the Stony Point Lighthouse, which now has an interpretive sign showing where the keeper's dwelling once stood, next to the tower.

According to the sign, various members of the Rose family (including two women) were keepers there for fifty-three years, during which time "there were no deaths from accidents on the water"—an impressive record for that treacherous stretch of the river, and one that underscores the dedication of those who kept the beacon burning during all kinds of weather.

Starting in 1856, the Stony Point keepers also were in charge of a bell, operated by a clock device, that rang every fifteen seconds on foggy nights. The bell originally was housed in a wooden tower near the now-demolished keeper's house, but in 1890 a better model was installed closer to the water. Visitors may take a trail down to the river's edge to view the bell, along with a still-operational beacon that was erected when the Stony Point Lighthouse was abandoned in 1926. But the newer models have none of the nostalgia of the old, and most visitors content themselves with viewing a 1923 Lighthouse Service bell on display near the park's excellent museum.

The full panorama of Hudson lighthouses is, of course, best perceived by taking a cruise along the river. For it is only from the deck of a boat that the Hudson's hazards—its narrows and shoals, rocky islets and irregular shores—are most evident. Sad to say, such a waterborne tour no longer can include the famous "leaning tower of Rockland," a dark-banded round lighthouse set on the dangerous Oyster Bed Shoal opposite Rockland Lake Landing. The Rockland Lake Lighthouse developed a decided tilt soon after it was built, in 1894, and the tilt worsened over the next three years, until it finally stabilized. The lighthouse remained a dependable, if somewhat off-beam beacon for nearly three decades after that, when automation took over and the lighthouse was torn down.

Nor is it possible nowadays to see the ornate wooden tower that in the 1870s guided ships around the tricky turn at Gees Point on the grounds of the U.S. Military Academy. More modern beacons have since been substituted for the West Point Lighthouse, but they are standard steel-frame affairs, with little to recommend them other than the reliability of their automated beams.

Much more interesting is the Danskammer Lighthouse, appropriately set on the flat-topped point jutting out from the west shore just north of Newburgh. Danskammer Point was given its name by a seventeenth-century Dutchman who spotted the Indians dancing around their nighttime bonfires at this important ceremonial site and decided it must be the Teufel's Danskammer—or the Devil's Dance Chamber.

Without those bonfires to warn of the projecting rock, the Danskammer was indeed a devilish threat to shipping, and in 1890 the steamer *Cornell* rammed into it. According to Arthur Adams (writing in *The Hudson: A Guidebook to the River*), the *Cornell* hit so hard that it broke off enough rock to form the base on which the Danskammer Lighthouse was built.

Colorful tales also are told about Fourmile Point, farther upriver on the west shore, where a cliff-top tower was in service until 1928. Next to the tower stood the keeper's quarters—a stone dwelling constructed by a sea captain who supposedly knew the location of treasure buried nearby.

Less dramatic but warmer reminiscences are recounted concerning the Stuyvesant Lighthouse south of Albany, which was a favorite among keepers, since it not only was one of the roomiest and had a small beach plus a garden, but also afforded ready access to the mainland by means of a footbridge. (Most lighthouses were accessible only by boat or, in the winter, by walking over the ice.) Memories are all that remain of the Stuyvesant Lighthouse, because the square, two-story structure was razed in 1933.

Not long after that, the lovely brick-and-stone Coxsackie Lighthouse (locally known as "Old Maid's Light" because of two spinsters who served as its keepers) was demolished after standing for more than a century on an islet now joined to Rattlesnake Island along the west shore of the Hudson.

Happily, the future seems more secure for the quartet of lighthouses that still stand guard over the river between Athens and Esopus. The northernmost of these is the Hudson-Athens Lighthouse, the first such structure in the region to be leased from the Coast Guard by a local preservation group. While the Coast Guard will continue to operate the light that warns river craft of the Great Middle Flats (shallows just north of the beacon), repair and maintenance of the century-plus red-brick building will be the responsibility of the Hudson-Athens Lighthouse Preservation Committee.

Next in line, heading downstream, is the Saugerties Lighthouse, separated from the west shore by swampland near the mouth of Esopus Creek. In the early 1980s, the Heritage Task Force of the Hudson River Valley joined forces with the Saugerties Conservancy to raise funds for restoring the three-story brick building, which has been rightly termed a "treasure."

Farther down the river, at Kingston, the cream-colored Rondout

Lighthouse (reachable via a short pier from the shore) is now open to visitors and features a museum—part of the impressive restoration of the city's riverfront area, where the Hudson River Maritime Center is located. The center, by the way, houses a marvelous miscellany of memorabilia that should be seen by any lover of Hudson lore.

The Esopus Meadows Lighthouse, the most southerly of the Athens-Esopus quartet, is perhaps the prettiest as well, despite a slight tilt. The tilt is the result of the foundation being banged into by both barges and the huge ice blocks that jam the river in bitter weather. One keeper, however, found the incline enticing for his pet parrot, as the late Ruth Glunt reported in her book *Lighthouses and Legends of the Hudson*. It seems the bird loved to chase a ball, and the tilted deck of the lighthouse was a perfect place to "keep the ball rolling."

Keeping the ball rolling is something that also can be said of the many people dedicated to preserving Hudson beacons. And thanks to those folks, the river's collection of old lighthouses will continue to illuminate the past for present and future generations.

II

PARKLANDS

5 IONA: VINTAGE ISLAND OF THE HUDSON

OF ALL THE HISTORY-STEEPED islands that hug the Hudson shores, none surpasses Iona's remarkable past or matches its superb setting at the scenic narrows of the river just south of the Bear Mountain Bridge. Yet few day-trippers driving along Route 9W pause to enjoy this unique part of the Palisades Interstate Park System, possibly because they simply don't know it's there. Indeed, that stretch of 9W is a sidewinder requiring a watchful eye, and the sign for Iona is purposely inconspicuous. So the marsh-bordered causeway linking the island to the shore remains a quiet lane, where wildflowers and waterfowl reign, and human beings somehow seem the strangers.

That is not to say the ambiance of Iona's arrow-straight entrance-way is inhospitable. Rather, the hushed, lush beauty is a gentle reminder of man's smallness in nature's overall scheme, despite his mighty impact on the now uninhabited island at the east end of the causeway.

That impact began at least three thousand years ago, when early Indians hunted and fished there, leaving behind a record of their presence in one of the island's shallow rockshelters. Those hunter-gatherers of the Archaic Period did not engage in agriculture, but the more settled Woodland Indians, who camped there later, may well have availed themselves of Iona's climatic advantages to plant their crops of corn and beans.

No trace of such prehistoric agricultural pursuits has survived the centuries, with the possible exception of some ceramic sherds recovered from a rockshelter. Those broken bits of pottery have been painstakingly fitted together, and the resulting cone-bottomed vessel with incised decorations is now on display at the Trailside History Museum in Bear Mountain State Park, along with other Iona Island artifacts.

As for its climatic advantages, Iona lies within the northernmost reaches of the sea breeze blowing upriver from the Hudson's mouth. This makes for milder winters, and springtime comes to Iona a full fortnight before it comes to Newburgh, only fourteen miles away. Yet it was not until the mid-nineteenth century that the island's longer growing season was utilized in any large-scale way. Prior to that time, Iona remained pretty much untouched, though it knew a succession of owners, and correspondingly was called by different names.

To the Indians it was Manahawagh, a variation of Manhattan, or "Island of the Hills"—an apt description, despite the fact that the highest elevation is no more than 60 feet above sea level. Multiple rock outcroppings, however, make for rugged terrain, and even today only about 40 of Iona's 118 acres are considered suitable for cultivation.

After Stephanus Van Cortland acquired the island in 1683, it became known as Salisbury (a name still attached to the marsh over which the present-day causeway passes), but by the time the Revolutionary War broke out in 1776, it also was being referred to as Selby's.

It was during the early days of the Revolution that Captain Thomas Machin drew up plans for fortifying the island against British attack. The stone ruins seen today at the Round Island end of Iona are often taken to be the remains of such eighteenth-century breastworks, but Machin's plan was never carried out, and in October 1777, British troops landed there unopposed.

Since the purpose of that "invasion" of Iona was only to provide a backup force for the main body of British soldiers then attacking nearby Forts Montgomery and Clinton, the Redcoats soon were sent elsewhere, and the island returned to its peaceful and primitive state.

Variously called Weyant's and Beveridge's Island in the succeeding decades, it was finally dubbed Iona by C. W. Grant, of Newburgh, who purchased the property in 1849. Newburgh, it may be recalled, was the home of Charles and Andrew Jackson Downing. And while the latter is better known for his landscape architecture, both brothers were actively engaged in horticulture, with Charles considered the leading pomologist of his day.

Dr. Grant, who knew the Downings, shared their interest in fruit growing, and when he found Iona's climate to be ideal for apples, pears, and grapes, he decided to turn his hobby into a business. Within two decades of moving there, Grant not only had built a handsome white mansion on the southeastern side of the island, but his extensive orchards and vineyards reportedly were producing the majority of commercially grown fruit in all the United States. Besides that, he had developed a new kind of grape—the Iona—which he advertised as being equally suited for the dining table or the vintner's vat.

Iona, by the way, does not take its name from the ancient Greek grape-growing islands of Ionia, as one tradition has it. Grant was of Scottish ancestry and surely named his island and his grape for Iona in the Hebrides—the "Cradle of Celtic Christianity" and the legendary burial place of Scottish kings.

It goes without saying that superior salesmanship was required to market the prolific produce coming from over 2,000 fruit trees, 20 acres of grapevines, and 11 greenhouses, but Dr. Grant had a talent for that, too—and therein lies one of Iona's more colorful tales.

In November 1864, New York City newspapers carried notices of a two-day "Convention of those interested in horticulture and rural homes," to be held that month on Iona Island. For the sum of $1 ($5 for those who wished meals and sleeping accommodations), convention goers would be taken up the Hudson by steamship to Grant's estate. There they would be treated to guided tours of the grounds and would listen to lectures by such luminaries as William Cullen Bryant, Horace Greeley, and the Reverend Henry Ward Beecher, all three of whom were avid amateur horticulturists. Charles Downing would be there too.

What could and should have been a great convention was at best a star-crossed gathering; at worst it was a deliberate deception. The steamer chartered to convey people to Iona never showed up at the dock in New York City—a fact announced in the morning newspapers only on the scheduled day of departure. But all was not lost: would-be excursionists were advised they could still visit the island that day by taking the train to Peekskill, where a ferry would bring them over to Iona.

About 150 people did just that. Or rather, they got as far as Peekskill, but the promised ferry wasn't there. It had gone aground a mile upriver and was awaiting high tide to float off. The hapless passengers had the choice of taking the next train back to New York or trekking more than a mile north along the railroad tracks to a point where they would be rowed over to the grounded ferry. Then at high tide, the freed ferry would take them to Iona.

Though none of them was dressed for a late-November hike along the Hudson, the majority trekked to the boat and eventually reached Iona. Once there, they were left to their own devices, for the highly touted guided tours turned out to be just another unkept promise. Even so, such hardy souls as Harriet Beecher Stowe enthusiastically explored the autumn-sered site, and everyone looked forward to an afternoon of oratory.

They weren't disappointed in that respect, for several truly stirring speeches were made, including an impassioned plea by Horace Greeley for New York to save its endangered Adirondack forest through the establishment of a preserve (something that wasn't done for another two decades). But before the oratory commenced, there surely was some disappointment in the discovery of what obviously was the underlying motive for the convention—the audience first had to sit through an auction of Dr. Grant's surplus grapevines!

Grant, it is said, made $10,000 on the sale. He probably made some enemies, too, especially when the weary travelers returned to the other side of the Hudson that evening and found they had to wait more than three frigid hours for the train to take them back to New York City.

The convention fiasco had little effect on the popularity of Grant's grapes, however, and while it is not as widely known as it was in the 1860s, the Iona can still be seen in some New York vineyards, for it makes a delightful dessert wine.

Another Iona first was the Trophy Tomato, developed by Dr. Grant's son-in-law, Robert Hasbrouck. But by the time Hasbrouck took charge of Iona, its golden days of agriculture were fading, and the property changed hands several times in the late nineteenth century. Eventually it became a private resort, then a public picnic ground and amusement park. Prizefighter John L. Sullivan supposedly trained on Iona during the 1880s and may have owned an interest in the park.

The two-story Grant mansion had by then been converted into a hotel, with a nearby Ferris wheel, a carrousel, and a large pavilion overlooking the wharf where weekend excursion boats could dock. Among them were such famous Hudson River steamers as the *Columbia,* the *Grand Republic,* and the *General Slocum,* but it was probably the smaller *Pioneer* from Peekskill that docked there the most often, since Iona was particularly popular with residents of that east-shore town. The *Pioneer*'s fare was affordable, too—10 cents in 1877.

The advent of the twentieth century changed all that. In an ironic reversal of the Biblical prophecy about plowshares and pruning hooks, peaceful Iona was turned into a major manufactory of war weapons.

The navy purchased Iona for $160,000 in 1899, whereupon construction commenced on a military complex that was to total nearly 150 buildings, plus an assortment of concrete bunkers and an underground tunnel that reportedly ran the length of the island. Gunpowder was never manufactured there, but all kinds of munitions were assembled, and practically all the bombs and ammunition used in the Atlantic sector during World Wars I and II came from Iona.

At one time during the 1940s, eight hundred men were working round-the-clock shifts at Iona, yet the facility maintained an excellent safety record: only one fatality during all of World War II, and a single serious accident in 1903, when seven men were killed in an explosion.

It was also in 1903 that the navy obtained an injunction against a colony of squatters who had a small quarrying operation on Round Island, a few hundred yards south of Iona. Thereafter, the abandoned drystone buildings fell into ruin, and the quarry was nearly forgotten about until 1942, when some tourists came across the tumbled stones. They excitedly reported they had found the remains of a Revolutionary War fort, while others—mindful of old legends placing Captain Kidd in the area—thought the ruins might be even older, and dug for treasure. Needless to say, nary a nickel's worth was found.

By this time, Round Island had been joined to Iona by means of fill, but the navy made no major changes there, other than to extend Iona's perimetric guard walk to include the additional knob of land. Five years later, the Iona munitions depot was declared obsolete, and the navy left in 1951, though the government continued to store rubber, copper, and documents there until the mid-1960s.

Iona was then acquired by the Palisades Interstate Park Commission, which began demolishing most of the buildings in preparation for a vast public recreational complex. That complex, however, never got past the blueprint stage and possibly never will, since Iona has now been declared a winter sanctuary for the endangered bald eagle.

Iona is now closed to everyone from December 1 to April 1, when eagles take refuge there. But even in the warmer months, only people with special permits for the PIPC's Pioneer Camp Site are allowed past the fence that parallels the railroad tracks and cuts off access to the major portion of the island.

It is the hope of many hikers and history buffs that someday soon the Park Commission will be able to open all of Iona to the public during those times when eagles will not be needing it, for there is no island with a richer heritage in the whole Hudson. Until that day arrives, the portion west of the railroad tracks may be visited via the causeway, where the rewards are great for bird watchers and wildflower fanciers.

But do tread gently, and please refrain from entering the fragile tidal marsh, which could easily be destroyed by heavy use. After all, man already has left enough of a mark on Iona.

6 HOW "MAD ANTHONY" GOT HIS NAME

MILITARY LEADERS ARE often given nicknames—not always complimentary ones. But in the days when insults were frequently answered by sword or pistol, calling a general a madman was literally taking your life into your hands.

Back in the early summer of 1779, just such an insult was hurled at Brigadier General Anthony Wayne for what was judged an irrational and foolhardy plan of battle. Worse yet, he was called a madman by fellow officers who considered Wayne beneath them because of his lack of formal military training. At any other time, the hot-tempered Pennsylvanian surely would have sought redress. In this instance, though, Wayne was more concerned about the latest crisis facing the beleaguered Continental Army. So he chose to ignore the verbal barb, little knowing he was destined to go down in history as "Mad Anthony."

The crisis involved the fortifications then being built at West Point, which George Washington felt were threatened by the presence of a British garrison at Stony Point, a dozen or so miles downriver. In order to protect West Point until its fortress was finished, Stony Point must be captured. But how?

Virtually impregnable, Stony Point's steep cliffs rose 150 feet above the Hudson on the east. On the west side, a moatlike swampland, flooded at high tide, presented an equally formidable barrier. Added to this were two rows of abatis (sharpened stakes set in the ground at an angle facing in the direction of possible attack), plus a ring of cannon protecting a series of earthworks with connecting tunnels. Night and day the only access route—a causeway across the marshland to the north—was zealously guarded by the British, while their sloop-of-war *Vulture* stood watch over the Hudson side.

Most of the military men Washington consulted were certain Stony Point could be conquered only by a long and expensive siege—something Washington had neither the time nor the troops and equipment to undertake. Yet the vital fortress at West Point was in grave jeopardy. If the British captured that, they would control all of the Hudson.

It was then that Brigadier General Anthony Wayne stepped forward with his daring plan. As the leader of a newly formed light infantry brigade made up of crack troops from Connecticut, Massachusetts, North Carolina, Pennsylvania, and Virginia, Wayne already had reconnoitered Stony Point and was positive he could successfully storm it.

Washington's staff listened in disbelief as Wayne outlined his plan for a surprise attack. Then came the derisive judgment: "Such an assault would be madness!"

Wayne's eyes flashed angrily, but before he could respond, Washington began to nod his head slowly. In direct opposition to his staff of military experts, the commander in chief approved the "mad" plan.

Wayne went on to describe how each movement had been charted, every possibility examined, even down to the gruesome if necessary step of an advance guard to silence all the farmers' dogs within the vicinity of Stony Point. This had to be done, Wayne felt, so that the dogs would not bark as the American force went past, thereby forewarning the British. Any inhabitant suspected of being sympathetic to the British would be taken into custody by the same advance guard. There must be no hint of the surprise attack. If there was—if the British had the slightest suspicion—then Wayne's 1,300 men would be sacrificed.

The other generals felt that the chance was too great to take, despite all the careful preparation, and they would not be dissuaded from their previous judgment. Wayne was insane, they insisted, and the storming of Stony Point would be just one more disaster in a long list of defeats. But Washington had made up his mind, and Wayne moved out with his men on the morning of July 15, 1779.

From their camp at Sandy Beach, near Highland Falls, Wayne's brigade marched 13 miles south, skirting the western slope of Dunderberg Mountain, to a spot about a mile from Stony Point. Here it was that "Mad Anthony" gave his men their orders.

The plan was simple enough: the assault force would be divided into three groups, one attacking from the left, the second from the right, and the third from the center. This the men could easily understand. What made them gasp was *how* they would attack. Except for the central force, their muskets were to remain *unloaded*. They were to take the British garrison at bayonet point!

Again and again, Wayne stressed the need for absolute silence (the unloaded muskets would help to ensure this) until the final assault. Once the men were over the barricades, however, they were to begin shouting as loudly as they could, "The fort's our own! The fort's our own!"

His subordinate officers stared incredulously at Wayne, and more than one must have silently echoed the accusation of "madman." Yet there were others who remembered a night almost two years before at the Paoli Tavern, in Pennsylvania, when Wayne himself had been the victim of just such a surprise bayonet attack. It was there that Wayne had learned how useless muskets were in hand-to-hand combat, the kind of combat he knew was necessary for storming Stony Point.

At midnight, Wayne gave the order for his men to enter the marshland to the west of Stony Point. While Wayne led the right-hand column through the waist-deep water, Colonel Richard Butler silently moved with the left-hand column over the causeway to the north. Meanwhile, a contingent of 150 men went ahead to chop through the dread abatis—those sharpened stakes that could skewer a man like a roasting pig.

From the two columns, an officer and twenty men had been chosen to lead the way through the breach made in the abatis. The troops, well aware of the odds against such a suicide squad, fittingly dubbed these men the "Forlorn Hope."

As quietly as they could, the columns moved forward. But total silence was impossible, especially for the men wading through the swamp. Within minutes, a British sentry discerned something more than the usual nighttime sounds coming from the marshy land below him. The alert was sounded, and in the flashes of their own muskets and cannon, the startled Redcoats could see the first of Wayne's men approaching the abatis.

Their silence was almost as disconcerting as their presence. With none of the usual battle cries, or the support of a steadily thumping drum—not even the shrill encouragement of a fife—the Americans moved on relentlessly, like men already dead. Like men who could not be killed!

Just as the axmen of the right and left columns reached the abatis, a thunderous barrage of musketfire erupted between the two points. It was coming from the only men of Wayne's infantry who had been allowed to carry loaded guns. Assuming this was the main attack force, the British commander, Colonel Henry Johnson, rushed half his troops to protect the center.

Meanwhile, to the right and left, Wayne's columns were beginning to squeeze through the hacked-out holes made in the first ring of abatis. Some fell victim to British fire—Wayne among them—but enough got through to begin chopping away at the second ring of abatis. Then on they went, over the earthworks and into the British encampment, bayonets flashing, with French Lieutenant Colonel François de Fleury leading the way.

Behind, supported by one of his men after being grazed by a musket ball, Wayne got to his feet and resumed his command, urging his previously silent men to now use their voices in an unremitting roar of "The fort's our own!"

As Wayne had planned, this sudden clamor further confused the already disorganized Redcoats, who began laying down their weapons, thinking the fortress had been overpowered. Even Colonel Johnson, who had been taken in by Wayne's diversionary fire at the center of the abatis, set aside his sword in surrender.

It had taken only thirty minutes for "Mad Anthony" to prove the sanity of his plan.

The news of his victory raced over the countryside, stunning the British and rallying the Americans, who had long been disheartened by the continued defeats suffered by the Continental Army. A grateful Congress soon awarded Wayne a gold medal, and prize money (equivalent to the amount of British equipment captured at Stony Point) was divided among the victorious assault force. As had been promised by Wayne, the first five men to enter the fort were awarded prizes ranging from $500 for the first men (Lieutenant Colonel de Fleury) down to $100 for the fifth man. The "Forlorn Hope" was not so forlorn, after all.

Even the British could not withhold their grudging admiration for the man who had stormed the unstormable Stony Point. And General Clinton was later to comment, "The success attending this bold... attempt... procured very deservedly no small share of reputation and applause to the spirited officer who conducted it."

Ironically, only two days later, George Washington decided that the isolated fort at Stony Point would be too difficult for the Americans to maintain. So, after stripping the site of all its guns and equipment, the Continental Army abandoned Stony Point. It had served its purpose, though, for the British had been demoralized by this stunning defeat, while the cooling embers of American hope had been rekindled.

The victory at Stony Point also served to etch a new hero's name indelibly into the minds of the people. For Wayne's own men now proudly took up the insult-turned-accolade, and the gallant Pennsylvanian was forever afterward to be known as Mad Anthony.

For more than a century after the Revolutionary War, the promontory on which the Battle of Stony Point took place was privately owned. Then, in 1895, the New York State Legislature voted in favor of establishing a preservation group called the Trustees of Scenic and Historic Places and Objects, dedicated to acquiring areas as well as artifacts, restoring them, and making them accessible to the public. Four years later, the trustees obtained a deed to three-quarters of the land that constitutes the present-day Stony Point Battlefield State

Historic Site, with an additional 11 acres acquired in succeeding years. Little work was done to improve the property until 1901, when the group became the American Scenic and Historic Preservation Society.

During this time, excursion boats often docked at the northern end of Stony Point, where a beach and small bathhouse had been built. Excursionists could then follow a path to the top of the promontory and enjoy the picnic facilities and small museum provided by the society.

Although the Stony Point fort had been dismantled, the battlefield itself had not been extensively altered, and as funds became available in the following decades, the site gradually was refurbished. Much of this restoration work took place during the Depression years of 1935–36, when a new museum was constructed along with the stalwart stone gate that still greets visitors entering the park by way of an access road from Route 9W.

In 1946, what was then called Stony Point Battlefield Reservation came under the jurisdiction of the Palisades Interstate Park Commission, which supervised a major restoration of the site to coincide with the 1976 bicentennial celebration of our country's founding. That restoration effort further enhanced the already lovely site, and it is now considered one of the best laid-out and best-maintained public parklands in the Hudson Valley. As you stroll the quiet footpaths through manicured lawns and past interpretive signs carefully constructed to blend in with the landscape, it is difficult to associate this peaceful place with the wild battle that earned "Mad Anthony" his name. But some old-timers say that if you sit by the brow of the promontory and listen long enough, the salt-tinged breeze from the Hudson below brings a whisper of *The fort's our own... the fort's our own....*

7 FROM BULLETS TO BIRDSONG:
THE STRANGE STORY OF BLAUVELT STATE PARK

BIRDSONG HAS LONG since replaced the whine of bullets whizzing across this mountainous area of eastern Rockland County, and wildflowers now camouflage a crumbling complex of concrete tunnels and target walls. But Blauvelt State Park's pre-World War I rifle range still provides an intriguing, if somewhat eerie, trek back through time to when National Guardsmen came here to practice target shooting—target shooting that was abruptly halted by a mysterious ballistic blooper.

Despite this colorful past and its equally impressive scenery, Blauvelt remains one of the least known of the state parks in the Hudson Valley. Part of its obscurity is due to its status as an "undeveloped park," which means that there are no signs to proclaim Blauvelt's presence other than some "posted" placards tacked onto trees along its perimeter. Nor are there any parking lots, only an occasional roadside turnoff big enough for two or three cars. As for public facilities such as rest rooms and drinking fountains, there are none. Yet this very primitiveness contributes to the beauty of Blauvelt, which isn't really hard to find if you just know where to look.

Lying southwest of Nyack, with some contiguous local or county parkland, Blauvelt is bounded (roughly) by Clausland Mountain Road on the south, Greenbush to the west, and Bradley Hill Road on the north, with Tweed Boulevard N. running through its northern and eastern edges. Wide and well-packed paths to the interior of the park can be found at various points along these border roads, but few of the paths are identified by trail markers. Notable exceptions are the blue-blazed Long Path, part of which follows one of the walls of the old rifle range, and the yellow-marked Piermont Trail, connecting Sparkill to Central Nyack. Thus, newcomers to Blauvelt should take care to keep their bearings.

Blauvelt, covering less than 600 acres, is one of the smallest of the public recreation areas administered by the Palisades Interstate Park Commission. It is the result of two separate land acquisitions. The first, a tract of 212 acres forming the northeastern section, was donated by the heirs of Stephen Rowe Bradley, of Nyack.

To quote from a Palisades Interstate Park Commission report made in 1912: "This land [the Bradley tract] is on the summit of the mountain and on its easterly side commands a magnificent view of the Tappan Zee Bay and the Hudson Valley; on the westerly side are equally extensive views of the back country and the Hackensack Valley. It is regarded as one of the most beautiful sights anywhere in the locality." It still is.

Not long after obtaining the Bradley tract, the Palisades Interstate Park Commission acquired a second, larger section to the southwest, and the combined tracts were named Blauvelt State Park.

In Dutch, Blauvelt means "Blue Grassland" or "Blue Field," and while there may be areas of the park that take on a bluish tinge at certain times of the day, that wasn't why it was called Blauvelt. It was named, instead, for some of the earliest European settlers in the area, the Blauvelt family, who also gave their name to the hamlet near the southwestern corner of the present-day park.

It was on land once belonging to the Blauvelt family that, around 1910, a rifle range was built for the New York National Guard. Solidly constructed, it was much more than just a series of target walls, for each battalion brought to Blauvelt would camp at the range for several days. The complex contained such structures as a mess hall, range office, headquarters building, and storage houses, in addition to high concrete target walls connected by safety tunnels.

When completed, the Blauvelt Rifle Range had cost half a million dollars—no small sum in those days. And at that price, it should have been a model of military endeavor, but it wasn't. It just didn't work right.

For some reason—probably the height of the land on which it was built—bullets that were supposed to hit the target area often overshot their mark and landed in South Nyack. Needless to say, this was somewhat upsetting to the folks over there, and it took only a few of these lead showers for the citizens of South Nyack to lodge a long and loud complaint.

Another $73,000 was spent to improve conditions at the rifle range. Large overhead screens were installed near the firing point to keep the bullets in Blauvelt instead of raining down on South Nyack. But the new screens didn't solve the problem, and rumor had it that the rifle range was cursed.

Whether it was cursed or just constructed improperly, the range became an embarrassment to the officials in charge, and they were only too glad to hand over their white elephant to the Palisades Interstate Park Commission. At that time—1913—the Blauvelt Rifle Range had been in operation less than three years. A mighty costly and short-lived white elephant.

During the next five years, from 1913 to 1918, the YWCA rented the land as a summer camp for New York City working girls, who paid $3.50 for a full week's vacation. It was a regimented vacation, however, for Camp Bluefields ("Bluefields" being the English version of "Blauvelt") followed the military theme of its predecessor. Campers were required to wear uniforms consisting of bloomers and middy blouses, they slept in tents, and their daily activities were signaled by bugle calls.

Then, in 1918, the property was turned into a state-run camp for the military training of young men between the ages of sixteen and nineteen. ROTC units used the site during and immediately following World War I, after which some members formed a "Comeback Club" and obtained permission to build summer homes at Blauvelt. For several summers thereafter, the rifle range was the scene of a gala "Fete Militaire" sponsored by the club, with the 1925 celebration featuring a costume ball in one of the camp buildings.

Such peaceful pursuits all too soon reverted to more serious maneuvers as it became evident that the "War to End All Wars" wasn't. In 1930, the army sent soldiers to Blauvelt for training (presumably without target practice, since the problem of the errant bullets never had been solved). And when World War II broke out, Blauvelt again became a training ground—this time for soldiers from nearby Camp Shanks—as well as an air raid post. But eventually the war clouds dispersed, the soldiers departed, and the deserted rifle range was subjected to the ravages of nature...and man.

Today, tree roots have collapsed several sections of the tunnel system, while other natural forces have been at work crumbling the concrete. None of these is as devastating, however, as the vandalism that had despoiled the complex and some of the peripheral areas of the park. Sadly, one of the most unusual natural features of Blauvelt—a huge boulder called Balance Rock, which had been a landmark for untold centuries in the northeastern part of the park—was callously destroyed in 1966 when vandals pushed it from its pedestal, sending it hurtling down the slope of a mountain.

Despite garbage and graffiti, the ruins of the old rifle range are still fun to explore, though special care should be taken in the shadowy tunnels, where the cracked floors are littered with beer cans and other debris. Ironically, the purpose of these tunnels was to provide safe passage for National Guardsmen going from one target area to another.

The main entrance to the park remains the old road that begins at the juncture of Greenbush Road and Route 303 (opposite Leber Road) in Blauvelt. Park in the space provided opposite utility pole #100 and follow the paved road that curves up to the plateau above. At the end of the pavement near the top of the hill, the trail straightens in a northeasterly direction, and the ruins of the massive mess hall and tower are just behind a stand of large fir trees on the left. About 150 yards farther along the trail, an embankment on the left, fronting on a large clearing, is part of the promenade and firing line.

The best preserved of Blauvelt's tunnels is closest to the southern end of Tweed Boulevard North, near its junction with North Clausland Mountain Road. Leave your car in one of the roadside turnoffs and take either of the two downhill trails that lead west.

A leisurely walk of about ten minutes will bring you to the 1,000-yard butts (target wall) and a tunnel, which is built partly below and partly above ground, with ventilation slits along one wall. The other tunnel wall, the one facing what had been the firing area, understandably has no openings.

You may walk on top of this tunnel, alongside it, or through it to what was an observation tower. The only safe way to enter the tower, however, is by walking through the tunnel—a distance of about 1,200 feet.

From the observation tower, a high wall (the 600-yard butts), paralleled by a concrete walkway, leads to another tunnel set at a right angle to the wall at its far end. On what was the lee side of each target wall can be found square concrete buildings, which were probably used to store targets and other paraphernalia.

If you keep following along the outside of the walls, you will come to a crumbling concrete stairway leading to an underpass at the western end of the complex. Here, target walls are smaller, both in height and length, and have small buildings at one end—buildings nearly hidden in summer by the rich flora of Blauvelt, which includes luscious blackberry bushes and a profusion of golden touch-me-nots.

Pause here for a few silent moments and you will be rewarded by the sight and sound of several kinds of birds—a fitting finale to your walk through time. For Blauvelt has come full circle: from birdsong to bullets and back to birdsong once more. With luck, it will ever remain so.

8 HAVEN IN THE HIGHLANDS

BACK IN 1983, when world-famous folk singer Pete Seeger appeared on TV screens to promote the I Love New York Summer Festival in the Hudson River Valley, many a local viewer recognized the ponderous profile of Storm King Mountain in the background and rightly guessed that the announcement had been filmed along the shore of Little Stony Point, not far from Seeger's home in Beacon.

What most viewers were not aware of, though, was that Seeger himself chose the location. For the long-time advocate of conservation not only was concerned about cleaning up the river that laps against this rocky knob just north of Cold Spring, but also acted as unofficial custodian of Little Stony Point, personally leading an annual campaign to clear the beach of debris.

Little Stony Point well merits such care, since it is as historic as it is scenic. What's more, it serves as an excellent introduction to the wide-ranging haven known as Hudson Highlands State Park, because Little Stony Point was the very first swatch acquired for that 4,000-acre patchwork of public land spreading down the river's eastern shore from Beacon to Garrison.

As is the case with most undeveloped state parklands, there are no signs proclaiming the presence of Little Stony Point, which is about one mile south of Breakneck Tunnel on the Putnam/Dutchess border. There are no formal parking lots either, though several gravel pull-offs parallel Route 9D, near where a short bridge spans the east-shore railroad tracks. At the other (west) side of this footbridge, paths meander off to the south and north; both lead down to the river's edge.

First-timers to Little Stony Point should try a full circuit of the small peninsula, following the path down the southern slope and passing secluded coves offering magnificent views of the Hudson. As this path veers west and then north along the perimeter, the granite mass that gave Little Stony Point its name rises almost perpendicularly from its wooded shoreline skirt. A T-shaped tunnel pierces its western face at ground level. This tunnel is thought to be the result of earlier mining operations, but now it is only a convenient shelter from a shower.

A better picture of the quarrying operations that once threatened the beauty of this section of the Hudson Highlands may be seen from and along the northwestern tip of Little Stony Point, where water 140 feet deep allowed barges to take on cargoes of crushed rock. The still-raw scars defacing Breakneck and Mount Taurus in the distance— along with nearby dregs of an old dock, rusted iron mooring rings, and a tall slope of tippled rock—are all silent souvenirs of that unfortunate era, which ended in 1966.

The following year, responding to the threat of further industrial development and aided by a grant from the Jackson Hole Preserve, New York State acquired Little Stony Point, and nature began masking the broken brown boulders and bone-white concrete foundations with eye-pleasing plumes of green.

Even more pleasant is the beach adjoining the old barge-docking area. This tree-studded sweep of sandy soil on the northeastern end of Little Stony Point is without question one of the most picturesque of all the Hudson-shore beaches—which is why it is usually crowded with swimmers and sailors during the warmer months. But when autumn arrives, the chill air chases such summer soldiers, and from then until late spring the beach attracts mostly hikers.

The cooler months are also ideal for a trek through the main body of Hudson Highlands State Park—an area extending from

Sugarloaf Mountain in Dutchess County south to Bull Hill (Mount Taurus) in Putnam.

All along Route 9D and adjacent roads in the area, trail heads can be found, including that of the aptly named Breakneck Trail (starting at the Breakneck Tunnel overpass)—a breathtakingly beautiful but sometimes perpendicular path that is definitely not for novices or anybody with acrophobia.

There is also the less strenuous Washburn Trail (leading off from Mountain Avenue in Cold Spring), which wends across 1,400-foot Mt. Taurus, and passes the legendary Table Rock. Supposedly, in precolonial days, an Indian spy leaped to his death from this rock, rather than surrender to Wappinger warriors.

For visual variety, however, the old Lake Surprise Road is unsurpassed. This paved road, which is now abandoned (at least that part of it within the park boundaries), meets Route 9D about a quarter-mile north of Little Stony Point. Again, there are no signs announcing access, but two tall cut-stone gateposts on the east side of the highway make it easy to spot.

From there, the road makes a gradual ascent, winding around the rocky western face of Mt. Taurus, then roughly paralleling the course of Breakneck Brook. For the first quarter-mile or so, fine views of the Hudson may be had (depending on the amount of foliage) from the quarry-stone curbing along the western side of this road, and there are interesting footpaths through the woods sloping down toward the river. But few who know this area tarry on these trails, for the most intriguing part of a trek on this old road lies just ahead, where a side lane arches off to the ruins of a large estate, then returns to the main road.

Roofless and vine-entwined, the solid stone walls of the estate's mansion are an eerie reminder of the opulent life once lived here in the early 1900s by Edward G. Cornish and his family.

As chairman of the board of the National Lead Company, Cornish could well afford whatever money might buy. And while he chose rough-hewn rocks from nearby Breakneck Mountain as building material, it is said that the interior of the mansion was as modern and commodious as the times allowed. So, too, was the rest of the estate:

there is a large swimming pool sequestered in a shaded vale on the west side of the mansion and an overgrown formal garden.

The more utilitarian aspects of the Cornish Estate can be equally interesting, including the shell of a greenhouse and a huge concrete cistern (farther up the main road), with its tall wooden tube still containing some of the charcoal used to filter the water. There is also the adjoining farm Edward Cornish owned, where an old barn is noteworthy for its chimney (most barns are not heated).

Just past the estate grounds, the road is not paved, but it still can be easily followed up to the concrete dam Cornish had built to form a large pond—a nice place for a picnic. History buffs, however, may prefer to turn off the main road before reaching the pond and take the Catskill Aqueduct Tunnel Path instead.

Although unidentified by any trail markers, this wide flat path is unmistakable, for it bisects the main road and runs northwest to southeast along the top of a massive earthen mound containing the water conduit. Hikers can go in either direction along this tunnel path, but for a short and scenic stroll, the northwestern section, heading toward Breakneck Ridge, is recommended.

There is probably no more pleasant and peaceful a walk in all the Highlands than this pathway, especially in late spring, when the abundant dogwoods are in full bloom. And though there are no far-off valley views to awe the eye, close-at-hand sights—varying from a large stone pumphouse to a tiny brass plate embedded in the top of the tunnel mound—hint at a construction story that borders on the incredible.

The Catskill Aqueduct was built in the early 1900s to carry water from the Ashokan Dam to New York City, but the Hudson almost halted it. Plans called for the aqueduct to cross the river, via an underground tunnel through the bedrock, from Storm King to Breakneck Mountain. The river's gorge, however—gouged out during the Ice Age—seemed bottomless. Finally, after four years of drilling, solid rock was struck 1,500 feet below the water level. The tunnel progressed, though not without other problems. One of the most perplexing of these was a phenomenon called "popping rock," whereby intense underground pressure caused pieces of rock to suddenly shoot off the tunnel wall, injuring anyone who happened to be in the way.

That the aqueduct ever reached Breakneck thus seems something of an engineering miracle; at the very least it is a monument to man's ability to surmount overwhelming odds. And all of it was accomplished in an era devoid of the giant earth-moving equipment that is available today—something that pedestrians might pause to ponder as they stroll along the embankment containing a water tunnel large enough for a locomotive to run through.

Anyone interested in a more detailed account of the Catskill Aqueduct should consult *In the Hudson Highlands,* a book of brief essays compiled by the nonprofit Appalachian Mountain Club, one of several hiking associations that help to maintain trails through this and other sections of Hudson Highlands State Park.

Those other sections include the former Hammond Brickyard, at Dutchess Junction; Bannerman's Island (off-limits to the public); Sugarloaf Mountain, just north of Breakneck Ridge; the Osborn Preserve, including Sugarloaf Hill and part of Canada Hill, in Philipstown; the marshland east of Constitution Island; Denning Point, at the mouth of Fishkill Creek; and a small parcel at Indian Brook Falls, in Garrison. All are scenic. Most are historically significant. And together with Little Stony Point and the Cornish/Aqueduct section, they make up what is a true haven in the Highlands.

9 HIDDEN TREASURE: MONSEY GLEN

WILLIAM BLAKE'S TIMELESS line about "seeing a world in a grain of sand" may be too great an exaggeration when it comes to describing a little-known Rockland County park called Monsey Glen. But a quiet stroll through this sylvan gem just a stone's throw off busy Route 59 certainly presents a panorama of Rockland's past, all tucked into a mere 24 acres.

Quarrymen, gandy dancers, gypsies, and landed gentry—all have left their mark on Monsey Glen. Its name harks back to the prehistoric inhabitants of the area, who discovered the sequestered ravine, which had been carved out by a stream. Utilizing some of the rockshelters in the sandstone walls, members of the Munsee branch of the Lenni-Lenape (or Delaware) Indians were the first human beings known to have enjoyed the site, which is so sheltered by surrounding foliage that even travelers along a nearby trail might remain unaware of its existence.

That seclusion is the same today as it was centuries ago. And since there are no signs announcing access to Monsey Glen, it is not surprising that many present-day passers-by also remain unaware of its presence. Because of the possibility of missing it entirely, would-be visitors might do best to head west along Route 59 from the hamlet of Monsey, then go south (a left-hand turn) on Saddle River

Road (Route 306). At the next corner, make a right on Fred Eller Drive, then another right at Summit Avenue. The dead end of Summit Avenue marks one entrance to Monsey Glen.

The other entrance (actually only a small gravel parking area) is located on the south side of Route 59, near where it passes over the railroad tracks about mile northwest of Saddle River Road. This entrance is more convenient to motorists coming from the direction of Suffern and also offers the best introduction to Monsey Glen—that is, if you're not turned off by the trash that clutters the pathways leading from the parking area. But the beer-can brigade rarely advances much past the park's periphery, and scenic rewards await those who persevere along the rutted dirt road gently sloping down to the ravine.

Once past the modern-day pumphouse, the road becomes more primitive, finally turning into a trail that may first have been defined by moccasin-shod feet. It follows a spring-fed stream coursing along the floor of a sandstone corridor carved out eons ago when the last great glacier was leaving the land.

In those ancient times, the now-gentle stream was much more forceful, and eventually it wore away the softer rock in the walls of the corridor so that several small caves were formed—ready-made shelters and storage rooms for the human beings who arrived on the scene many millennia later.

The largest of the glen's rockshelters was 49 feet long, 6 feet high, and 6 feet deep when archeologists first measured it in 1936. Then, when they removed an artifact-bearing layer of dirt in front of the shelter, they found a huge sandstone slab, which at one time had been part of the roof overhang. This showed the shelter originally had been even bigger. It also revealed that Indians had used it for a much longer time, too. For while the dirt layer on top of the slab contained pottery sherds and other artifacts associated with Woodland Indians (from around 1000 B.C. to A.D. 1600), the dirt beneath the slab yielded tools and projectile points more than 3,000 years old.

Construction of the New York State Thruway in the late 1950s reportedly destroyed much of that particular rockshelter. Some artifacts which were found there, however, can be seen at the

Trailside Museum in Bear Mountain State Park, where an excellent diorama by Richard Koke shows how the shelter and its inhabitants must have looked in prehistoric times.

Prior to the 1936 archeological discoveries at Monsey Glen, its rockshelters had been commonly called "bear dens." Not to worry, though. The only furred four-leggers found there today are of a much smaller size (muskrat, skunk, opossum, and such), and it is doubtful that any bear has set foot in the glen since the eighteenth century. It simply was too busy a place after the end of the Colonial era.

By the mid-1800s, the Piermont Branch of the New York and Erie Railroad was being built along the glen's northern edge, with an army of gandy dancers laboring to lay the 6-foot-wide track. Even earlier, the ring of sledgehammers splitting rock had resounded through the glen as local builders availed themselves of the fine-grained sandstone.

According to Eloise K. Hoffman, who lived in Monsey for over seventy years, there is a stone house on nearby Saddle River Road that was constructed of this comely and convenient material. The sandstone also served well for fireplace mantels, flagging, and tombstones. The quarry at Monsey Glen was never a large one, however, and as soon as it was abandoned, nature began masking the scars left behind by the rock reapers. Nowadays, there is barely a trace, with the possible exception of some steps carved into an outcropping of rock near the center of the glen.

These steps are something of a mystery, in that there is no record of when they were carved or by whom. Suffern history buff Josephine Watts, who for many years helped conduct Boy Scout hikes through the park, thinks the steps are surely the result of quarrying. On the other hand, there is a story that these are "Indian stairs," though why native Americans might trouble themselves to chisel out toeholds in easily traversed terrain is an even greater mystery.

Since the steps occur in an amphitheater-like area that has been a favorite family outing site for a century or more, some folks figure the step carving was undertaken merely to accommodate long-skirted ladies during Victorian-day picnics. Yet William Heidgerd, whose family owned the land from the mid-1800s until the early part of this century, believes the steps predate that era; at least they were a well-known feature of the glen when he played there as a boy around 1908.

Heidgerd grew up in the family's Glen House, just north of the railroad tracks that form the upper boundary of the present-day park, and though he later moved to his grandparents' home on Upper Main Street in Monsey, the picturesque ravine remained one of his favorite haunts.

Heidgerd's grandparents' house, incidentally, was known to fly the largest American flag in the county. Intensely proud of his adopted country—which had provided him and his brother Diedrich with the opportunity to become successful woolen jobbers—the first William Heidgerd had a flagmaker create an enormous banner with stripes a full 8 inches wide. On appropriate occasions, this flag—now housed at the Historical Society of Rockland County in New City— was hung from the attic windows so that it draped the front of the Main Street mansion.

Gypsies also found Monsey Glen to be to their liking, and during the early part of the present century the clearing at the head of the glen served as a campsite for the Romany wanderers. Heidgerd and his older sister, Marguerite Hartwell, never forgot their childhood fascination with the gypsies, whose horse-drawn wagons were as colorful as their costumes.

"They were just as if you took them out of a storybook," Mrs. Hartwell reminisced shortly before her death in 1985. "And this made it almost impossible for we children to heed the warning of our parents never to go near the gypsy camp!" Gypsies reputedly stole children as well as horses, but no such mishap befell the Heidgerds. Mrs. Hartwell did believe, however, that a special watch was kept at the family farm during the short time each summer that the gypsies camped at the glen.

The Heidgerd farm (now the southern section of the park) was never a large agricultural operation, but more the project of a gentleman farmer whose fields were sown mainly to supply food for his carriage horses and a small complement of barnyard animals.

The fields and pastures of the old farm have long since been taken over by undomesticated growth, and in all but the coldest months a bounty of wildflowers greets walkers along the paths that lead through the park. Trailing arbutus occurs there as well—one of the few places in Rockland County where this rare species of plant life can be found.

Marguerite Hartwell recalled that in bygone years her sisters always relied on the glen to provide whatever flowers they needed for home decorations, as well as for "a drink of the coolest and most refreshing water you've ever tasted."

Several springs feed into the brook flowing through Monsey Glen, but the one the Heidgerd girls visited was probably that which is near the "amphitheater" with the carved steps. It was there that the Heidgerd family held their picnics, and a section of brookside sandstone was chiseled into a trough to retain the delicious springwater. The remains of this rustic reservoir may still be seen, though hikers should refrain from sampling the water.

On the other side of the brook, a footpath leads west past two more springs, one of which is situated by a large rock overhang that is a welcome umbrella for hikers caught in a downpour. This side of the glen is steep, however, and even properly shod explorers should watch their step on the damp, moss-covered rocks.

The best bet is to remain on the main trail, especially in the area just past the overhang, where an old dam impedes the stream and the ravine opens into a pond now clogged with vegetation. In the days of the Heidgerds, the pond was clear of such growth, but children were cautioned not to swim there because of quicksand on the bottom. Possibly this was just a story made up by protective parents, but a recent report of a hiker encountering "quaking mud" in that area should be reason enough for staying away from the pond.

The bordering high banks are much more interesting anyway, with a perfectly safe path offering fine views of the pond. This pond almost became part of a land developer's dream, for there was a period in the not-too-distant past when the primitive beauty of Monsey Glen was threatened by businessmen who envisioned a host of modern houses abutting the ancient shelters of the Indians.

Fortunately, that dream never became a reality, and in 1976, Rockland County acquired the property for a park.

The fact that it has managed to survive the depredations of quarrymen and gandy dancers, then the threat of developers, makes Monsey Glen even more precious—a hidden treasure now guaranteed to remain intact for discovery by all the generations which follow ours.

10 TAKING COMFORT IN WINDING HILLS

THE OLD ADAGE about never judging a book by its cover certainly holds true for Winding Hills, a little-known parkland treasure in Orange County. The park's two access roads—both on Route 17K, about two miles west of the village of Montgomery—are marked by unobtrusive, chocolate-brown wood signs, beyond which the traveler sees little more than a thick stand of trees. Neither of these downward-sloping lanes reveals much, even when they converge at the entrance gate to Winding Hills and a single paved road can be seen leading uphill past a small pond. But anyone who perseveres for another few hundred yards along the tree-lined avenue will be rewarded by the sight of a sparkling blue lake that is only one of the many fine features of the 500-acre park.

At this point, a turnoff on the right-hand side of the road allows visitors to park awhile and stroll across the road to where a flagpole bracketed by several benches overlooks the lake. There is no better place to get your bearings, for the full extent of this long body of water is evident here, including the public boat launch at its southern end.

If boating or camping is on your mind, then backtrack a bit down the road you came in on until you reach a side lane leading off to the west. This will take you to the dock area, where you may launch your own boat (nonmotorized craft only) for free or rent a canoe, paddleboat, or rowboat during the warm-weather months. There are no swimming facilities, but if you have a New York State permit, fishing is allowed, either in the lake or at the two ponds elsewhere in the park. And if you manage to hook a bass, perch, or pickerel—to name only three of the varieties available—you can cook it right there, for the campsites all have fire rings and the free picnic area features charcoal grills at each table.

However pleasant the southern end of Winding Hills may be, it is the section north of the flagpole lookout that comprises the greatest portion of the park and offers its greatest attractions. At least that is how many people view it, since the less-developed areas are a haven for hikers and history buffs, with two main trails that bond the present to the past and serve as marvelous outdoor classrooms.

The northern area has its amenities, too, however, and picnickers will find a 20-acre grove there with plenty of tables, as well as rest-room facilities, fresh water, and a pavilion for large groups. There is also a Nature Center full of exhibits, which range from fossils and bones to nineteenth-century artifacts found in the park and even a see-through beehive.

Getting back to the two trails mentioned earlier: both are relatively easy to traverse, and cover a distance of about a mile. Before hiking, it's a good idea to stop off at the ranger's office or the Nature Center and obtain a brochure that describes the numbered stations along each trail.

For anyone interested in history, the Heritage Trail is a must. The trail was built by 4-H Club members over a five-year period and opened in 1979. It begins at the ranger's house located at the first parking lot north of the flagpole lookout. This lot is small, and if you find it full, just follow the main park road a short distance north to a second, larger lot by the picnic grove, then walk back to the trailhead.

A sign standing by the big tree near the ranger's house points the way west, down a path through the trees to the lake shore. From here to the northern tip of the lake (approximately 300 yards), the Heritage Trail is wide and level, so that handicapped people may enjoy this quieter and more primitive part of the park, where wildflowers abound in season and the many different kinds of birds seem almost tame.

The Heritage Trail crosses the northern end of the lake by means of a floating footbridge, and although handrails are provided, wise parents would best keep a firm hold on their youngsters' hands. Along the way, there are several platforms extending out into the water that serve both as fishing stations and observation posts. At these points you can really key into the vast changes that occurred at the lake over the eons since the Ice Age.

As the great glaciers retreated, this area was covered with water as it is now. But eventually the water drained off, leaving behind a swampy bed of rich organic sediment in which vegetation flourished. This sediment, not true soil, is called "black dirt." Mastodons roamed here 10,000 years ago, and in seeking to satisfy their voracious appetites, some may have become enmired in the swamp, as happened in similar areas. A few miles east of Winding Hills, a historical marker at the corner of Route 17K and Bailey Road records a mastodon excavation undertaken in the early 1800s by the famous painter Charles Willson Peale, who displayed the bones in his Philadelphia museum of natural history.

Cotemporaneous with the mastodons, nomadic Paleo Indians prowled the borders of the Winding Hills swamp and may have hunted the elephant-like beasts. These early native people were succeeded by Indians of the Archaic and Woodland Period, and at the time the first European settlers arrived, in the nineteenth century, what was to be known as Winding Hills was the home of the Delaware (or Lenni-Lenape) Indians.

There is no record of what the Indians called the highlands surrounding the swamp, and its first known name was Comfort Hills—not for its cozy terrain but because that was the name of a family who farmed here. Indeed, the rocky slopes were far from a comfort to those homesteaders, whose efforts to clear the land are still evident in the stone fences that cross the hills west of the lake.

The Heritage Trail makes an elliptical loop through this section, with markers pointing out old house foundations and fields, as well as natural features and wild plants important to the pioneers. In those days, only a small part of the lake bed was dry enough for cultivation. The rest was a mosquito-infested mire with pockets of quicksand that could quickly swallow up a wandering cow or an unwary man—the legend is told of a farmer who went into the swamp one day and never returned. Stories of his ghost—abetted by the natural phosphorescence and mists associated with any such bogland—likely were retold by housewives in an effort to keep children out of Kelleher's Swamp (the name given to it for a family that farmed here in the mid-1800s).

Drowned trees and other vestiges of the swamp can still be seen as the Heritage Trail winds back along the west shore of the lake, but the forest hides what little remains of a remote shack that was the home of the mysterious recluse of Winding Hills. This character was a cultured man of British descent who chose to live alone with only his sheepdog for company, and his story is now part of the local folklore.

As you recross the floating bridge, take a look to the north, where dead tree trunks poke up from the water; birdhouses and feeders have been attached to some of them, and you're apt to spot a number of waterfowl, including Canada geese and a resident great blue heron. Take another look, too, toward the south, and see if you can make out the vague rhomboid shape that prompted turn-of-the-century inhabitants to call the lake bed Diamond Valley. By that time, more of the lake bed was dry and the fertile black dirt was producing crops of onions, celery, and lettuce.

All that changed in the 1930s when someone—assisted by beavers—built a dam that caused Diamond Valley to once more fill with water. That dam later deteriorated, but the lake bed never again was used for farming, staying instead a swampland until Orange County established Winding Hills Park and dug out the lake you now see. So in a way the property has come full circle: it is much as it must have been millennia ago, when glacial meltwater still covered the ground.

In addition to the Heritage Trail, which runs through the northwestern portion of Winding Hills, there is a scenic Nature Trail that will take you through the eastern sector and is well worth the walk. Unlike the Heritage Trail, this path can be picked up at several different points, including the picnic grove and the large parking lot north of the ranger's house. However, for the full circuit—and if you wish to follow the numbered sites in order—proceed to the trailhead just north of the Nature Center. From there, the Nature Trail circles around to the northeast, then south past a shale bank and a wide variety of identified trees and other flora.

At the trail's southernmost point, thee is a fine view of the white-rocked Shawangunk Mountains (to the north and west of Winding Hills), and at this point a footpath off the main trail will take you to the highest point in the park (780 feet), which is topped by an airplane beacon. The Nature Trail then turns back north to a serene spot called the Upper Pond. Here you can either cross the footbridge to the picnic area or follow the trail that circles the pond. The latter route, though a little longer, is recommended, for this is one of the loveliest and most peaceful places in Winding Hills, and you can also fish here.

Upper Pond seems so much a part of the natural surroundings that it is hard to believe that it is man-made, having once been a cow pasture where local children played baseball in the 1930s. In fact, Bob Kimball, whose family summered in the two-story house that is now the ranger's quarters, reminisced that he and his playmates used cow "flops" as bases for their ball games!

Another pastime was called "sliding down the birches," in which youngsters would climb up one of the slim gray birches on the nearby hill until the tree bent over. Then the climber would slide down to another birch and continue the process all the way down the hill. Needless to say, park rangers would frown on such frolics today, but in any event the gray birches of half a century ago have all but disappeared from the hillside.

Other trees have taken their places, including a thick stand of pines near the Upper Pond. This forest was planted by Boy Scouts back in 1930, under the leadership of a man named Clarence W. Hunter, who did much to preserve the beauty of Winding Hills—a beauty that was threatened in the 1960s by developers who wanted to dot the landscape with dwellings.

Fortunately, Orange County purchased the property in 1972, ensuring that present and future generations can enjoy the old Comfort Hills. You too can take comfort in Winding Hills—just be sure to keep a sharp eye out for those access signs on Route 17K, and don't judge the book by its cover!

11 THE DUTCH GARDEN

A HALF-DOZEN MILES northeast of Monsey Glen, there is another parkland treasure hidden away in the center of Rockland County's bustling New City. It is there, masked by the modern cubes of concrete and steel, that the Dutch Garden poignantly commemorates the past and one woman's dream of preserving it.

Although it's been there since the 1930s, not many Hudson Valley dwellers are aware of its existence. And even those who do know about the Dutch Garden may have a hard time finding it the first time they try, unless they keep an eye out for the remains of a red-brick wall in back of the New City Courthouse. (There is also a rough footpath leading to the Dutch Garden from the parking lot behind the post office, just south of the courthouse.)

Nor is the approach to the Dutch Garden especially inviting. Vandalized brick bordered by unchecked underbrush gives the impression of an abandoned estate on which you are trespassing. But don't be deterred: the park is public, and once you are past its perimeter, the interior of the Dutch Garden is a visual treat.

Thanks to a local garden club, the flower beds are maintained, though today they only hint at the horticultural magnificence that earned this spot first prize in a nationwide contest for the 1934 Garden of the Year. That past honor is briefly recorded on a bronze

78

plaque at the north entrance of the Dutch Garden, where a now-crumbling set of curved steps leads up to an intricately bricked teahouse.

The teahouse bricks themselves offer a history lesson to the observant visitor. Nearby Haverstraw, with its massive deposits of clay conveniently contained in the hills abutting the Hudson, was for many years a leading producer of brick. To distinguish their product from those of the dozens of other companies in operation, manufacturers would mark their bricks, usually with initials. And if you look closely enough around the Dutch Garden, you supposedly can find bricks bearing fifty different trademarks.

This wide-ranging representation of Haverstraw's once-thriving industry was no accident. For in addition to commemorating the county's early settlers with the kind of garden the Dutch planted, the park's designer wished to portray other aspects of Rockland's development. Thus, as visitors explore the teahouse, they are confronted with an amazing and often amusing assortment of symbols.

Peter Stuyvesant is represented, as is Henry Hudson's ship the *Half Moon,* along with an Indian, a windmill, a river sloop, the Ramapos—even Popeye and Betty Boop!

Why these cartoon characters? Probably because they were so popular at the time the Dutch Garden was being built, and the chief mason (evidently a man of humor as well as skill) faithfully followed his orders to record the present along with the past. He even included the Colonial female figures that were the trademarks of Old Dutch cleanser and Baker's cocoa.

Some visitors might regard these commercials as being at odds with the more formal carvings found on the teahouse walls: roses and lilacs, along with the Dutch word *bescischap* (meaning "progress") inscribed over the fireplace, or even an unidentified gargoyle-like face terminating one of the doorway arches. But the overall effect is actually cohesive: like a local library with divers titles, the teahouse carvings are a collection of different topics, all of which relate in some way to Rockland County.

The garden itself stretches south from the porch of the teahouse, forming a long rectangle of several large flower beds interspersed by walks and bordered on one side by the remains of a latticework wall of almost unbelievable delicacy. This wall was considered a marvel of masonry when it was completed by a Garnerville mason named Biagio Gugliuzzo. Other masons had scoffed at Gugliuzzo's plans, saying the wall was much too delicate to stand. But stand it did—that is, until vandals accomplished what natural forces could not.

For some reason—perhaps because of its singularity and secluded setting—the Dutch Garden has been a particularly favored target of vandals, who have battered down many of the brick structures that once provided pleasant retreats for strollers. But enough remains—including a pavilion and an arbor, plus a quaint table-and-bench grouping—to testify to the talent and tenacity of the remarkable Rockland woman who turned a drab back lot into a colorful commemorative.

Mary Mowbray-Clarke was already something of a local legend when, in 1928, at the age of fifty-four, she went to work as a landscape architect and consultant for the Rockland County Board of Supervisors. She was a bit of a bohemian, and her stone studio, called the Brocken, had long been a gathering place for fellow painters, writers, and the politically disenchanted, who were welcome to stay in a quartet of lean-tos that she and her husband had constructed on their old farm off South Mountain Road near Nyack.

Mary Mowbray-Clarke was well known in New York City, too, where her Sunwise Turn shop on Forty-fourth Street not only sold books but also served as a publishing and publicity center for avant-garde artists in the post–World War I period. The bookshop—never very successful in financial terms—did not last long after that (nor did Mary's marriage). But the mistress of Brocken remained the visionary she had always been.

It has been said that only Mary Mowbray-Clarke could have created the Dutch Garden, which began as a WPA project during the darkest days of the Great Depression, when the present was too forlorn for many people to envision future beauty. Mary, however, could and did—and she was willing to work harder than any hod carrier to accomplish her goal.

An example of this was the "chauffeur service" she initiated when she found out that Biagio Gugliuzzo did not own a car and had no other means of regular transportation to New City. Mary was determined to have this master mason assist her in building the Dutch Garden, so each workday morning for eighteen months she drove up to Garnerville to pick up Gugliuzzo and bring him to New City, then took him home in the evening. She was also the one who stood behind his plan for the latticework wall when his fellow masons scoffed at the design.

There were other problems as well, not the least of which was the resentment some of the workers showed over a woman giving them orders. In time, the unintimidated Mary managed to win them over, just as she was able to convince government officials to allot the funds she needed, and by 1934 the Dutch Garden had become a reality.

Framed and defined by rich red brick, the beds of tulips, herbs, and roses were complemented by flowering shrubs set amidst Himalayan pines and lilac bushes—a carefully planned profusion of plants that proved Mary Mowbray-Clarke to be as fine a landscape architect as she was an artist and teacher. And as soon as it was opened to the public, the Dutch Garden became one of the most popular outdoor places in the whole Hudson Valley.

It became even more popular in 1934, when it received the award for Garden of the Year. Out of 1,500 entries, the Dutch Garden won first place in the nationwide contest held by *Better Homes and Gardens* magazine, which, in its May 1935 issue, ran an article about Mary Mowbray-Clarke and her dedication to beautification and preservation projects.

It was also around this time that President Franklin Roosevelt's wife Eleanor made a special trip just to see the Dutch Garden—an imprimatur that, it might be thought, would have helped assure lasting fame for the site.

Public fancy is fickle, though. The flocks of visitors became fewer as time went on, and desuetude—combined with a lack of funds for maintenance—invited deterioration.

This went on for nearly three decades, until 1964, when the local Chamber of Commerce joined forces with the New City Garden Club to restore and maintain the Dutch Garden. Then, in 1968, the property became part of a county park encompassing the adjacent Demarest Kill picnic grove and historic mill site (reachable by a path at the western edge of the garden), adding the attraction of a streamside ramble to the more formal features found within the Dutch Garden itself.

Unfortunately, Mary Mowbray-Clarke did not live to see the refurbishing of her beloved garden; she died at the age of eighty-eight, two years before the restoration began. But her spirit still pervades this lovely place, especially during May and June, when the many varieties of lilacs are in bloom and their heady fragrance fills the air. If there is a breeze coming off the Demarest Kill, the thickly clustered lilac blooms, so heavy that they bend their branches, will bob gently—almost as if Mary Mowbray-Clarke is nodding her approval.

12 CLIMBING THE INDIAN LADDER TRAIL

HAVE YOU EVER heard of the Helderbergs? A surprising number of New Yorkers haven't, even though this range of limestone hills overlooking Albany are in many ways the most remarkable of all the mountains that bracket the Hudson Valley. The Helderbergs are a geological wonderland. Their unique properties have wooed scientists and spelunkers for two centuries, while their hidden recesses and soaring heights have been the setting for some of the region's most dramatic scenes, both historic and aesthetic.

It was in recognition of aesthetics that the Helderbergs were named; "clear mountain" is a loose translation, but one that aptly describes the view from their summits. From the eastern escarpment, Albany looks like Lilliput. And thanks to a philanthropic former mayor of that city, the breathtaking cliffside and part of the upper plateau are now public property—the little-known but unforgettable John Boyd Thacher State Park.

Born in 1847, John Boyd Thacher is best remembered as one of New York's most public-minded officials. He served as a state senator from 1884 to 1885, then was twice elected mayor of Albany. But Thacher was a scholar, too, and his love of natural history prompted him to make sure the property he owned in the Helderbergs would be preserved as a park that future generations could enjoy.

Over the years, Thacher's original gift of 350 acres—presented to
New York by his widow, Grace Treadwell Thacher—was added to by
state purchases of adjoining lands, so that now the park covers nearly
1,700 acres.

The chief feature of the park is its Indian Ladder Trail, which
follows the contour of the cliff midway down its eroded face of
multilayered limestone. Sturdy stone steps now allow travelers to
scale the escarpment, but there once was an actual Indian ladder that
was the only route. As the nineteenth-century historian Verplanck
Colvin reported: "In 1710, this Helderberg region was a wilderness;
nay all westward of the Hudson River settlement was unknown.
Albany was a frontier town, a trading post, a place where annuities
were paid, and blankets exchanged with Indians for beaver pelts.
From Albany over the sand plains... led an Indian trail westward.
Straight as the wild bee or the crow the wild Indian made his course
from the white man's settlement to his own home in the beauteous
Schoharie Valley. The stern cliffs of these hills opposed his progress;
his hatchet fells a tree against them, the stumps of the branches
which he trimmed away formed the round of the Indian Ladder."

At the time Colvin wrote this, in 1869, a regular road had
replaced the Indian trail, slanting steeply upward at the spot where
the old tree-trunk ladder had stood. But the road, too, was done
away with after the park was established in 1914, and visitors now
have a much better view of the escarpment's more distant past.

That past dates back millions of years, to the Paleozoic Era, when
a shallow sea covered the surrounding area and layers of sediment
containing an abundance of marine life were gradually accumulating
on the sea bottom. In time, the land was uplifted and the sea drained
away, leaving behind a plateau that was subjected to eons of erosion.
Water wearing away softer rock beneath overlying layers of limestone caused large blocks to fall from the top of the plateau, so that
its face (or escarpment) gradually "retreated" from just south of the
Adirondacks to its current location outside of Albany. Meanwhile,
over the millennia, water filtering down through cracks and fissures
in the surface of the plateau honeycombed the interior with caves
that would one day provide refuge for an assortment of fugitives.

A plaque attached to the escarpment face near the bottom of the first flight of stone steps lists the many scientists, both European and American, whose pioneering researches in the Helderbergs resulted in what is known as the American school of stratigraphy. You don't have to be a geologist, however, to appreciate why early nineteenth-century scientists considered the Helderberg escarpment to be "classic ground" for anyone studying stratigraphy (the arrangement of rocks in layers or strata).

Nor will fossil fanciers need to be told that the Helderberg plateau is "one of the richest fossil-bearing formations in the world." One needs only to look at the ancient shells embedded in the dense Coeymans limestone that forms the uppermost portion of the escarpment. Beneath this overhanging ledge, at the base of the steps, can be seen a softer type of limestone known as the Manlius formation, which is also studded with the remains of marine life—from fossils that look much like modern-day mussels to sharp-pointed icicle-shaped shells. Both the Manlius and Coeymans formations are made up of multiple layers ("ribbon limestone") averaging from 1 to 3 inches thick and varying in color, which makes for a pleasant pattern, especially when the morning sun strikes it. The names of the formations, it should be noted, come from the places where they were first identified: Manlius is a small town in Onondaga County, and Coeymans is closer by in Albany County.

Between the Coeymans and Manlius formations is a band of softer waterlime that has eroded away to form a ledge known as the Upper Bear Path—though it is unlikely any bear would brave the uneven narrow walkway, which is also off-limits to the public. Instead, walkers along the Indian Ladder Trail follow a wider ledge farther down the escarpment face. This is called the Lower Bear Path, and it is only from this vantage point that the escarpment's many features can be seen close up.

It is much like walking around the inner side of a huge bowl, although this isn't immediately apparent to first-timers awed by the rugged rock wall looming high above them. Huge vertical fissures bisect the horizontal limestone layers, making it appear as if the overhanging rocks are on the point of falling—a spine-tingling speculation that gains strength if one looks down from the opposite edge of the path, where untold centuries of tumbled rock have

formed a steep talus slope. But park rangers carefully check the
stability of the escarpment's face before opening the Indian Ladder
Trail each season, and visitors can be sure of their safety even when
venturing into one of the fissures accessible from the perimeter of
the path.

Fenced-off areas should be respected, however, including Tory
Cave. The entrance can be seen at the base of the Manlius formation
about midway along the path. One of the many springs in the
sieve-like limestone issues from the 25-foot-wide entrance to this
cave, which in days gone by was also known as Tory's Hole or the
Tory House because it was the reputed meeting place of local
Loyalists during the Revolution. This tradition is backed up by the
fact that a British spy named John Salisbury was apprehended here in
1777. Had he not lit a campfire, Salisbury might well have eluded
capture, for the cave entrance is not visible from the top of the
escarpment. But smoke from Salisbury's fire filtered up through one
of the natural chimneys in the overlying rock, alerting pursuing
patriots to his presence.

The cave itself is shallow and otherwise unremarkable, except for
a fragment of latter-day lore that credits it with being the inspiration
for "the first man-made snowstorm in history." According to the late
author-spelunker Clay Perry, artificial snow was invented in 1946 by
Vincent J. Schaefer, who, after viewing ice stalagmites in Tory Cave,
proceeded to seed a cloud with dry ice, inducing snow to fall over
Mount Greylock, in Massachusetts.

Nearby Fool's Cave is simply that: a long (1,000-foot) but confin-
ing mud-filled corridor that only a fool would want to crawl through.
Its chief value is as an example of the way most of the water from
surface streams courses through the interior of the Helderberg
plateau, issuing at the base of the escarpment, rather than washing
over the edge of the precipice. Still, there are two small but lovely
waterfalls that can be seen along the Indian Ladder Trail: Mine Lot
and Outlet.

Together, the creeks feeding these falls carved out the amphitheater-
like curve (embayment) in the escarpment, though this is hard to
conceive of, considering the paucity of the present-day flow. In fact,
Outlet Creek is often dry by midsummer, but visitors can see its bed

after they climb up from the Indian Ladder Trail and follow the park path along the rim of the Helderberg plateau. It is from there that the full scope of the escarpment can be appreciated, along with far-ranging views of the Adirondack foothills, Vermont's Green Mountains, and the Berkshires of Massachusetts.

The hills closer at hand are once again richly forested, after being denuded of most of their trees during the centuries preceding the establishment of the park. And a well-marked nature trail now offers an instructive look at the complexities of this forest community, including trees and shrubs used by the Indians for medicine and food. There is even a sign pointing out sapwood rot—a fungus that destroys birch trees but was put to good use by Indians and early settlers, who collected it for carrying fire from one place to another (hence its other name, "tinder fungus").

The nature trail (only one of several rewarding footpaths through the park) begins near the Paint Mine picnic site, called that because of a local tradition that Indians made paint or dye by burning certain rocks found in that section. Although no tangible evidence has ever been unearthed to support this story, the names of other parts of the park are based on documented sources and together form a capsule account of the area's history following the arrival of European settlers in the late seventeenth century.

For instance, Stone Lot and Mine Lot refer to the time when Helderberg rock was quarried for building material, as well as burned in an on-site kiln for its lime content. Knowles Flat and LaGrange Bush refer to past property owners, with Hop Field and Pear Orchard recalling the attempts of farmers to till the rocky soil. As for Yellow Rock, that commemorates the day a large portion of the ledge slid down into the valley below, revealing a fresh mustard-colored rock face. (Helderberg limestone is more commonly dark blue when cracked open.)

But of all the evocative place names in John Boyd Thacher State Park, that of Hailes' Cave is the most significant for anyone at all interested in the spelean history of the Helderbergs. For although Hailes' Cave is not as large or as complex as some other caverns in these honeycombed hills, it represents a long-gone era when speleology was in its infancy and intrepid individuals explored caves with only a flickering lantern to light their way.

Such an individual was Theodore C. Hailes, an Albany teacher whose underground investigations during the late 1880s focused worldwide attention on the uniqueness of the Helderbergs. Hailes, however, did not discover the 2,800-foot cavern that now bears his name. Considering its proximity to the Indian ladder, it certainly was known about by early settlers, if not native Americans, and reputedly it served as a hideout for rebellious tenant farmers during the Anti-Rent War of the mid-1880s. At that time it was called Helmus Pitcher's Cave; later this was changed to Sutphen's, then Thacher's Cave when it became the property of John Boyd Thacher.

Unfortunately, park officials have deemed it necessary to prohibit visitors from entering Hailes' Cave, and even the trail leading up to it is off-limits. There are some dangerous conditions, which include flooded passages and slippery ledges that in the past cost at least one person her life. And park officials are well aware of the incident in 1933 when a group of college students got lost in the cave and remained there until a rescue party found them the next day. But it is possible that at some time in the future a portion of Hailes' Cave will be reopened, since it is so symbolic of the vast underground honeycomb of the Helderbergs.

In the meantime, visitors to the park are welcome to climb the historic Indian Ladder Trail, as well as to walk the rim of the escarpment or to wander the woodland paths of the plateau top— and that is an enriching enough experience to make any Helderberg visit one of the most memorable outdoor trips you've ever taken.

13 GOOSEPOND:

AN UNREMARKABLE MOUNTAIN, A REMARKABLE STATE PARK

FOR MOST MOTORISTS zipping along Route 17 between the Orange County towns of Monroe and Chester, Goosepond Mountain is merely an unremarkable profile against the southern sky. And even those who are aware of its status as a state park are not apt to stop there, since few realize the extent of this undeveloped area—ranging from mountain to marshland to meadow—or know of its many attractions, including a rich history replete with at least one unsolved mystery.

Goosepond Mountain is one of the lesser-known public lands administered by the Palisades Interstate Park Commission, partly because of its relative newness. The property was acquired between August 1962 and March 1964, when New York State bought up one parcel of land after another along a 2-mile, east-west stretch of Route 17M (which parallels Route 17), plus other lots extending nearly 3 miles to the south, for a total of 1,542 acres.

Then, except for a few buildings retained for use by a resident ranger, all structures standing on the new parkland were demolished: old farmhouses on Lazy Hill Road (which is now the main path through the park), as well as the quaint cobble dwellings along Route 17M, including one building that had served as a speakeasy during the days of Prohibition.

Ironically, after all this demolition and displacement of human beings (some of whom had fought the Eminent Domain decree that forced them to sell their homes), there was no development of the land as a public park. Nor are there any plans for doing so in the near future, supposedly because the state lacks the money. Yet this could be a blessing in disguise, for if the park were fully developed, the subsequent increased usage might well disrupt the delicate natural balance that now makes Goosepond a wonderland of wildlife.

Though bear and elk have long since disappeared from the park, a host of other critters still call it home, including deer and smaller animals. The amphibian and reptilian orders are well represented too, but the true bonanza is the bird population.

According to Orange County Community College Biology Professor John P. Tramontano, at least sixty-five species of birds breed in Goosepond Mountain State Park, and another seventy-five species migrate through it in spring and fall. The mountain, of course, was named for the migrating geese that, along with several types of ducks, still visit the area. However, most of them now settle in the marshy area bordering Seely Brook instead of on the mountain itself.

An excellent but unmarked trail that skirts the edge of the marsh can be found just west of the bridge crossing Seely Brook on Route 17M. The trail (actually an abandoned roadway) can be seen through the trees at the edge of the parking area (just a bare-dirt space on the south side of 17M). Within a few hundred feet, the old concrete road comes to an end, but hikers can continue along the woods road curving to the right. From this woods road, other trails ascend the eastern slope of the mountain, where several clearings afford superb views.

Two other primitive parking areas can be found farther west along Route 17M. Both have trails leading up the mountain, but the westernmost one is probably the best traveled and therefore offers the easiest walking. This trail goes past a pond that in earlier days was used both for fishing and ice harvesting, with an earth-covered stone dam that provides a picturesque place for picnicking.

In this sylvan setting, where the only sounds are those of nature, it is difficult to imagine you are just a few minutes away from a busy highway—or, for that matter, from the site of a Goosepond Mountain mystery. It was not far from this pond that, in the 1940s, an eerie discovery was made. In the course of clearing some land, men from a neighboring farm chanced to move a huge boulder. Under one edge they found a pair of ancient handcuffs... with human wrist bones still locked within the rusted iron loops.

Who was the unfortunate person whose manacled hands had been pinned beneath the boulder? Was it murder, or did the boulder accidentally fall on the victim? And why the handcuffs? Was the victim an escaped prisoner? A slave who had been fettered by his master?

No answers have been found, nor was the rest of the skeleton ever recovered. All that is surely known is that the cuffs are hand-made and very old, possibly dating back to Revolutionary War times, when Goosepond provided refuge for the legendary "cowboy" Claudius Smith. ("Cowboy," in those days, meant a guerrilla Loyalist who supplied the British with cattle stolen from the Americans.)

Local tradition says that Claudius Smith used to hide out in a rockshelter on the other side of the marsh—a rockshelter that also has yielded artifacts of the prehistoric Indians who lived there for thousands of years before the first white settler arrived in the area.

Dozens of projectile points—some dating back to 3500 B.C., others believed to be even older—hundreds of pottery sherds, and an assortment of other artifacts and animal bones have been excavat-ed from this ancient Indian village site and are now in the collection of the Trailside History Museum in nearby Bear Mountain State Park. A visit to this small but excellent museum (open daily, year-round, and free of charge) is well worthwhile, since its permanent Indian exhibit features items from several local rockshelters, including the one at Goosepond. Those from Goosepond bear the identifying number "14-0."

A deservedly popular place, the museum at Bear Mountain hosts more than half a million people each year. In contrast, Goosepond Mountain State Park probably is visited by less than one-hundredth that many people and is for that reason ideal for anyone whose main purpose in walking through woods is to get away from the madding crowd. Even the main trail through the park—the now abandoned Lazy Hill Road—is peaceful, with pedestrians few and points of interest plentiful.

The entrance to Lazy Hill Road is on Route 17M, almost directly opposite its junction with Oxford Road. Cars may be parked in the dirt lot across from Lazy Hill Road, which is chained off to prevent vehicles from entering the park—but the chain is not meant to keep out hikers.

To walk the full length of Lazy Hill Road takes over an hour one way if you are traveling at a leisurely pace, but more time should be allowed if you intend to explore any of the many small trails and farm lanes that branch off from the main road.

One short path you surely should take is found on the first slope of the gentle caterpillar-like humps of Lazy Hill, where Orange County Community College began building an astronomical observatory in the early 1970s. Unfortunately, the project was abandoned upon the death of the professor who proposed it, and all that remains is the shell of the observatory "silo."

From this silo, or farther up the hill where the presence of evergreen trees and lilac bushes marks the site of now demolished farmhouses, there is a wide-ranging view of the verdant Chester Valley. As you continue along Lazy Hill Road, however, the distant valley view gives way to one of Goosepond Mountain, rising more than a thousand feet above Seely Brook, which runs a curving course through the marshland at its base.

During the warmer months, myriad wildflowers and mammoth mushrooms are to be seen in these bottomlands, but care should be taken to stay on existing paths, for the deep mud of the marsh can be treacherous.

All along Lazy Hill Road, long lines of stone fences tell a silent story of the labor it took to clear the land for the farms that began there more than two centuries ago. Indeed, this section of Goosepond is like a ghost town, with only rocky reminders of the past: a set of carefully curved steps, flanked by pillars constructed of river cobbles, which lead to a nonexistent house; an old kiln, its drystone inner walls encrusted with burned lime, standing alone in a now fallow field; the ruins of a stone-lined spring, where the water still runs cool and clear....

As might be expected in any area that has known continuous human habitation for over 5,000 years, legends abound in Goosepond.

Not far from where Booth Road meets Lazy Hill, there is an old house where treasure supposedly was buried in the yard during the tumultuous time of the Revolution. And there is still the mystery of where Claudius Smith hid some of the silver he is said to have stolen—though that treasure, if it exists, could be anywhere in the Ramapos, since Smith had hideouts throughout the region.

There is also the story of a cave somewhere in the park where old burlap bags were found hanging across the entrance—a cave the Revolutionary "cowboy" might have used, in addition to the aforementioned Indian rockshelter. No one seems to know the exact location of that cave or even if it still exists, but a likely spot would be among the fractured rocks high on the eastern flank of Goosepond Mountain (best seen from the southern section of Lazy Hill Road).

Anyone interested in such sites should be aware of two things: first, poisonous copperheads are common in the less-traveled, rocky parts of the park, and second, it is against the law to deface or in any other way damage state park property—and that includes dumping debris and digging for Indian artifacts or treasure. In other words, leave nothing behind but footprints; take nothing but pictures.

Admittedly, whatever pictures you do take of the mountain itself are apt to be lacking in dramatic appeal, for Goosepond presents, as mentioned before, a rather unimpressive profile from afar. But for nature lovers and history buffs, that unremarkable profile is the symbol of a remarkable state park.

14 THE PLEASURES OF "PARKING" IN SARATOGA SPRINGS

MENTION SARATOGA SPRINGS to most folks and you evoke the image of sleek horses on a picturesque racetrack, or the mammoth marble bathhouses that once made this literally sparkling community a world-famous spa. As for aficionados of Victorian architecture, the preponderance of well-preserved old buildings is a never-ending delight, while the academic-minded are sure to think of the sylvan campus of Skidmore College on the north end of the broad concourse bisecting the city.

But Saratoga Springs is a paradise for park lovers, too—something that is not so widely publicized as its other attractions and therefore easily overlooked by out-of-towners unfamiliar with the area.

Mineral springs are, of course, what made the city famous, and tracking down those that still spout can be an enlightening adventure, leading from mini-parks like the one on High Rock Avenue to the massive Saratoga Spa State Reservation.

Local legend credits Sir William Johnson, Superintendent of Indian Affairs in the Mohawk Valley, as being the first white man to drink from a Saratoga spring. Suffering from an old war wound and other ailments, Johnson reportedly was led there in the late 1760s by Indians, who for untold centuries had considered the waters of High Rock Spring to be curative.

Whether or not Johnson was helped, he lived for nearly a decade after his visit to the tall cone of rock built up by sediment in the mineral-laden spring, and word spread of the Indians' restorative waters. Eventually more than forty different springs were discovered, and by the late 1800s, people were flocking to Saratoga to take the cure.

Since that Victorian term "the cure" is at best a broad one, perhaps this is a good place to describe what Saratoga's famous springs are—and aren't. First of all, no two springs are exactly alike, although all are naturally carbonated. Mineral content and concentration vary, as do taste and smell, but the springs can be divided into two general categories: alkaline (which is soothing to the digestive tract) and saline (containing a high percentage of mineral salts).

Newcomers to Saratoga should be wary of imbibing too freely of the saline kind, lest they wind up with a case of minerally motivated "turista." A word to the wise: Old Hathorn fountain, at the corner of Spring and Putnam Streets, has the most saline water of all. A less potent and more potable drink can be had at the Peerless public fountain, just off Circular Street, north of Lake Avenue.

Of course, Saratoga's famous waters are for external use, too, and visitors might like to stop by Big Red Spring on the grounds of the racetrack, where the city's first bathhouse was built, in 1784. Claims were made that Big Red's waters could cure a variety of ailments, from arthritis to acne. But while such claims remain just that, there is no doubt that skin disorders and aching bones often are relieved—if only temporarily—by immersion in the city's effervescent springs.

These natural bubble baths are great tension relievers, too, and for anyone who has the time, a 90-minute respite (incorporating private bath, massage, and rest between hot sheets) at one of the state-run bathhouses can be better than a bottle of tranquilizers—and a whole lot healthier and cheaper! The baths are great for weary feet as well, so park explorers might like to plan such a therapeutic session as a finale to their woodland tours.

Although certainly not a woodland in the strict sense of the word, 20-acre Congress Park is a great place to start exploring, since it offers an overall introduction to Saratoga Springs. The park is bounded by Broadway, Spring Street, and Circular Street, and its pillared white pavilion shades the sparkling spring that is credited with bringing worldwide renown to Saratoga.

There is an old joke that Congress Spring was so named because it had an "unpleasant effect upon the system similar to that produced by reading Congress speeches." But the name actually goes back to the year 1792, when U.S. Congressman Nicholas Gilman was on a hunting expedition in the wilderness of Saratoga. When the congressman came across some water spouting from the ground, a local boy became so excited that he ran back home shouting, "The Congress found a spring!" The boy's abbreviation of Gilman's title stuck, and from then on the spring was known as the Congress.

The site was not fully developed, however, until 1826, when John Clarke purchased it and began shipping bottled "Congress Water" all over the country. In addition to his bottling plant, Clarke also constructed a pavilion at which the public could drink all the water they wanted for a penny. The cent was for the services of "dipper boys," all of whom were dressed in Sunday suits!

That "Golden Age" of Saratoga is still evident in the solidly handsome structure known as the Casino, just across the greensward from Congress Spring. It was built by world champion prizefighter John Morrissey and once catered to the gaming instincts of society's elite, but it is now the home of the Historical Society of Saratoga Springs, with exhibits pertaining to all aspects of the city's colorful past.

For those who enjoy formal gardens, there is the Canfield Fountain and the Italian Garden adjacent to the Casino. Meanwhile, on the other side of the park, the Trask Fountain provides a lovely place to sit on summer afternoons when the rectangular reflecting pool emphasizes the graceful lines of a bronze statue created by Daniel Chester French in honor of Spencer Trask.

Although Spencer Trask is best known for his association with the nearby artist's retreat of Yaddo, he also was prominent in preserving Saratoga's once-threatened springs. At the turn of the century, carbonic acid gas companies were rapidly drilling wells to pump out the naturally carbonated water, from which carbon dioxide could be inexpensively extracted for use in soft drinks and for other industrial purposes. And as the pumping increased, the level of underground water decreased, until concerned citizens mounted a campaign to halt what they viewed as the inevitable destruction of Saratoga's greatest resource.

Fortunately, their campaign was successful. Most of the springs eventually were put under state protection, and the 2,000-acre Saratoga Spa Reservation was established in 1909.

Before talking a word-walk through that park, however, we should return a moment to the aforementioned Spencer Trask, whose Yaddo estate lies along Union Avenue. The majority of the estate is private, but the formal gardens are open year-round to the public and are well worth a visit.

The grounds bordering the roads through Saratoga Spa Reservation are equally well kept but less formal. Several magnificent old bathhouses are located here, along with the handsome Gideon Putnam Hotel, plus picnic areas, swimming pools, an eighteen-hole golf course, and several roadside fountains with signs describing the type of mineral water they offer. A network of pleasant footpaths meander through the forested areas, and a main trail along the Vale of Springs should not be missed.

The Vale of Springs is located where the park road crosses Geyser Creek, next to a stone well containing Hayes Spring. Cut into the side of the well is a "breathing port"—but be careful how deep you sniff or quaff, for the smell is as strong as the heavily saline water.

A few hundred feet down the trail past Hayes Spring is a midstream island looking much like a flattened rock mushroom, which was built up by minerals in the geyser spouting out of the top. You are welcome to walk over to the island, but caution should be taken, for the carbonated waters leave a slightly oil-like film on the rock (on skin, too), and a misstep can land you in the creek.

Many people turn back at this point, thinking that the geyser is the Vale's main attraction. The most spectacular feature, however, occurs farther down the trail, where a multicolored mound of moist rock, called Orenda Terrace, covers one side of the Vale. It is a continually growing curtain of tufa deposited by the mineral-laden waters of Orenda Spring spilling down from high above.

For sightseers who might like to do some freshwater swimming or fishing, Saratoga Lake (situated southeast of the city proper, along Route 9P) is a scenic spot with two separate parks: Brown's Beach on the eastern shore, and Kaydeross on the western side, the latter containing a kid-pleasing collection of amusements.

Considering the many park pleasures to be found within Saratoga Springs, it might seem superfluous to add a few others that are further afield. But there are three other parks only a short drive from the city that are decidedly different from all the others, and it would be a disservice not to describe them.

The most extensive is Saratoga National Historical Park, which lies along the heights of the Hudson southeast of Saratoga Springs. In keeping with the standard of excellence for which properties administered by the National Park Service are justly known, this site of the 1777 Battle of Saratoga provides an unforgettable lesson in the history of our country. Actually, there were two battles: one at the Freeman Farm on September 19, and the second at Bemis Heights on October 7. Both sites are incorporated in the park.

Were it not for Saratoga and the defeat of British General "Gentleman Johnny" Burgoyne, the American fight for independence might well have lasted considerably longer or even been lost altogether. For it was the victory at Saratoga that provided a much-needed morale booster and convinced the French to support the cause of the colonists.

Saratoga is also the place where the eventual traitor Benedict Arnold performed heroically and was wounded by a musket ball in his leg. And near the Breymann Redoubt, within the park, can be found what is surely one of the most unusual military monuments ever erected: on a thick slab of stone is carved the replica of a boot, in honor of Arnold's injury.

A complete tour of the park takes about four hours by car, allowing for stops along the 9-mile circuit road, but it is certainly worth the time spent. Each of the ten main sites is furnished with interpretive signs and audio boxes. Wooden stakes painted blue for Americans or red for British also mark the soldiers' positions at various points. The scenery is magnificent, especially at Bemis Heights.

Those who do not have time for a complete tour of Saratoga National Historical Park can still enjoy the excellent exhibits in the

Visitor's Center (just off Route 32), which also offers a short film describing the conflict.

Fossils, rather than battlefields, are the main feature of the two other parks near Saratoga Springs that provide a unique experience for lovers of the outdoors. Both are located west of the city on Route 29, where a road leading north points the way to the Petrified Sea Gardens, a National Natural Registered Landmark.

The property is part of an underwater reef that was formed 500 million years ago, with the now exposed ledges covered by huge cryptozoon plant fossils, locally known as "stone cabbages." There also are such geological points of interest as glacial crevices and potholes, while the rest of the park has a miscellany of attractions, including an outdoor museum devoted exclusively to sun dials.

The Petrified Sea Gardens are usually open daily during summer, but if you arrive there to find the gates closed, all is not lost. Just drive a little farther along the road, where Lester Park is open to the public year-round, free of charge. Be careful, though: it's easy to pass right by Lester Park. Keep an eye out for the marker on the east side of the road which points to a layer of stone cabbages.

After viewing these examples of ancient algae, look across the road, where a footpath leads up a stony bank to an opening in the trees bordering the top. This path leads through an old quarry and along the edge of an exposure of Hoyt limestone, with enlightening if somewhat eroded markers describing this Upper Cambrian formation that contains smaller cryptozoon fossils and occasional fragments of trilobites.

Needless to say, Lester Park may be more for fossil fanciers than the general public. But with the variety of outdoor attractions in and around Saratoga Springs, there are certainly parks aplenty for people of all tastes and ages.

III

OTHER
PLACES

15 MAYA-ON-HUDSON

ONE OF THE Hudson's most unusual landmarks lies on a tiny island off the shore of northern Dutchess County, where the stubs of dark stone arches are all that remain of a pocket of Mayan culture that once dominated the scene.

Mayans on the Hudson? No, that ancient Mesoamerican civilization never extended this far north. But for seven decades, starting in the mid-1800s, a sampling of its exquisite sculpture stood on South Cruger Island—a silent monument to one of the world's greatest explorers, and the tragic termination of his most cherished dream.

That man was John Lloyd Stephens, who might have lived out his life as a New York City lawyer and politician were it not for a quirk of fate. Stephens was only twenty-nine years old in 1834, when he was stricken with a severe throat infection that did not respond to conventional treatment. Convinced that his condition was being exacerbated by long hours of speech making, doctors advised Stephens to take an extended European vacation.

If Stephens' doctors thought travel meant rest and relaxation to this handsome bachelor, they were wrong. Instead of a slow-paced round of spas, sightseeing, and soirées in "civilized" Europe, Stephens included some out-of-the-way places that were as dangerous as they were physically demanding. He was, for instance, the first American to visit the ancient and abandoned city of Petra in the rockbound wilderness of southwest Jordan—a journey that required him, for safety's sake, to go disguised as a Turkish merchant. Then a debilitating bout with dysentery halted his wandering, and in 1836 Stephens headed home.

During his two-year absence from New York City, Stephens had corresponded with Charles Fenno Hoffman, who printed the richly detailed letters in his *American Monthly Magazine,* despite Stephens' insistence that he was not writing them for publication. To preserve his friend's anonymity, Hoffman gave each letter the byline "An American Traveler." Still, the author's identity did not remain a secret for very long, and Stephens arrived home to find himself launched on a new career—that of a travel writer.

His first book, *Incidents of Travel in Egypt, Arabia, Petraea, and the Holy Land,* appeared in 1837 and met with immediate success. That success was spurred, to great extent, by a 12-page paean in the *New-York Review* written by none other than Edgar Allan Poe, who capped his praises of Stephens by saying, "We hope it is not the last time we shall hear from him."

Indeed, it wasn't. A year later, Stephens published *Incidents of Travel in Greece, Turkey, Russia and Poland* (a deadly title, perhaps, but a delightful narrative), and his place among New York's literati was assured.

Meanwhile, the artist-architect Frederick Catherwood had moved to New York from London and established a public exhibit called the Panorama at Broadway and Prince Street, only a short distance from Stephens' home on LeRoy Street. The gallery opened with a showing of Catherwood's painstakingly precise depiction of Jerusalem—only one of several panoramas of ancient cities that the talented young artist created after a decade of on-site study in the Mediterranean and Middle East.

Catherwood had met John Lloyd Stephens during the latter's trip abroad, so it was only natural that the two like-minded men promptly renewed their acquaintance. It was a friendship that lasted a lifetime and, in the process, drastically altered archeological attitudes about Mesoamerica.

His research into ancient Mayan ruins might never have happened had it not been for a rebuff Stephens received in 1839. Still active in politics, Stephens had worked with Governor William Seward in convincing the State Legislature to appropriate funds for gathering up early New York records then housed in Holland. Stephens had hoped to be given this prestigious mission, but the Legislature appointed J. R. Brodhead instead.

Disappointed but undaunted, Stephens convinced Catherwood to accompany him to Central America in search of the ruined cities they had read about in sketchy reports of earlier explorers. Before their departure in October 1839, word arrived that the United States Ambassador in Central America had died, so Stephens applied to President Van Buren for the post, figuring he could combine diplomatic duties with his personal search into the distant past. Van Buren obviously thought so too, and promptly gave Stephens the position.

One job proved to be as dangerous as the other, for Central America was in a turmoil of civil strife, and Stephens had as much trouble tracking down heads of government as he did in finding the ancient stone structures rumored to be hidden deep within the dense forests and jungles of the disease-ridden land. Amazingly, he accomplished both goals, though not without paying a terrible toll.

Repeatedly, Stephens and Catherwood were felled by agonizing ailments; the dampness so crippled Catherwood with rheumatism that at times he could not draw the spectacular structures they came across. On another occasion, Stephens woke up to find both his feet horribly swollen from insects that had burrowed beneath his toenails. And there were always the intestinal problems caused by poor food and water, plus the health-sapping heat. But worst of all was the ever-present anopheles mosquito, which brought on recurrent attacks of malaria—the disease from which Stephens eventually died at the age of forty-seven.

The perseverance of Stephens and Catherwood was as monumental as their work, which took them from Palenque, in Mexico, to the ruined city of Copán, in Honduras, then on to Uxmal, on the Yucatán peninsula, and dozens of points in between. While Catherwood sketched each site, Stephens busied himself examining and measuring the ruins, taking careful notes for the detailed descriptions he would record every night, along with the varied adventures that befell them.

One of the more fortuitous of these adventures was a chance meeting in Mexico with a young traveler who hailed from—of all places—the Dutchess County town of Rhinebeck. Though untrained in archeology, Henry Pawling was excited by the idea of discovering lost civilizations and immediately offered to help his fellow New Yorkers with their work.

It was Pawling who labored long hours in making thirty plaster casts of carvings at Palenque, only to have them smashed by local inhabitants who resented the presence of the foreigners. The destruction of those casts sorely disappointed Stephens, who dreamed of building a museum to house all the relics he planned to bring back to New York. In fact, he already had raised $20,000 for his proposed Museum of American Antiquities and was counting on his next book to encourage even more financial backing.

He began work on that book as soon as he and Catherwood reached New York on July 31, 1840, following a near-fatal voyage aboard a sailing ship that became becalmed (a New York-bound sloop rescued them). *Incidents of Travel in Central America, Chiapas and Yucatan* appeared the following summer—a quick-paced, engaging narrative covering every aspect of Stephens' year-long adventure, from cholera, cockfights, and mind-boggling carvings, to his purchase of the ancient city of Copán for a mere $50.

"Perhaps the most interesting book of travel ever published," was the way Edgar Allan Poe described it in a review for *Graham's Magazine*, and the public concurred, making Stephens one of the most widely read writers of his day.

Stephens, however, wasted no time basking in the limelight. Current thinking was that any ancient ruin in the New World had some Old World origin (Roman, Egyptian, Phoenician, etc.), but now Stephens wasn't so sure that theory was correct. And so when Secretary of State Daniel Webster offered him a diplomatic post in Mexico, Stephens refused. He and Catherwood wanted to go back to Yucatán, and they did in October 1841.

On their earlier journey, they had stayed only briefly at the Mayan ruins of Uxmal. This time they studied the structures thoroughly, while selecting examples of artwork, including an unusual carved lintel made of sapote wood, to be carefully wrapped, then carted to the coast by Indian porters, and from there shipped by boat to New York City. The items would then be exhibited in Catherwood's Panorama, since Stephens' own Museum of American Antiquities was still but a dream.

On this trip they visited more than forty ruined cities in Yucatán before returning home in June 1842 with a treasure trove of Mayan artifacts. These, too, were placed on exhibit in Catherwood's Panorama.

One month later, on the night of July 31, 1842, a devastating fire swept through the Panorama. The Mayan artifacts, along with Catherwood's paintings, were reduced to ashes—a sight that prompted Stephens to say, "We seem doomed to be in the midst of ruins; but in all our explorations there was none so touching as this."

Though his dream of a Museum of American Antiquities had been destroyed with the irreplaceable items, Stephens forged ahead with his next book, *Incidents of Travel in Yucatan*, for he was anxious to present his own theory on the origin of the ancient architecture. The structures, he stated, were strictly Mesoamerican, the work of a native culture, with no Old World influence whatsoever. It was a startling challenge to the theories of the days, but Stephens was so convincing that his conclusions were generally accepted.

It was also in the Yucatán book that Stephens sadly noted the fire at Catherwood's Panorama, but not the fact that a dozen Mayan sculptures they had collected escaped the conflagration. These lime-stone carvings (including two massive doorjambs, a feather-plumed death's-head, and a Mayan bust atop an intricately incised, drum-shaped seat) had been delayed in transit and thus missed being part of the Panorama exhibit. The sculptures were too few to build a museum around, so Stephens gave them to an old friend, John Church Cruger, possibly in repayment for Cruger's past patronage.

Cruger's country home was on an island in the Hudson near Annandale, where the heavy sculptures were shipped via river steam-boat. At the south end of Cruger's Island, separated from it by a narrow channel, rose a round, rock-ribbed knob of land. It was this solitary islet that Cruger chose as the setting for the sculptures, and he proceeded to build an arched stone "ruin" to house them.

The combination of pewter-colored Hudson Valley rock and bone-white Yucatán limestone may seem contradictory, but it must be considered in the context of its time. During the mid-nineteenth century, ruins were the rage—a preoccupation with the past spurred, in part, by discoveries such as the Rosetta Stone (the key to hitherto undecipherable Egyptian hieroglyphics), and the Venus de Milo (a second-century B.C. Greek masterpiece found in 1820).

The Hudson Valley reflected this trend, especially along the wealthier eastern shore, where medieval castles were constructed, ancient ruins replicated, and statuary transplanted from Greek and Roman sites. Contemporary artists also were caught up in this "romance of the ruins," including Thomas Cole of the Hudson River School. And it was Cole's 1834 painting "Moonlight" (showing a round stone tower atop a bleak hill) that supposedly influenced Cruger's fanciful framework for the Mayan sculptures. That local tradition is reinforced by another story, which says Cruger used to take houseguests on moonlight cruises to view his "ruins."

It is not known whether John Lloyd Stephens was present on any of those excursions, for his few remaining years of life were spent busily pursuing a multitude of new projects. He was elected to the State Constitutional Convention in 1847 and soon was engaged in building a railroad across the isthmus of Panama—a monumental feat of engineering that contributed to his death. Working in the mosquito-infested jungles, his old enemy, malaria, flared up again. This time his liver became infected, and Stephens died in a coma on October 13, 1852. There were various memorials to him—a steamship named in his honor, a statue in Panama, and a stained-glass window in a Lower Manhattan church—but none as fitting as the Mayan "ruins" on South Cruger Island.

Today, the crumbling stonework may still be seen by boaters during the season of least foliage, but the Mayan sculptures are gone. They were purchased in 1919 by the American Museum of Natural History and shipped back to New York City.

There is an unsubstantiated story that one sculpture was left behind and is now somewhere in the Wappingers Falls area. Possibly this is only wishful thinking. Or perhaps the "leftover" is the same uncarved chunk of limestone recovered by Columbia University students during an archeological investigation of South Cruger Island in the 1960s. But if one of the sculptures does still exist in the region where they first found refuge, perhaps someday it will be rediscovered, thereby adding a welcome footnote to the strange story of "Maya-on-Hudson."

In the meantime, the other sculptures may be viewed at the American Museum of Natural History, where they now grace the second-floor gallery of Mexican and Central American artifacts.

In a way, the dream of John Lloyd Stephens came true after all.

16 OPUS 40

THE ANCIENT SCULPTURES that once adorned South Cruger Island may be long gone from their riverside ruin, but the Mayan touch has not been totally lost to the region. Almost directly across the Hudson, and less than a dozen miles inland, an old Saugerties quarry is the site of a huge environmental sculpture that offers a modern version of Mayan grandeur, with just a hint of déjà vu. It is the work of a single man, Harvey Fite, who labored nearly four decades and ultimately gave his life to achieve a masterpiece covering more than six acres.

He called it, simply, Opus 40.

Like its creator, Opus 40 is a complexity of views and visions, offering an unforgettable experience to all who wend their way westward from the Hudson to the Ulster County hamlet of High Woods.

Although Harvey Fite didn't plan it that way, the approach to High Woods is an excellent introduction to Opus 40. Travelers may take the Glasco Turnpike west from the Mount Marion exit of Route 9W, or Route 212 out of Saugerties (Exit 20 on the New York Thruway). Either way leads past many mementos of the bluestone industry that once flourished in the Catskills. Indeed, it sometimes seems that no other building material was used, for the smooth blue-gray stone is seen in everything from doorsteps to dams, and dozens of abandoned quarries pockmark the rock-fenced hillsides.

Take the time to look at some of these old excavations, with their heaps of tumbled rock thrusting through a tangle of underbrush and scrawny second-growth trees, and you will have some idea of what was facing Harvey Fite when he began turning an overgrown quarry into an environmental sculpture of Mayan proportions.

Keep that picture in mind as you continue to the end of Fite Road, where the trees surrounding the parking lot of Opus 40 prevent any preview of Harvey Fite's long years of labor. From the parking lot, a wooded lane bordered by layers of bluestone leads to what can only be described as a breathtaking experience. For as you emerge from this sylvan corridor, you are suddenly in a wide-open space of meticulously laid stone ramps and stairs, pools and platforms, secluded nooks and subsurface passages. Their gracefully curved lines are independent yet coordinated, all culminating in the focal point of the 6-acre complex—a rough-cut bluestone monolith reaching for the sky.

Most people find it hard to believe that all this is the work of one man; it is even more difficult to conceive of him doing much of it while holding down a full-time teaching position and pursuing a career as a sculptor. But that is exactly what Harvey Fite did, in addition to building a house and studio overlooking his quarry, plus a museum to house tools and other memorabilia of the bluestone industry. And that is why, to fully appreciate Opus 40, you must first appreciate the unique man who created it.

Harvey Fite was born on Christmas Day, 1903. Three years later, his family moved from Pennsylvania to Texas, where Fite spent his boyhood, and in 1923 he entered Houston Law School. The lawyer's life was not for him, though, and eventually he transferred to St. Stephen's College (now Bard) on the banks of the Hudson in northwestern Dutchess County.

Although he had gone to St. Stephen's to study for the ministry, it was theater that Fite found most fascinating, so after three years he left St. Stephen's to join a traveling company of actors.

Fite never lost his love of the theater, but he could not abide the periods of backstage idleness that are part of putting any production together. Therefore, one day, while waiting for a costume fitting, he happened to pick up a dressmaker's discarded wooden spool and began whittling on it just to while away the time. The shaping of that wooden spool shaped the rest of his life as well. Shortly thereafter, Fite quit the theatrical troupe to become a sculptor.

Although at that time he had no formal training (he later studied sculpture for two summers in Italy), Fite's natural talent earned him enough of a reputation within the next few years for Bard College to offer him, in 1933, the job of organizing its new Fine Arts Division. Fite agreed, with the understanding that in addition to establishing a drama department and building a theater there, he could also open a sculpture studio for undergraduates. The arrangement worked out well: Fite remained at Bard for more than thirty years, teaching the history and theory of sculpture in addition to conducting studio classes.

When Fite first became affiliated with Bard, he was still living at the Maverick artists' colony in Woodstock. But in neither place did he have his own studio, so he readily accepted the invitation of fellow artist Tom Penning to work at his studio a few miles from Woodstock, at High Woods. By then, Fite was working in stone as well as wood, and he soon realized one of the area's abandoned bluestone quarries would provide him not only with plenty of space but with an ample supply of excellent raw material.

In May 1938, Harvey Fite purchased the old Benny Myers' quarry, scenically situated on a hill where Overlook Mountain dominates a dramatic backdrop of the purple-blue Catskills.

The first order of business was to build a house and studio along the eastern edge of the quarry, but before Fite could complete these projects, he accepted an assignment from the Carnegie Institute to help restore some Mayan artifacts in the ancient Honduran city of Copán.

A century earlier, explorer John Lloyd Stephens had rediscovered these ruins of the Mayan civilization—something Harvey Fite surely knew about, and which gave his restoration work at Copán an interesting thread of coincidence. For South Cruger Island, where the sculptures brought back by Stephens were first installed, lies just offshore of the Bard College campus in Annandale. Although Fite did not begin teaching at Bard until long after the Stephens sculptures had been removed from the island, it is fairly certain he knew of their existence and he may well have visited the layered stone ruin that had been built to house them there. Fite also may have seen the sculptures on one of his trips to New York City, since the American Museum of Natural History is not far from the Whitney Museum, where one of Fite's own carvings is now in the permanent collection.

As for Copán, Fite's work there took only one winter, but it was enough to reinforce his reverence for Mayan architecture—a reverence that is reflected throughout Opus 40, though Fite did not have that in mind when he began building the complex. In fact, he had formulated no master plan whatsoever when he began clearing his quarry in the spring of 1939.

Initially, Fite was thinking of an outdoor showcase for his large sculptures (now placed around the periphery of the main complex). However, as he worked at fitting together thousands of smooth-sided slabs of the fossilized sedimentary rock called bluestone, the showcase became a giant sculpture in itself.

Except for occasional assists by visiting friends, Fite worked alone, utilizing ancient construction techniques, including a mortarless method for setting stone. This involves the careful placement of large keystones that are supported by smaller slabs so that no cement is needed. The resulting construction can endure a thousand years, as did that of the Maya.

When asked to give his project a name, Fite decided to call it Opus 40, since he felt he had about four decades left in his life when he would be physically capable of working with heavy stone. Yet Opus 40 could conceivably have been continued long after that, for Fite's creative ideas seemed as endless as the massive deposits of bluestone in his quarry.

Sadly, Harvey Fite's work was ended one year short of his 40-year goal. In May 1976, at the age of seventy-two, he was killed in a fall from the quarry wall. Opus 40 therefore remains unfinished, though not in the eyes of the thousands of people who visit the site, exhilarating in its flowing lines and the ever-changing interplay of light and shadow on stone.

Until her own death in October 1987, Fite's widow, Barbara,

worked unceasingly to preserve Opus 40, which is now a not-for-profit corporation, with a cadre of volunteers who serve as guides. The dedication of these guides is one of the things that makes Opus 40 such a special place, for practically every corner has a story of its own, and the guides enthusiastically point out interesting aspects to tourists, augmenting the excellent slide show that is presented on those warm-weather weekends when the site is open to the public.

Visitors are also welcome to tour the gallery displaying some of Harvey Fite's other work, as well as to enjoy the Quarryman's Museum he built to house his collection of tools and other items pertaining to the life of nineteenth-century stoneworkers in the Catskills. Though it covers only a single bare-board upstairs room, this folk museum is one of the finest around. Its floor, walls, and even the rafters are covered with all kinds of domestic and quarry-related implements—from drills and draglines to a leisuretime set of handmade dominoes. Meanwhile, outside the museum, huge chains hang from the weathered eaves, and well-preserved examples of powerful rock-moving machinery share ground space with some small sculptures that reveal Harvey Fite's wry sense of humor and resourcefulness.

Merely reading about it, one may find this miscellany incompatible with the massive Maya-like complex nestled in the nearby quarry, but seeing it shows that everything at Opus 40 has a marvelous way of melding. Such was the magic of the master artist Harvey Fite, who left this great legacy to the Mid-Hudson region.

Long before Route 97 became a paved highway leading west from Port Jervis, this photograph was taken of Hawk's Nest, named for the avian predators that nested there. At the top of the cliff is Lifting Rocks, where Tom Quick and Cahoonzie rained down flaming boulders on a band of Delaware Indians camped below.

Toward the end of his life, the mysterious wanderer known as the Leatherman accepted the gift of a few articles of warm clothing. Prior to that time, his costume consisted solely of rough leather garments he had sewn together with thongs, and which were worn—winter or summer—over bare flesh.

The "Sage of Slabsides," John Burroughs, sat for this family portrait on a summer day at Riverby in the early 1900s. With him is his only son Julian, Julian's wife Emily, and the daughters Elizabeth (with doll) and Ursula. (*This Underwood & Underwood photo courtesy of Elizabeth Burroughs Kelley.*)

Right, a familiar figure in his "ice-cream suit" and shock of white hair, Mark Twain was in his seventies when he began visiting the exclusive Orange County enclave of Tuxedo Park. Shown here in front of the home of one of his Tuxedo Park hosts, Twain was much in demand as a storyteller, and once read passages from *Tom Sawyer* and *Huckleberry Finn* to schoolchildren assembled at the local library.

Below, this cave in Harriman State Park, east of Tuxedo, was the main hideout of Revolutionary War "cowboy" Claudius Smith. An interior tunnel leads to the top of the cliff, where Smith and his band kept watch over the Ramapo Pass.

Much older than the Victorian-age stonework decorating its entrance, Ellenville's Sun-Ray Tunnel is also called the Spanish Mine in recognition of legends that it was excavated either by members of Ponce de Léon's party seeking the Fountain of Youth, or by sixteenth-century gold-seekers from Spain. Several hundred years later, it was developed as an excursion site and its exceptionally pure water bottled for sale across the country. *Below,* among several similarly named and supposedly haunted sites in the region, Rockland County's Spook Rock is distinctive not only because of the efforts that have been made to preserve it, but because of its prominence along what was once a major Indian trail.

Above, an engraving shows Goshen's church of St. John the Evangelist as it looked at the time its legendary first Midnight Mass was celebrated in 1847. (*Photo reproduced by permission of the Cullen family.*)

Left, as affable as he was handsome, wealthy shipping merchant David Crawford so loved his early nineteenth-century mansion on Newburgh's Montgomery Street that it is said he never left there—even after death.

Left, sculptor Harvey Fite single-handedl[y] labored for nearly forty years to turn an abandoned Saugerties quarry into a work [of] art. He is seen here setting a capstone during the early days of Opus 40, when th[e] site was still filled with tons of tumbled bluestone discarded during nineteenth-century quarry operations. *Below,* the foc[us] of Opus 40 is a rough-cut monolith, benea[th] which stretches the massive outdoor sculptu[re] that Harvey Fite created, and which ultimate[ly] caused his death. (*Photos courtesy of Opus 4[0]*)

An old photograph in the Bard College Library collection shows one of the twelve Mayan sculptures given by explorer John Lloyd Stephens to John Church Cruger in 1842. Cruger installed them on the Hudson River island he owned opposite Annandale, first building a stone "ruin" to showcase the ancient artifacts.

Below, a year before his death—to mark the centennial of the capture of Major John André (alias John Anderson)—Tarrytown millionaire tobacconist John Anderson donated this statue of John Paulding, leader of three militiamen who apprehended the British spy. The tobacconist could not have missed the curious irony in John Anderson, the haunted, commemorating the capture of John André, the hunted.

The "Spirit of Life" statue sculpted by Daniel Chester French is the focal point of the Trask Fountain in Saratoga's Congress Park—a handsome memento to one of the men who mounted a campaign to save Saratoga's springs from destruction during the early 1900s.

Rather than his treachery, the heroism of Benedict Arnold is recalled in this odd monument in Saratoga National Historical Park. The boot represents the leg wound Arnold suffered during the 1777 battle in which his zeal earned him the nickname the "Madman of Saratoga."

17 THE BLACK GOLD OF ORANGE COUNTY

IT CAN BE capricious and cruel, but it is compellingly beautiful, while its dark depths harbor a prehistoric treasure matched only by its present-day surface bounty. Men have called this land a variety of names: from "muckland" and "meadows" to "drowned land" and just plain "black dirt." But of all the names given it, "black gold" perhaps best describes this area in Orange County, for it boasts some of the most fertile farmland in the world, with an equally rich history that is in many ways the story of America in miniature.

That story began more than a century of centuries ago when parts of Orange County lay beneath the waters of a lake created by the last of the great glaciers (the Wisconsin), which blanketed the Northeast during the Ice Age. Eventually the waters of the lake receded, and some of its thick bed of organic sediment became a swamp where vegetation flourished—enough vegetation to satisfy the voracious appetites of the multi-ton mastodons then roaming the land.

Yet the swamp was as life-threatening as it was life-sustaining for these huge herbivores, many of whom became trapped and died when they ventured into the thick ooze. Covered by succeeding layers of silt, which preserved their bones, the entombed mastodons remained untouched for thousands of years until Colonial settlers first tried taming the treacherous swamp.

"Treacherous" is no exaggeration either. For even today, pockets of quicksand are known to exist in some black dirt fields, and from time to time whole stretches of road have been swallowed by the unstable soil. But none of these risks—including dust storms that can turn noon into night, fires that sometimes smolder beneath the soil's surface, and periodic flooding of the low-lying fields—has ever stopped men from seeking the rewards the black dirt can bestow.

As early as 1759, a Colonial assemblyman named Henry Wisner introduced a bill to finance a series of ditches to drain the section of black dirt through which the Wallkill River flows. (That section is the largest of the scattered patches of Orange County black dirt, covering about 55 square miles in all and occurring mainly in the southern part of the county.) But it was not until 1767 that these original ditches were laid out, and when they were finally dug, some of them produced more than just drainage.

It was during a ditch-digging operation on a farm near the Wallkill that in the early 1780s a discovery was made that focused nationwide attention on Orange County. The bones of a "very surprising animal" were unearthed, and while at first they were thought to be those of an elephant, further investigation proved them to be the remains of a prehistoric mastodon.

Public interest ran high and wide. Though the Revolutionary War was going on, George Washington took the time to view the ancient bones. So did the physician general of the Hessian forces, Frederick Michaelis, who was so intrigued with the discovery that he excavated the remains of still another mastodon, which he took with him when he returned to his native Germany.

But it was the artist Charles Willson Peale who is perhaps the most responsible for publicizing the mastodons of Orange County. Hearing about the discoveries, Peale journeyed to Orange County, where he participated in the recovery of two mastodon skeletons, one of which was displayed at his museum of natural history in Philadelphia. Then, in 1806, Peale began work on his famous painting "The Exhumation of the Mastodon"—a dramatic depiction of the recovery operation that is still a favorite of gallery visitors.

According to a leaflet published by the Orange County Community College in Middletown (where one of the finest mastodon specimens ever found is on display), "more mastodon remains have been recovered from Orange County than from any other locale in the Northeast." And not all the mastodons found in the county have been dug up. There are at least three others still remaining in the ground, which brings the total count to over forty—and there are probably more as yet undiscovered.

As intriguing as these ancient animals may be, it is the agricultural aspect of the black dirt that has been its main attraction since man first realized its potential for prolific farm produce. That realization did not come at once, however. The Paleo-Indians who inhabited the area at the same time as the mastodons were hunters and gatherers rather than tillers of the soil. As for the later white colonists, they were apt to regard their black-dirt acres as woodlots—something that is reflected in place names like Cedar Swamp and Pine Island.

Other settlers were more far-seeing, including the famous writer Michel-Guillaume-Jean de Crèvecoeur (also known as J. Hector St. John de Crèvecoeur), who penned the classic *Letters From an American Farmer* and *Sketches of 18th Century America.*

Although a Frenchman by birth, Crèvecoeur was an American by choice, and had it not been for the Revolutionary War, this soldier-turned-farmer probably would have lived out his life at Pine Hill, the land he bought on what is now Route 94 in the town of Blooming Grove. A roadside marker now points out the site of Pine Hill (a mile or so north of Chester village). But the sign gives no hint of Crèvecoeur's plans for the black dirt—nor of the tragedy that forced him to abandon his beloved farm.

From 1769 to 1776, Crèvecoeur and his family lived in happiness at Pine Hill. During this time he helped launch a project for controlling the Crommeline Creek so that it would adequately drain the Greycourt Meadows, a substantial strip of black dirt that extends north from the village of Chester into the town of Blooming Grove. For the Frenchman envisioned cultivated fields replacing the wild vegetation then growing on the rich lowlands east of Pine Hill. But with the outbreak of war, the drainage project died, as did the rest of Crèvecoeur's dreams.

Crèvecoeur was married to the former Mehetable Tippet of Westchester County, whose family was pro-Tory. The pacifist Crèvecoeur tried to remain neutral in a region that was decidedly rebel, but it couldn't work—and it didn't.

For two years, Crèvecoeur endured the distrust displayed by his patriot neighbors. Then, in 1778, he fled to British-held New York City, leaving friends to care for his family at Pine Hill. But the British did not trust Crèvecoeur either, and what followed was a nightmare: imprisonment, poverty, physical and mental breakdown, then a long recuperation in Europe.

It was not until the Revolution ended in 1783 that Crèvecoeur was able to return to America, only to find Pine Hill burned to the ground, his wife dead, and his four children missing. And although he eventually was reunited with what remained of his family and enjoyed a modicum of success both as an author and a diplomat, Crèvecoeur never went back to Pine Hill, or his black-dirt project.

There is a story still told on the Greycourt Meadows about a ghostly white horse and rider that were seen crossing the black dirt from time to time in years gone by. Some people speculate it was Crèvecoeur returning to view the land he once sought to reclaim. If so, he must have been pleased, for the weed-tangled muckland has been turned into carefully tilled fields where, in season, parallel rows of plants—mainly onions, lettuce, and celery—form an impressive parade of every shade of green imaginable.

Surrounded by the softly rounded, blue-green hills, with an occasional brick-red barn or chalk-white dwelling, the scene is so breathtakingly beautiful that it is easy to understand the love so many people—artists and farmers alike—have felt for this land, despite its potential for perversity.

That perversity was clearly demonstrated to the army of immigrant Irish laborers hired by the Erie Railroad in the late 1830s to lay tracks across the Chester black dirt. Hundreds of tree-trunk pilings had to be sunk into the spongy sediment before it would support the railbed, and in some places the black dirt was reported to be bottomless. More modern measurements have shown that while Orange County black dirt fields vary in depth—from a mere 18 inches of sediment to well over 40 feet—none is actually bottomless.

When the railbed was finished and the Erie pushed farther west, many of those Irish laborers remained behind. For the Chester black dirt, with its underlying layers of peat and gray clay, reminded them of Ireland. They became the next wave of farmers on the Greycourt Meadows, first working as sharecroppers until they had enough money to buy fields of their own.

At one time, these families were so numerous that the northern end of Chester's Meadow Avenue was called Irish Town. But as was so often the case with the various immigrant groups that have enriched America, the children did not always follow in the footsteps of their parents, and after several generations, the Irish presence gave way to a new set of European arrivals—the Italians, who currently farm much of the black dirt in the Chester vicinity.

Shortly after the turn of the century, still another nationality settled on the black dirt, when a nucleus of a dozen Polish families bought a tract known as the Mission Lands in the southwestern corner of Warwick, near the New Jersey border. Other Poles soon joined the original group, and their community has spread out into adjoining black dirt areas.

Poles, Irish, Italians—these are only three of the nationalities that have made the black dirt of Orange County a miniature American melting pot. Or maybe "salad bowl" would be a better term, since such crispy crops are the main ones raised there now, with the onion the undisputed king of the black dirt. In fact, about half of all New York State's onions come from Orange County black dirt.

In addition to the localities already mentioned, Pumpkin Swamp Road (which meets Route 17A just east of its junction with Route 94 in the village of Florida) provides marvelous vistas of the black dirt, as do Pine Island Turnpike to the south and the Pulaski Highway to the west. Near where the latter road meets County Route 68, a limestone outcrop known as Mount Lookout looms high above the black dirt. There, in the 1960s, a cave was found to contain some of the oldest remains of man ever located east of the Mississippi. With evidence like this suggesting that the black dirt has been nurturing humankind for 10,000 years or more, it is no wonder that it is called the black gold of Orange County.

18 THE CANAL THAT DIDN'T DIE

TEXTBOOKS MAY TELL YOU that the Delaware and Hudson Canal died back in 1898, but don't believe it. The old transportation artery still pulses in places like the Ulster County hamlet of High Falls, where a company of caring people are dedicated to preserving the canal and its past, and in the process have transfused new life into the whole community.

Why have these people worked so hard to prevent the demise of what might seem to be merely a decaying and outdated old ditch? That question can best be answered by backtracking through time to the early nineteenth century, when this country was not yet crisscrossed by a network of modern roads and railbeds, and rivers were the principal routes of transportation.

Wherever there were no natural or navigable corridors connecting these watery highways, canals were constructed to facilitate the movement of both freight and folk—a slow but economical means of travel that was especially suited to shipments of heavy nonperishable goods such as cement and coal.

It was the latter product that prompted the building of the Delaware and Hudson Canal. As its name implies, the D&H connected those two rivers, running 108 miles from Honesdale, Pennsylvania, to Kingston, where coal could then be shipped south down the Hudson to New York City.

If that seems like a somewhat circuitous route, it was literally cheaper in the long run—an economy envisioned by Maurice and William Wurts, for whom Wurtsboro is named. In need of a mass market for coal from mines they owned near Honesdale, the brothers managed to convince a bevy of New York bankers that a profitable canal could be built along the relatively flat land of various river valleys stretching north through Sullivan, Orange, and Ulster counties. In July 1825, construction began.

The vision of the Wurts brothers was matched only by that of a man from Port Jackson (now Accord), who supposedly predicted the coming of the canal long before it was a reality. Tradition says the man was out walking one day when he spied a boat filled with people floating toward him across dry land. Unnerved by the experience, the man related it in detail to a number of people, who recalled it years later when construction crews reached Port Jackson. For it seems the canal was following the exact same route the man's imaginary boat had taken!

Whether fact or folklore, the tale exemplifies the colorful character of the D&H that inspired area authors like Manville Wakefield and Dorothy Sanderson to chronicle its past. For although it never was as famous as the longer and older Erie, the D&H Canal had its share of historic happenings—including the construction of four aqueducts designed by John August Roebling, of Brooklyn Bridge renown.

One of Roebling's canal aqueducts was built at High Falls, where the D&H originally crossed Rondout Creek by means of a twin-arched stone bridge. But when increased commerce necessitated the enlargement of the D&H in 1847, the stone span could not accommodate the widened canal, and Roebling's aqueduct was built right beside it.

The aqueduct, a long, water-filled wooden trough anchored to stone abutments on either side of the creek, must have presented an eye-arresting picture as canal boats floated through the trough, at right angles to the rushing Rondout below. Unfortunately, that is a picture it is no longer possible to view, though the site of the aqueduct—demolished not long after the canal closed down in 1898—still provides a scenic stopping point for visitors to High Falls.

In his classic study of the D&H, called *Coal Boats to Tidewater,* the late Manville Wakefield called High Falls a "lock-dominated village," and it still is. The remains of nearly a dozen canal locks are all within walking distance of the main street, including the beautifully preserved Lock #16.

Little of this is obvious, however, to travelers zipping along Route 213. For while the road passes through the northern end of the hamlet, High Falls doesn't announce its attractions on the kind of bold billboards that can ruin the ambiance of an historic area. Instead, the people of High Falls savor their heritage with a quiet pride, but it is a pride that is enthusiastically and freely shared with anyone interested enough to seek out the off-highway treasures nestled in the folds of this hillside hamlet.

The first stop on any High Falls ramble should be the D&H Canal Historical Society Museum, a block south of Route 213 on Mohonk Road. Open from May to November, the museum is housed in a beautiful, century-old deconsecrated church. Of course, the emphasis of the museum is on the D&H and its relationship to High Falls, but the rest of the canal is not neglected, nor is the story of the surrounding countryside, its industries, and its people.

Several times a year, the D&H Canal Historical Society conducts long guided tours to canal-associated sites, including old cement mines, in the vicinity. And on any day visitors are welcome to take a short trail the society has marked out, starting at Lock #16 and passing a part of the canal containing four other locks.

Adjacent to Lock #16 is the handsome Depuy Canal House, which well deserves its National Historic Landmark status. This stone structure, built in 1797 as a tavern, has undergone painstaking restoration, and now serves as a restaurant.

Just across Route 213 from the Depuy House, a path leads north to the nearby Rondout Creek and the remains of Roebling's aqueduct. But since parking is often tight in this part of High Falls, drivers might prefer to continue a few blocks east along Route 213 and then turn north onto the Boiceville Road. A few minutes' drive will bring you to a parking area on the left-hand side of the road, with paths leading down to the shelving white rocks along the shore of the Rondout. A good view of the remains of Roebling's aqueduct can be had from here, but for a comprehensive view of the High Falls section of the waterway and its industrial history, visitors should backtrack to Route 213 and proceed a short distance west to where the road crosses Rondout Creek.

At the northeastern end of the bridge, a driveway leads down to a small parking area overlooking the lovely cascade for which High Falls was named. A hydroelectric generating plant enclosed by a tall wire fence somewhat obscures the falls. At first glance, the fence seems to prevent further exploration, but a closer look reveals a stile-like entrance and a sign that invites visitors into the linear park that was recently made available to the public through the joint efforts of the High Falls Civic Association and the Central Hudson Gas and Electric Corporation. Understandably, the two hydroelectric buildings are off-limits, but visitors are welcome to walk along the broad lane that leads down along the southern bank of the Rondout from the upper cascade.

If the falls seem familiar even to those who have never visited this area before, that may be because they recognize the setting from the movie *Splendor in the Grass*. For it was here, in a strangely augural scene, that actress Natalie Wood played the role of a teenage girl who nearly drowns at the base of the falls. (Twenty years later, in 1981, Miss Wood drowned in a boating accident off Catalina Island.)

In springtime, when showers and winter runoff from the mountains add to the volume and velocity of the Rondout, the falls are spectacular, and it is easy to understand why an overhead aqueduct was needed to carry D&H canal boats across the creek. Unfortunately, the site of the aqueduct is not within the bounds of this excellent linear park, but footpaths off the paved lane lead to scenic vistas, among them a smaller cascade called Lower Falls. Along the way, well-placed signs point out the historic and geological significance of the area, as well as the ruins of an old cement mill that provided not only mortar for building the D&H but also cargoes for the boats later plying the completed canal. Although coal was the initial reason the D&H was constructed, the canal also was used to transport a host of other commodities, including bluestone, with High Falls serving as a shipping center for that once-famous building material.

Before leaving the linear park, one of its most thoughtful features should be noted: a portage for canoers, who can exit the Rondout via a ramp just above the upper cascade then carry their craft down the paved lane and re-enter the waterway beyond the Lower Falls, to continue past the site of Roebling's aqueduct and the twin-arched bridge that preceded it.

Oddly enough, the earlier (1826) bridge outlived its replacement by a good many years. But eventually the sturdy stone span was judged to be dangerous (not because it might fall down but because people might fall off), and it was sentenced to death by dynamite. The keystone was salvaged, however, and now stands at the entrance to Lock #16. Its placement there—a fragment of something demolished, framed by the lock that has been preserved and is scrupulously maintained—serves as a silent message that we must all be mindful of our heritage, lest it be lost. Fortunately the folks in High Falls have taken that message to heart and are doing their best to see that the old D&H doesn't die.

High Falls isn't the only place where dedicated people are working to preserve the D&H Canal, and anyone interested in the old waterway should also visit the western Orange County community of Cuddebackville, where a little-known but lovely park is well on its way to becoming a showpiece of historic preservation.

Until recently, it was only too easy for drivers along Route 209 to zip past the country lane that was the only access to the D&H Canal Park, where the Neversink Valley Area Museum is located. Then, in 1988, a new road was extended to meet Route 209 at the place where it crosses the Neversink River, and an easily spotted sign was erected on the northwestern side of the bridge, so that first-time visitors now have no trouble finding the park. Yet despite the new road's scenic shoreside entry, there is still something to be said for the older route, which may be a bit longer and more bumpy but in some ways serves as a better introduction to the nineteenth-century canal community.

To take this older route, drivers should keep their eyes peeled for the turn onto Hoag Road, just south of where Route 211 meets 209 in Cuddebackville. Evidence of the D&H Canal is not apparent until the narrow lane climbs a wooded rise, and then the waterway can be seen serenely curving off to the right, its tree-bordered towpath tempting would-be trekkers to take a canal-side stroll right there and then. Parking, however, is not permissible at this point, and drivers should continue along the lane, passing by a large boulder bearing a commemorative plaque, then a white house with an adjacent barnlike structure.

From there, the lane slopes downward, past a now defunct (but maybe someday restored) hydroelectric plant and the new visitors' center (with plenty of parking), and on to where the D&H Canal once crossed the Neversink River by means of an aqueduct built by John A. Roebling. On the verdant bottomland by the river, a cluster of old houses can be found—the nucleus of the D&H Canal Park and a lesson in living history that helps make the past part of the present. For these houses are representative of the many small enclaves of tradesmen that provided essential services along the 108-mile length of the D&H during the latter half of the nineteenth century.

The monumental task of keeping canal traffic flowing is not readily conceived by computer-age minds, which is why it is recommended that visitors first stop by the museum in the restored Blacksmith House, a short distance from the parking lot at the end of the lane. The interior of this rustic structure is jam-packed with exhibits that tell the story of the D&H from its construction in the 1820s to its closing in 1898.

These exhibits spill over into the barn across the lane in back of the museum, and in an adjacent field there can be found the full-size replica of a canal boat that serves as an outdoor classroom. Smaller models of the kind of craft that plied the canal can be seen on the lawn between the museum and the adjacent Carpenter's House (another building slated for full restoration), while interpretive signs placed at strategic points on the park grounds add to the enjoyment of an outdoor jaunt.

One of those signs—set up across the road from the Blacksmith House—directs attention to a trail leading down to the Neversink River and the remains of Roebling's aqueduct. This short trail is somewhat steep and stony, but it is well worth the walk for nature lovers as well as history buffs, since this is one of the most scenic spots along the river. Fishing is great here, too! On either side of the narrow Neversink, the aqueduct's massive gray-stone foundations rise above the trees. The span that carried the canal over the river is missing, but the square channel cut into the top of each foundation gives a good indication of how the huge water-filled wooden trough was placed.

The Cuddebackville section of the canal is an appealing area with a colorful heritage that can best be appreciated by taking one of the guided tours that are held on Sunday afternoons throughout the summer. The park, by the way, is administered by Orange County and contains the longest section of the D&H still holding water.

As walkers wend their way past waste weirs, feeder ditches, and guard gates to the broad bank of the towpath, tour leaders patiently explain the way canal locks worked and what happened when boats going in opposite directions met. This section of the D&H is unique in that it is the only place along the canal where the flow of water was against the barges carrying coal from Honesdale, Pennsylvania, to Kingston. Another singularity concerns the specially designed ropes known as Neversink Locks lines, which were needed to haul the heavy coal barges—some as long as 90 feet and carrying 140-ton loads—onto the nearby aqueduct.

Speaking of locks, a highlight of each tour is the aforementioned barnlike structure near the lane leading into the park. This building served as a combination store and home for the tender of Lock #51—perhaps the most famous of the canal's 108 locks. Lock #51 was long ago filled in, but memories remain of a lady named Mary Casey, who sold baked goods so delicious that appreciative canal men dubbed this stop the Pie Lock.

Tales also are told of fights that erupted among "canawlers," of their frequent raids on nearby farm fields, and of the rowdy tricks they played to relieve the tedium of traveling a mere 3 miles an hour. A favorite pastime of some was to poke their long canal poles into any privy along the bank that happened to be occupied at the time of their passing. Such incidents incensed property owners along the canal, as did the bawdy behavior of bachelor boatmen upon meeting a comely maiden.

But residents were not without their own form of retribution. A widely practiced custom during the warmer months was to swim in the canal, with the more daring of the local youths hitching a ride by hanging on to the end of the loaded canal barge. Convinced that the added drag impeded their already slow progress, hot-tempered boatmen would hurl chunks of coal at the hitchers. Few were hit, but many a canal-side home was heated in winter by the chunks of coal summertime swimmers retrieved from the bottom of the 6-foot-deep canal.

Then there was the time in 1873 when two impatient boatmen got into an argument with a local lock tender named Griffin. After beating up the elderly tender, the bullies climbed aboard their boat and continued south along the canal. But there was a glitch in their getaway: namely the slow-moving boat. For by the time they reached Port Jervis, the injured lock tender already had arrived there by traveling overland, and the local police chief was waiting to arrest the boatmen.

But man-made mischief was the least of the troubles that could and often did disrupt canal operations. "Painters" (panthers) were a threat in the more remote sections, while a prolonged or severe winter might delay the spring opening of the canal for several weeks, until all the ice had melted. Water—too much or too little—was also a problem.

Company planners, of course, had provided the D&H with an extensive system of water sources to maintain the level of the canal. In fact, such Sullivan County lakes as Masten, Yankee, Wolf, Wanasink, Marie-Louise, and Loch Sheldrake all served as canal feeders, with some of those lakes merely ponds or swamps prior to being dammed by D&H developers. Yet even with all the streams and lakes that fed it, during drought years the level of the canal might fall too low to support traffic, and there were times when as many as several hundred boats were detained en route—a hardship for independent boatmen whose profit (or loss) depended on the number of trips they made per season.

Floods could be even worse, particularly since they put added strain on any weak section of the canal wall. Unless detected in time (and special watchmen were employed for just this task), weak sections were wont to give way—and did in April 1869, when a 600-foot gap opened up in the canal just south of Cuddebackville. The water rushing through the rent took two boats with it, but the sturdy craft managed to survive the sudden detour and were hauled back into the canal as soon as it was repaired by a crew of three hundred men.

Stories like this are what make tours of the D&H Canal Park so interesting, and visitors are often surprised to learn how much of the waterway still exists. As reported in *Towpath Chatter*, the newsletter of the Neversink Valley Area Museum, a mid-1980s survey of Orange and Sullivan counties "documented almost 350 individual sites, ranging from something as elaborate as a lock to something as simple as a waste weir that allowed the canal to be drained if repairs were needed.... An incredible stretch of the canal is in the Bashakill Wildlife Preserve. A drydock there looks as if, after only a little work, you could pull a boat in and repair it."

Fortunately, New York State now owns the Bashakill—a 2,200-acre wetland paralleling Route 209 just north of Cuddebackville—which means the D&H sites there will be preserved for future generations. So, too, will be a 9.5-mile strip of land running north from the Port Jervis city line to the D&H Canal Park, then continuing on the other side of the park to Port Orange Road in Westbrookville. This ribbon of land, no more than 60 feet wide at any point, contains the old D&H towpath, which was used as a route for power-line poles in the decades following the canal's closing. In recent years, however, the historical significance and recreation potential of the property was recognized by the utility company that owned it, and the land was donated to Orange County.

Plans call for the property to be developed as a linear park, much like the Croton Aqueduct Trail in Westchester County, and eventually it will be possible to hike more than 10 uninterrupted miles along the refurbished towpath, for the two segments of the linear park link up to the mile of towpath within the D&H Canal Park.

Meanwhile, in conjunction with the Neversink Valley Area Museum, the D&H Canal Park continues its impressive program of research, restoration, recreation, and other activities that highlight the rich history of the region.

One of the most popular of these public events is the annual D. W. Griffith film festival. During the early 1900s, the pioneer filmmaker shot many of his silent movies in Cuddebackville, and the museum owns twenty of these short (15- to 20-minute) films. Each summer a selection is shown to audiences, who delight in seeing movie greats like Max Sennett and Mary Pickford acting out their parts—accompanied by the tinkle of an old-time player piano—against still-recognizable backdrops such as the D&H Canal Store on Oakland Valley Road.

Among the favorites of the museum's film collection is *A Squaw's Love,* which made movie history in more ways than one. The film, produced in 1911 and starring the legendary Mabel Normand, is the first in which more than one camera was used to shoot a scene. It was also a film in which the star, Miss Normand, refused to use a double for a dangerous scene—that of jumping off a cliff into a river. And she is shown shivering and shaken—but surviving—after plunging into the Neversink River near the museum, with Roebling's aqueduct in the background. What was not recorded on film but is preserved in the folklore of the film industry is the story that the drenched star called for a bottle of brandy the minute she was pulled ashore and downed the contents in a single draught.

Folks who enjoy such local lore won't want to miss another of the museum's annual events, called "Canal Country Ghosts," which offers an evening of Halloween-type tales told by some of the region's best storytellers.

But no matter the time or the season, a visit to the D&H Canal Park is an enriching experience. Indeed, the D&H hasn't died and it won't, as long as there are present-day people dedicated to preserving the past for the future.

19 YADDO

It all began in 1784. After seven years of civil strife, the newborn American nation was returning to normal, as discharged veterans spread out over the land in search of the peaceful future for which they had fought.

One of those Revolutionary War veterans was German-born Jacobus Barhyte, who had seen action at Bemis Heights and came back to buy 200 acres in the wilderness west of that Hudson-shore battleground in Saratoga County. Settling on a high knoll from which he could view the landscape of his former soldiering, Barhyte proceeded to build a log house, which he later converted to an inn when the pond at the base of his hill gained fame among fishermen.

But it wasn't only fishermen who flocked to Barhyte's. For anyone who fancied fine trout—including the one-time King of Spain, Joseph Bonaparte—Barhyte's inn was the favored place to dine when in Saratoga Springs. And like the proverbial "man who came to dinner," guests sometimes stayed on, especially writers, for whom the evergreen-shaded setting seemed to exert a strange and powerful pull.

It is said that Edgar Allan Poe composed the first draft of his immortal poem "The Raven" while strolling along the wooded shoreline of Barhyte's trout pond. By that time (1842-43), Jacobus

Barhyte's son John was operating the inn with his wife Ann. An accomplished author in her own right, Ann Barhyte reportedly helped Poe with his masterpiece, though she did not live to see its publication.

Ann Barhyte's untimely death in 1844 marked the first of a series of tragedies that seemed to accentuate the long shadows cast by the tall evergreens surrounding the inn—an umbra that was, in part, responsible for the property eventually being named Yaddo.

Unable to live amid the scenes that he associated with his beloved wife, John Barhyte sold the estate to a trio of partners interested only in cutting the timber. Oddly enough, the partners never touched the tall stand of pines near the inn; nor did Richard Childs, who purchased the property in 1854, though he moved the old Barhyte house to another location in order to make room for the Queen Anne villa he built.

This ornate villa, so out of place in its woodland setting overlooking the pond, was to see its share of sorrow. Within fifteen years, the wealthy Dr. Childs had lost all his money and the house was sold at auction, after which it remained empty for nearly a decade.

Perhaps it was the mournful mien of the desolate and decaying villa that prompted a grieving New York City couple to rent it during the summer of 1881. For Katrina and Spencer Trask had recently lost their firstborn son, and the "perfectly hideous house surrounded by a wild wilderness" (as Katrina later described it) symbolized their gloom, while at the same time holding out the hope of better times ahead.

Seeing what could be, rather than what was, the Trasks decided to buy the property and refurbish the dilapidated dwelling—a decision reinforced by something their small daughter said one day during the long months of real-estate negotiations.

Asked what she would like to call the pine-shaded villa that was to be her summer home, four-year-old Christina astonished her elders by answering, "Call it Yaddo, for it makes poetry. Yaddo, shadow—shadow, Yaddo! It sounds like shadow, but it's *not* going to be shadow."

Thus was born the name of Yaddo, from a perceptive child's

mental melding of two dark images—tree shadows and the mourning clothes her family wore—which she verbally revised to reflect her own bright optimism.

And for the next seven years, Yaddo was just that: a place of unshadowed happiness and ever-growing beauty, as Spencer and Katrina restored the house and grounds. At first intended only as a summer retreat, Yaddo soon gained favor over their Brooklyn home, especially when two more children—Spencer, Jr., and Little Katrina—were born. But Spencer's position as a financier required his presence in New York City for at least part of the year, so the Trasks continued to spend the winter months in Brooklyn.

It was there, in 1888, that tragedy touched them again.

Katrina came down with diphtheria, and the children were allowed to visit the sickroom. No one realized that the contagious stage of the disease had not yet passed. One by one, the children developed diphtheria; one by one, they died. Their heartbroken mother survived, though with permanently impaired health.

Bereft of all four of their children, the Trasks were soon enough beset by more misfortune. In the spring of 1891, as Spencer Trask lay ill with pneumonia in their Brooklyn home, word arrived that the Yaddo villa had been destroyed by fire. Rather than enervating the already ailing man, however, the news spurred Spencer's recovery, for he knew how much Katrina cared for Yaddo, and he was determined to build an even larger and lovelier mansion for his wife.

Phoenix-like, the new mansion arose from the ashes of the old; only this time the building on Barhyte's hill was more suited to its setting, since architect William Halsey Wood had given it the semblance of an English country house. The interior, though, was opulent with Tiffany glass, richly carved wood, and imported furnishings all comfortably accommodated in spacious chambers, including a two-hundred-seat music room.

Friends and fellow artists of the literary-minded Katrina, as well as Spencer's business and political associates, were soon flocking to the handsome home of the Trasks, whose parties became one of the highlights of the summer season at Saratoga Springs.

Even more important, visiting writers and musicians frequently reported an almost uncanny catalysis of their creative output during their stay at Yaddo. Katrina did not find this surprising, since as an author she had experienced Yaddo's influence and was also aware of its earlier literary associations. What did come as a surprise to her was the sudden revelation, one day in 1899, of what must be the future of the estate.

She and Spencer had been taking a late-afternoon stroll along a hillside path paralleling the pond when Katrina envisioned a host of city-weary artists being succored and inspired by the same serenity she was experiencing. And as soon as he heard Katrina's description of her vision, Spencer agreed that Yaddo should become an artist's retreat.

Up until the time of this decision, Katrina and Spencer had not proceeded in the further development of Yaddo, since they no longer had any children to inherit it. But once the couple realized how Yaddo could contribute to future generations of creative artists, they set to work in earnest.

The magnificent rose garden was laid out during this period, as was the rock garden and some of the ancillary buildings that now serve as studios for the artists who stay at Yaddo. As for Barhyte's pond, Spencer divided it into two smaller lakes. He then joined these to some other ponds so that a quartet of lakelets embraced the base of Yaddo's knoll like a shimmering necklace—each bead bearing the name of one of his dead children.

While such a memorial may seem somewhat morose to modern tastes, that was not the mood Trask intended, nor is it the mood that prevails. Instead, these four peaceful ponds, bordered by a shaded footpath, encourage the kind of introspection that brings forth the best in many of the artists who are invited to Yaddo.

Officially, Yaddo did not become an artist's retreat until nearly three decades after Katrina and Spencer conceived the idea, because of financial reverses suffered by Spencer during the depression of 1907, followed by his death in a train wreck two years later.

The widowed Katrina was then a permanent invalid, but she carried on the dream she and Spencer had for Yaddo, only at a slower pace. In order to conserve money, she closed the mansion and moved into one of the estate's smaller houses, while at the same time constricting Yaddo's master plan to conform to her reduced means. Work went on, however, and in the summer of 1926 Yaddo welcomed its first group of artists.

Unfortunately, Katrina did not live to see that triumphant time, though her indomitable spirit pervades Yaddo to this very day. That spirit is evident not only in the respect for nature and serene loveliness of the estate, but in the lifestyle, too. For Yaddo is not a resort, but a retreat, where guests can escape mundane responsibilities in order to devote full attention to their work.

A typical day begins when a communal breakfast is served at 8:00 A.M., after which guests pick up their lunch pails (lined up on a bench outside the dining room door) and return to their studios. The hours between nine and four are reserved for work, with no intrusions (such as phone calls or visitors or even a loud lawnmower) to disrupt concentration.

Does such a regimen work? This is the question most frequently asked about Yaddo. And while a host of affirmative quotes could be culled from Yaddo's files (including Philip Roth's succinct remark that Yaddo is "the best friend a writer ever had"), the most convincing answer is found in the administration building's library.

Lining the walls are hundreds of books, all of which were penned (at least in part) while their authors were guests at Yaddo. The bindings read like a Who's Who in American literature: James T. Farrell, Truman Capote, Katherine Anne Porter, Irving Stone, James Baldwin, Flannery O'Connor, Carson McCullers, John Cheever, William Carlos Williams, and Sylvia Plath—to name only ten.

Then there are the paintings, sketches, photographs, and other art works that appreciative guests have bestowed on Yaddo throughout the years—gifts that the public rarely sees, since Yaddo must, by its very nature, retain its privacy. However, there are periodic fundraising events that the public may attend, and the extensive gardens are open free of charge throughout the year.

Visiting these gardens is like a trip through time, for all along the driveway from Yaddo's main entrance on Union Avenue, the eye is treated to variegated vistas representing the centuries since Jacobus Barhyte first settled these verdant hills: the pond site where Poe roamed, the path leading past the mansion-crested hill, and of course the towering evergreens casting their long shadows.

But just as tiny Christina Trask insisted so long ago, these shadows are neither somber nor mournful. How could they be, when so much of value has been—and still is being—accomplished at this unusual place?

Bravo, Yaddo. May your inspiration continue for many centuries more!

20 OPEN HOUSE AT HURLEY

A RAMBLE THROUGH the Ulster County hamlet of Hurley is an enriching experience at any time of the year, but the second Saturday in July is especially rewarding. For that is when Hurley holds its annual Stone House Day—a community-wide celebration that has as its center-piece the greatest concentration of old stone houses in the United States.

Each year since 1950, the owners of a dozen or so of these private dwellings agree to open their doors to the public for one day, and touring the interiors is like strolling through several centuries of Hurley's history. It has been an eventful history, too, despite the hamlet's seemingly out-of-the-way setting in the foothills of the Catskills west of Kingston.

That Hurley exists at all can be attributed to the tenacity of its earliest settlers. Burned out by Indians in the spring of 1663, those hardy Hollanders and Huguenots took temporary refuge in Wiltwyck (present-day Kingston), from which a search party was sent out to rescue women and children taken captive. By late fall, all the prisoners had been found and freed, except for one woman who chose to remain with the Indians. The rest were reunited with their families, and in time they returned to rebuild their homes

136

in the settlement originally known as Nieuw Dorp, or "new village."

With the advent of English rule, the name was changed to Hurley—not for the ancient Celtic game, but in honor of the British governor's ancestral home—and the succeeding century saw the construction of many of the stone houses that now qualify the community for National Historic Landmark status.

Hurleyites are intensely proud of their heritage, but it is a hospitable pride without a hint of snobbishness—something strangers sense the minute they turn off Route 209 on Stone House Day and a friendly wave directs them to the free parking area. Hurley's narrow streets are best-suited to pedestrians, who find that most of the houses open to the public are within easy walking distance. It's more fun to amble along, savoring the ambiance of this picturesque community and enjoying the many other events that are held in conjunction with Stone House Day—a country fair, Colonial craft demonstrations, a Continental Army encampment, plus book and antique sales, to name only some.

As for those outlying houses included in the tour, free bus service is provided at regular intervals from the high-steepled Hurley Reformed Church, which stands in white simplicity at the end of the old main street. This mid-nineteenth-century fane is a focal point in more ways than one, for Stone House Day is organized by its congregation, with tasty meals served throughout the day in the basement cafeteria. The Ulster County Genealogical Society simultaneously hosts an open house at their headquarters in the church's adjacent Schadewald Hall. Visitors are welcome to consult the society's extensive records, in addition to touring the interior of the church. Don't miss the swinging wooden doors on the once privately owned pews.

Hurley was founded in 1661, and was later the home of abolitionist leader Sojourner Truth, who was born around 1797 and spent the first eleven years of her life as a slave at the Colonel Gerardus Hardenberg house—not to be confused with the other Hardenberg house in Hurley, which was built in 1818.

Anyone interested in the subject of slavery during the early days of Hurley should also stop by the Crispell house (now the church parsonage), where a narrow stairway leads to the cramped quarters once allotted to slaves. On the other hand, the Ten Eyck house, directly across the street, has a long-held tradition of harboring escaped slaves in pre-Emancipation days. Supposedly, the Canada-bound fugitives would arrive via an underground tunnel connecting the dwelling with the nearby church—a story seemingly borne out in modern times when the earth in back of the house caved in and a tunnel-like depression was discovered.

Nor is that the only intriguing tradition associated with the beautifully maintained Ten Eyck house, which was built in 1780 and still displays a defensive gunport in one of its shutters. A different kind of defense can be seen in the upper panel of a main-floor door, where two glass "bull's-eyes" were installed to ward off witches.

As any fan of Hudson Valley folklore can attest, witchcraft was as feared here as in the infamous Salem, the only difference being that old-time Hurleyites preferred an ounce of prevention to a pound of punishment. A broom would be set diagonally in a doorway to deter witches from entering, and the Polly Crispell cottage even sports a set of iron spikes inside its chimney to snag any witches sliding down. (How poor Santa Claus got past those "witch catchers" is anybody's guess.)

In the case of a possible witch already indoors, a pinch of salt placed beneath the suspect's chair was considered a reliable test, for salt was thought to immobilize practitioners of black magic. That was the way a Hurley women name Betsy Conway was proved innocent one day while visiting the Hotaling house. Despite the salt beneath her seat, Betsy had no trouble getting up when it was time to go—or so the story is told.

Betsy reportedly lived near the Wynkoop residence, which began as a small dwelling in 1676, before a larger structure was built around it at a later date. It was here that Revolutionary War hero Colonel Cornelius Wynkoop was killed by a slave in 1792, but the gracefully gabled house seems to harbor no haunts. Incidentally, visitors may well experience a sense of déjà vu, since the Wynkoop house was the setting for some scenes in the Dustin Hoffman movie *Tootsie*.

For ghosts, tour takers are directed to the three-story Abram Elmendorf house, which is one of the youngest (circa 1790) of

Hurley's stone structures, and utterly English in architecture. (Most of the older dwellings are Dutch-derived.) Inside this handsomely appointed home, there is a stairwell door that had to be secured against a restless ghost. According to legend, a lady known as Aunt Nellie died when she tumbled down the steps, and from that day on, the stairwell door never would stay closed. As for whether Aunt Nellie still roams the nether regions of the house, tour guides will not comment other than to say that all old structures have strange sounds.

Some of those in Hurley have secret chambers, too—a feature that came in handy when the Council of Safety decided to hide documents at the Jan Van Deusen house during the Revolutionary War. Built in 1723, this sturdy building on Hurley's main street became the temporary capitol of New York after the British burned Kingston in 1777. It was also during 1777 that the landed Loyalist Cadwallader Colden, Jr. was kept here under house arrest.

Colden could well consider himself lucky, for just down the street, another prisoner was briefly incarcerated at the DuMond dwelling, also called the Guard house or Spy house. Convicted of spying when a silver bullet he carried was discovered to contain a British communiqué, Lieutenant Daniel Taylor was hanged from a nearby apple tree on October 19, 1777. The tree is long gone, but the site of Taylor's grave can still be seen along Schoonmaker Lane.

In addition to the buildings already mentioned, the Stone House Day tour often includes:

• DuBois Home. After inheriting his father Jacob's farm along the Esopus Creek on the west side of Hurley, Johannis DuBois built a one-room residence, which in 1780 was enlarged to the well-proportioned structure seen today.

• Jonathan Elmendorf House. Not to be confused with the Abram Elmendorf home mentioned earlier, this Colonial manor house was constructed in the 1780s and is considered "a fine example of a wealthy burgher's residence."

• Newkirk House. An eighteenth-century dwelling located on the banks of Preymaker Brook (named for a local Indian chief) not far from Ten Eyck Bowerie.

• TEN EYCK BOWERIE. A ten-room house with an attic that was used to store grain grown on the rich farmland between the brook and Esopus Creek.

Corn has been raised in the Hurley area since Indian times and still constitutes its major farm product, but in the past, several other industries thrived here. Besides the expected gristmills, there was a distillery and a brewery, plus a woolen mill, a brickyard, and tan pits to process animal hides. Though these early industries have not survived, the sites of their operation make interesting stops for anyone taking a driving tour of the rest of Hurley's impressive architectural heritage. In all, Hurley boasts twenty-six stone houses, amid many nineteenth-century homes made from other materials.

As previously noted, the Stone House Day itinerary varies from year to year, with the same buildings not always open to the public. An exception is the Hurley Patentee Manor, a mid-eighteenth-century mansion in the Georgian style that originated as a small cottage in 1696. Containing a number of interesting features (including animal pens in the cellar), the manor usually can be visited from mid-July through August.

Even when these houses are not open, Hurley offers many outdoor attractions to those interested in the heritage of the Hudson Valley. For instance, a grooved slab set on the front lawn of the bank is a memento of the bluestone industry that once flourished in the region. Wagons hauling the heavy slabs traveled along a special track paved with bluestone, and over the years deep ruts were worn into the roadbed, a section of which has been saved by history-minded Hurleyites.

Another evocative site is the old Hurley Burying Ground, at the end of a picturesque lane that branches off from the main street, between the Polly Crispell cottage and the Petrus Elmendorf house. Situated on a wooded knoll, the cemetery is noteworthy for its concentration of unusual tombstones, the earliest decipherable date being 1715, and many markers that are simply tall spires of uncarved local stone similar to the monumental menhirs of Europe.

But, of course, the historic homes of Hurley are the hamlet's chief attraction. So try to get to Hurley on Stone House Day, when you can enjoy the interiors as well as the exteriors of many of these marvelous old homes. It's an excursion into Hudson Valley history and hospitality that has few equals.

21 LANDMARKS ALONG THE TREASON TRAIL

HISTORIC ROUTES CAN BE fascinating to follow, and none more so than the Hudson Valley's Treason Trail, which traces the betrayal of his country by Benedict Arnold and the tragic price paid by his co-conspirator John André.

But before starting out on the Treason Trail, it's best to backtrack a bit in time to Philadelphia in 1778 and the meeting of Benedict Arnold and Margaret (Peggy) Shippen. Arnold, twice the age of the eighteen-year-old beauty, was quick to propose, but Peggy put him off until April 8, 1779, when they were finally married. By that time, Arnold, crippled from a leg wound sustained in the Battle of Saratoga, was disillusioned with the American cause and soon would face court-martial for alleged illegal activities as an officer in the Continental Army.

Though her father was an avowed neutral, Peggy Shippen Arnold made no bones about her Loyalist sympathies. These were engendered in part, perhaps, by her romance with a handsome young British officer who had been a frequent visitor to the Shippen home during the British occupation of Philadelphia in the winter of 1777-78.

Even today it is not known whether it was Benedict Arnold or his wife who first proposed his defection to the British side. But by the summer of 1779, Arnold began corresponding, through intermediaries, with Sir Henry Clinton's headquarters in New York City. Chief among the negotiators was Clinton's Adjutant-General, the same officer who had been Peggy Arnold's admirer—twenty-eight-year-old Major John André.

Negotiations stumbled along through coded correspondence (with Arnold assuming the name of Monk—after the Scottish general who helped restore the British monarchy in 1660—and André calling himself John Anderson). It all had finally bogged down in August 1779: Arnold had named his price—£10,000—but Clinton would not, or could not, agree to it.

It was an entirely different matter, though, when a year later Benedict Arnold was given command of the understaffed, incompletely fortified West Point. Well aware of the advantage of controlling this critical Hudson River fortress, General Clinton quickly agreed that a plan for surrendering West Point to the British was well worth £20,000.

On September 21, 1780, the British sloop-of-war *Vulture*, with André on board, anchored in the Hudson off what is now Croton Point. Before long, a messenger sent by Benedict Arnold arrived, bearing a pass for "Mr. John Anderson." André was then rowed to the west bank of the Hudson near Haverstraw. Arnold was waiting, and the two conversed there until dawn. A marker commemorating this meeting is on Route 9W just north of Haverstraw.

The conspirators then repaired to the nearby home of Joshua Hett Smith, a British sympathizer who was privy to Arnold's plot to betray West Point. Smith's house was located on what is now the grounds of the Helen Hayes Rehabilitation Hospital in West Haverstraw, and it was from the windows of Smith's hilltop home that the conspirators watched as a patriot shore battery opened fire on the *Vulture*, still anchored in the Hudson awaiting André's return. Lieutenant Andrew Sutherland, in command of the *Vulture*, was forced to weigh anchor and sail out of range of the patriot guns. It may have been at this time that Sutherland ordered the shot that pierced a headstone in a cemetery on the eastern store. This red sandstone marker, with a plaque commemorating the event, can still be seen at the top of the hill in Sparta Cemetery, on Route 9, just south of Ossining.

Since it was now impossible for André to return to New York City on the *Vulture*, he spent the afternoon of September 22 hiding at the Smith house, hoping the ship would return under cover of darkness. But when night fell, Smith argued against an attempt to row André out to the *Vulture*. It would be safer, he insisted, to take André overland to the British lines. Arnold was in agreement, pointing out that patriot spy boats were certain to be plying the river.

In direct opposition to an admonition given him by Clinton, André was persuaded to change his uniform for civilian attire and to hide the maps and other information Arnold had given him in his boot. Then he and Smith proceeded to King's Ferry at Stony Point, where they crossed the Hudson to Verplanck, on the eastern shore. The old King's Ferry landing is down the hill in back of the museum at Stony Point Battlefield State Historic Site.

From Verplanck, André and Smith made their way to Montrose, then northeast to Peekskill, where they spent the night at the Andreas Miller house (no longer standing), then went on to Yorktown. After André and Smith had breakfast at the Underhill house (see the marker on the building at the northwest corner of California and Hanover Streets, south of Yorktown Heights), André went on alone to White Plains, where he would find a British outpost. But André, following a circuitous route, got no farther than Tarrytown.

Come all you brave Americans,
And unto me give ear,
I'll sing you now a ditty
That will your spirits cheer
Concerning a young gentleman
Who came from Tarrytown
Where he met a British officer,
A man of high renown.

So begins an old ballad that describes the plight of John André when, on the morning of September 23, 1780, he encountered a man wearing a Hessian coat, which caused the young British officer to think he was in friendly hands. John Paulding, however, was an American militiaman, who was soon joined by two others, Isaac Van Wart and David Williams. The three militiamen then forced André to undress in order to search him and found the incriminating papers concerning West Point secreted inside André's stocking. The site of André's capture is marked by a tall monument in Patriots' Park, on the west side of North Broadway just below College Avenue in Tarrytown. Not far from there, on Grove Street, the Historical Society of the Tarrytowns features a Captors' Room containing one of the best collections of material pertaining to the Arnold-André plot.

The three militiamen took André to the nearest American post, at Sands Mill (now Armonk), which was commanded by Lieutenant Colonel John Jameson. There is a stone marker at the site of Jameson's headquarters at the confluence of High, Cox, and Greenway Roads, near Route 128. Although Jameson's loyalty has never been questioned, it is known that he was a friend of Benedict Arnold. As such, he might have recognized the traitor's handwriting on some of the captured documents, which could account for his otherwise unaccountable action at this point. For Jameson sent André under guard *to Arnold*, while he dispatched the documents to George Washington, who was then returning to West Point from a visit with General Rochambeau at Hartford, Connecticut.

A few hours after André was sent off to Arnold, Major Benjamin Tallmadge arrived at Jameson's headquarters and tried to persuade the latter to recall the party. Though Jameson agreed to bring back the prisoner, he allowed an accompanying letter to go through to Arnold.

André was returned late that night and in the morning was sent to Colonel Sheldon's headquarters at the Gilbert house in South Salem. (Though the house is no longer standing, there is a marble slab in the stone wall on the west side of Main Street, south of Bouton Road.) It was there that André penned a letter to George Washington, explaining what had happened and hinting that he should not be considered a spy, even though he was in civilian clothes when arrested.

Ironically, Washington was to have spent the night of September

24 with Benedict Arnold at his headquarters in the Beverly Robinson house on the east bank of the Hudson south of Garrison. (See the marker for the Robinson house on the east side of Route 9D south of Route 403.) However, Washington was delayed and sent two aides to inform Arnold of the fact.

On the morning of September 25, Arnold was just sitting down to breakfast with these aides when Jameson's letter arrived concerning André's capture. Arnold excused himself to the aides on the pretext of having to check on something at West Point, and told them he would return shortly to greet Washington when the commander in chief arrived. But instead of crossing the Hudson to West Point, Arnold ordered his men to row down the river to where the *Vulture* was anchored off Ossining. Once aboard, he was quickly taken to Clinton in New York, where Peggy Arnold later joined him.

When George Washington arrived at the Robinson house later that day and was told that Arnold was at West Point, he paused to have something to eat. Then, leaving behind young Alexander Hamilton, Washington crossed the river to West Point, only to be told that Arnold had not been there for the past two days. Washington returned to the Robinson house, where he was confronted by Hamilton, who, in the meantime, had received Jameson's message and André's letter.

"Whom can we trust now?" was the stunned Washington's only remark.

The fleeing Arnold had not taken his wife Peggy along, and she was left at the Robinson house to confront Washington. In what has been called "one of the most impressive fits of hysterics in American history," Peggy Shippen Arnold insisted that she'd had no part in the treason of her husband, and the ever-chivalrous Washington said he believed her.

During a drenching rainstorm in the early morning of September 26, André was brought to the Robinson house by Major Tallmadge. Though Washington inquired about the prisoner, he refused to see him, and that night André was taken to West Point, where he remained incarcerated until the morning of September 28.

André was later brought by barge to Stony Point, then overland southwest to Tappan, where he was held prisoner in the Yost Mabie

Tavern, now known as the '76 House. The now public building is on the west side of Main Street in Tappan, just south of where Old Tappan Road meets Washington Street.

George Washington ordered a Court of Inquiry, made up of thirteen generals, to convene in the Reformed Dutch Church at Tappan. (The Reformed Church of Tappan, on Main Street between Old Tappan and Greenbush Roads, is the third church on this site, the second having been the one used for André's trial.) No defense counsel was present and the decision of the court was in the form of a recommendation: "Major André, Adjutant-General to the British Army, ought to be considered as a spy from the enemy, and... agreeably to the law and usage of nations... he ought to suffer death."

André had maintained that he was not a spy and should be treated as a prisoner of war, since he had been in American territory and had been told by Arnold—the commanding American general— to change his uniform. This the board would not consider, though there was much sympathy for André among the Americans, including Washington himself.

Therefore, on September 30, 1780, it was with reluctance that George Washington, while headquartered at the De Wint house, approved the recommendation of the Court of Inquiry and ordered that André be executed at 5 P.M. the following day. (The De Wint house, located at Livingston Street and Oak Tree Road in Tappan, is open to the public.)

There was only one hope for André: that General Clinton would return Arnold to the Americans. André's execution was thus delayed until General Greene, who had presided over the Court of Inquiry, could confer with Clinton's representative, General Robertson. As much as he wanted to save André, Clinton felt he could not go back on his word to Arnold. The British commander could only make dire threats against those American prisoners he held, should André be executed.

At noon on October 2, 1780, André, dressed in a scarlet coat, was escorted from the Yost Mabie Tavern by a contingent of 500 troops, followed by a baggage wagon containing a black coffin. To the tune of fifes and drums, they marched a half mile west on Old Tappan

Road to the top of the prominence now known as André Hill. There, at a gallows made of two forked trees with a third laid across, the procession halted.

"I have borne everything with fortitude," André was heard to say, "but this is too degrading." However, when he was told to climb in the baggage wagon and stand on top of the coffin, he did so bravely.

The hangman—a Tory named Strickland then under arrest—had disguised himself by smearing his face with bootblack. When André saw this hideous figure, he refused to let Strickland touch him and placed the noose around his own neck. His last words were: "I pray you bear witness that I met my fate like a brave man." Then a colonel named Scammell lowered the point of his sword, signaling the horses harnessed to the wagon to step forward, and André came to the end of the Treason Trail.

For more than forty years, André's remains lay beneath a heap of stones on the hill where he was hanged. Then, in 1821, the Duke of York, through British Consul James Buchanan, requested that André's body be removed to London's Westminster Abbey. The petition was granted, and André was returned to his native England.

The monument that now stands on André Hill in Tappan was dedicated in 1879, and though it bears many inscriptions, perhaps the most fitting is the one that records George Washington's sympathetic judgment: "He was more unfortunate than a criminal."

As for Benedict Arnold, though he escaped capture and was given a commission in the British Army, the taint of his treason was ever upon him. He died impoverished in England in 1801, a tragic figure mistrusted by both the Americans he had betrayed and the British who had bought him.

IV

CURIOUS
CHARACTERS

22 THE OTHER JOHN ANDERSON

ALTHOUGH MANY PEOPLE visit Patriots' Park in Tarrytown and pause to admire the statue marking the site where British Major John André was captured on a fogbound September morning in 1780, few take the time to read a small inscription at the base of the monument: *This statue a gift of John Anderson.* Fewer still are aware of the irony of the inscription. For André's code name was John Anderson, and at first glance it would seem that the captured had erected a monument to his captors.

The true irony, however, is hidden away in the little-known story of the real John Anderson, a Tarrytown millionaire tobacconist whose success was overshadowed by a specter from the past.

In 1837 the dark-haired Mary Cecilia Rogers first appeared behind the counter of John Anderson's tobacco shop a few blocks from the New York City Hall. The presence of the seventeen-year-old beauty created an immediate sensation, for it was the first time a "seegar girl" had been employed in the city.

Though the use of a young saleslady in a strictly male establishment was frowned on by society in general, Mary must have found her job exciting, for Anderson's store was a favorite with Broadway dandies and gamblers, newspaper reporters and editors, as well as such literary greats as Washington Irving and James Fenimore Cooper. Edgar Allan Poe probably patronized the shop at that time, too, for he lived only a short distance away.

Mary continued to be the popular attraction of Anderson's shop until the middle of 1839. At this time a rise in the Rogers family fortunes allowed her widowed mother to buy a boardinghouse, and Mary no longer had to work outside her home. After she left Anderson's employ, she faded from public notice into a more respectable obscurity—but only for two years.

On Sunday, July 25, 1841, Mary disappeared. Two days later, her body was found floating in the Hudson River near the Weehawken shore. A coroner's jury convened that evening concluded merely that the lovely cigar girl's death had been precipitated by "violence committed by some person or persons unknown." But the investigating doctor's report had been more detailed. The hapless girl, he said, had been bound and gagged, then raped by at least three men, after which she had been thrown into the Hudson. The actual cause of death, Dr. Richard Cook added, was from strangulation caused by a thin strip of lace torn from the victim's own clothing and wound tightly around her neck.

Since there were many gangs known to frequent the resort area, called the Elysian Fields, near where Mary's body had been brought ashore, the investigation proceeded along these lines—and got nowhere.

Three weeks later, when there was still no clue to Mary's murder, a Committee of Safety was formed. Its members raised $500 reward money; among them was John Anderson, Mary's former employer, who gave one of the largest contributions, $50.

By September, the reward fund had swelled to $1,250 and police were confident of a break in the case, when Frederica Loss, who operated the Nick Moore Inn, near the New Jersey shore at Weehawken, reported that her son had found some women's clothes in a thicket. The clothes were those of Mary Rogers. Mrs. Loss also said she remembered hearing screams coming from the woods on the day of Mary's disappearance, so it was assumed that the site of the murder finally had been determined.

If public interest had been running high before, it now became rabid, with boatloads of people crossing the Hudson to view the supposed site of the murder. However, by late September, when no further progress had been made in the investigation, public interest again died down—though not for long.

On October 8, the body of Daniel Payne, Mary's fiancé, was found on the beach where Mary's body had been brought ashore. In a nearby thicket was an empty laudanum bottle and in Payne's pocket a note: "To the World—Here I am on the spot; God forgive me for my misfortune in my misspent life."

Could the note mean that Payne killed Mary? This was seriously considered, since the police had already begun to investigate the possibility that Mary had been murdered by a single person, rather than a gang. Nor was Payne the only man suspected. In addition to the usual crackpot confessions that sensational murders always elicit, the police had received many anonymous letters concerning the crime. Rumors of who the murderer might be were numerous, ranging from Mary's ex-fiancé, one Alfred Crommelin, to a mysterious naval officer, and even her employer, John Anderson.

Why John Anderson? Well, Mary had worked for him in the past, and she *was* beautiful, and John Anderson *was* only twenty-five years old...so went the speculative whispers. There had been talk of an affair between them, with the New York *Herald* of August 3, 1841 flatly stating that "three years ago [Mary] lived with Anderson, the cigar man."

Along with many others, John Anderson was interrogated by the police, and though he was subsequently released, there remained the shadow of suspicion that he might in some way be implicated in Mary's death. Anderson was tormented by the whispers and stares that followed him wherever he went, and he knew this would continue until Mary's killer was caught. Yet the case was no closer to a solution than it had been when Mary's body was found. What if it were *never* solved?

On the other hand, what if the case were solved by someone other than the police? Considering the clientele of his store and the fact that the newspapers were conducting investigations as intensive as those of the authorities, it would only have been natural for Anderson to think of a journalist as someone who might possibly help him.

Earlier that year, an unusual short story by Edgar Allan Poe had appeared in the April issue of *Graham's Magazine*. Based on an actual occurrence, "The Murders in the Rue Morgue" concerned a citizen solving a case that had baffled the police—a solution that had freed a man wrongfully accused of murder. What if Poe used the same technique to solve the murder of Mary Rogers in the form of fiction?

There is no concrete evidence that John Anderson ever approached Edgar Allan Poe with such an idea; obviously, it was not the kind of proposal that would have been committed to paper or made public. But the idea has persisted down through the years, and there is proof that Anderson and Poe were in each other's company on at least one social occasion. In addition, a decade after Anderson's death, a witness under oath was to recall that the tobacconist said Poe had stopped by his shop "to get points" on the Rogers case.

What may be the best evidence, though, is found in John Anderson's advertisements in a short-lived newspaper called the *Broadway Journal*. Poe began to edit this weekly journal in March 1845, and in October 1845 he purchased it. The *Broadway Journal* was by no means a success, yet for some reason Anderson suddenly chose to place advertisements in it, beginning with the issue of November 8, 1845, and in all subsequent issues. Was it because Anderson was repaying an old debt?

Whether it was at Anderson's urging that Poe decided to write "The Mystery of Marie Roget" (setting the Mary Rogers case in France), or whether Poe merely decided to take up the challenge of an unsolved mystery, may never be determined. Nor was the tale destined to clear John Anderson's name, however much Poe strove to show Anderson's innocence, even going so far as to give him the fictional name of Le Blanc, meaning white or spotless. For prior to the appearance of the second and final installment of the tale, the Mary Rogers murder was to be "solved" by the ravings of a dying woman. The embers of the case were thus fanned into a scandalous inferno that was to burn into the very soul and sanity of John Anderson.

On the first or second day of November 1842, Frederica Loss—who operated the New Jersey inn near where Mary Rogers' clothes had been found—was shot by one of her sons. The fatally injured woman was soon delirious, though she did not die until November 10. During that time her rambling words assumed a certain pattern—a pattern the family physician soon associated with the ill-fated Mary Rogers.

Rumors began to spread, but Dr. Gautier, who attended the dying woman, insisted that Mrs. Loss knew nothing more about Mary's death than had appeared in the newspapers a year before. It was possible, some thought, that Mrs. Loss's memories of the bizarre case had been revived by the first installment of "The Mystery of Marie Roget" in the November issue (on sale about the middle of October) of the *Ladies' Companion.*

At the inquest, held on November 11, the coroner exonerated her son by concluding that Mrs. Loss's death was accidental. But four days after that, the deceased Mrs. Loss and all three of her sons were accused (in an affidavit filed by a Hudson County, New Jersey, justice of the peace) of complicity in the death of Mary Rogers, as well as with disposing of the corpse.

The New York newspapers, which days earlier had picked up the scent of the rumors hovering over Weehawken, soon had what was purported to be the full story. The New York *Herald* bluntly stated that Mary Rogers had been the victim of a bungled abortion, rather than dying from strangulation following a gang rape, as first believed. The illegal operation supposedly had been performed by an un-named doctor at the inn owned by Mrs. Loss. After trussing the corpse to make it look as if Mary had been attacked and strangled, the body was dumped into the Hudson and some of the clothes thrown into a nearby pond. Later, the clothing was retrieved and strewn in the thicket near the Nick Moore Inn.

On November 19, 1842, a hearing was held in Jersey City. But there had been no actual deathbed confession by Mrs. Loss—at least none that had been committed to paper. Nor was there any evidence or witnesses to link her three sons with the crime. And though one newspaper feebly promised, "The magistrates are on the scent and these investigations will not end here," the hearing was, indeed, the end of the Mary Rogers case—at least the official part of it. For John Anderson, it was far from over.

Although there were no more developments in the mystery, from time to time the name of Mary Rogers came before the public eye. In 1844, J. H. Ingraham wrote a fictional account called *The Beautiful Cigar Girl*, and in 1851 there appeared a sensational piece of trash titled *A Confession of the Awful Bloody Transactions in the Life of the Fiend-like Murderer of Miss Mary Rogers*. Then, eighteen years later, an incident in Andrew Davis' *Tales of a Physician* once again recalled the Rogers case.

If these sporadic reminders bothered John Anderson, he did not reveal it—at least not publicly. Nor did his association with Mary Rogers seem to affect his business, which eventually made him a millionaire, for Anderson's Solace Tobacco became known all over the country. Its popularity was due in great measure to the fact that Anderson was the first to maintain the freshness of tobacco by wrapping it in tinfoil. Later real estate dealings increased his fortune, much of which he gave away in a series of philanthropic acts, including his donation of the Tarrytown monument erected in 1880.

By that time, Anderson had been a resident of Tarrytown for nearly a decade, having built a mansion on North Broadway that was noteworthy for its massive steel shutters. When closed, these shutters made the house look like a fortress, as if its master felt the need of such safety. But steel provides no protection against the supernatural, and stories survive about a ghost seen in the shuttered mansion. Those old tales do not tell whose ghost it was, for although John Anderson "had his peculiarities" (as mentioned in Scharf's *History of Westchester County*), the story of his obsession was not brought out until a decade after his death, when in 1891 a bitter legal battle was fought by the heirs to his fortune.

As this trial progressed, it was revealed that not only had Anderson been questioned by the police in regard to the death of Mary Rogers, but he had also been arrested and later released due to lack of evidence. Since several influential people knew of his arrest, Anderson had felt that it severely injured his reputation. In fact, once, when walking with his business partner Felix McCloskey, Anderson had pointed to Mary's former home at 126 Nassau Street, calling it the "damned house" that had driven him "out of politics" and had "kept him from advancing."

Even years later, when Fernando Wood approached Anderson

with the suggestion that he run for mayor of New York City, Anderson flatly refused, giving as his reason the Mary Rogers mystery, which he felt still besmirched his name.

Colonel Edward C. James testified at the 1891 trail that Anderson was never able to "shake off" this impression, "which, when his faculties began to fail and old age to creep upon him, lent a controlling force which undermined his intellectual powers." James's statement was backed up by various witnesses, including one-time State Senator Abner C. Mattoon, who told the court that Anderson said Mary Rogers had "appeared to him in the spirit from time to time." Anderson was so convinced of these ghostly visitations that he even began to dabble in spiritualism, believing Mary advised him on business investments and talked to him about the circumstances of her death.

Modern-day psychologists might view Anderson's many acts of philanthropy as an attempt to assuage his guilt over Mary's death. But of what was Anderson guilty?

At the 1891 trial, his partner testified that Anderson told him, "I want people to believe I had no hand in her [Mary] taking off." Then McCloskey went on to say that Anderson "assured me that he *hadn't* anything *directly, himself,* to do with it."

The key word in this denial surely is *directly,* for another witness was to tell the court that Anderson admitted "an abortion had been committed on the girl—the year before her murder took place, or a year and a half... and that he got into some trouble about it.... Outside of that there was no grounds on earth for anybody to suppose he had anything to do with the murder."

Though there had been talk of an affair between Anderson and his lovely employee, there is no evidence to convict his of impregnating Mary—either a year and a half before her death or in 1841. As for James Gordon Bennett's besmirching remark in the New York *Herald* that Mary had lived with Anderson, this was true, but not in the way Bennett meant for it to be taken. Later investigation brought to light that a close friendship had existed between Anderson's wife and Mary, and that the "Beautiful Seegar Girl" *and her mother* went to live in the Anderson home prior to the purchase of the Rogers boardinghouse.

Considering his generosity and obvious regard for the girl, Anderson may well have arranged—or at least provided funds for—an abortion a year or so before Mary's death. If this were so, then he might well have felt that he had helped her along the "road to ruination" that had resulted in another affair and the subsequent bungled abortion. It is also possible that Mary, having been aided once before by Anderson, again approached her former employer when she found herself pregnant in 1841. Responding either to threat or compassion, Anderson might have given her the money to terminate the pregnancy or even arranged for the abortion. Had he done so, he would have felt some responsibility for her death, though he had not been *directly* involved in it.

Whatever the case, the steel-shuttered mansion on North Broadway became a ghost-ridden prison for John Anderson, whose release came only with his death in November 1881. In time the house itself was demolished, so that today the only material memento of the man in Tarrytown is the handsome statue in Patriots' Park. A much better way to recall the other John Anderson—for his generosity, rather than for the dark mystery that haunted him to the grave.

23 THE LEATHERMAN

HE WAS A WANDERER without much wealth or warmth, and so uncommunicative that even today we are not certain of his real name. Yet a century after his death, this mysterious marcher continues to capture the imagination of young and old alike, just as he did when people first dubbed him "The Leatherman."

They called him that because of his ungainly garb. Winter or summer, he wore a heavy, below-the-knees coat made of leather patches he had crudely stitched together with thongs of the same material. Completing the handmade outfit were long leather pants and hat, plus a pair of leather-topped wooden-soled shoes resembling sabots. All these were worn without benefit of any undergarment to buffer the rub of leather against flesh—which is one of the reasons it is thought the Leatherman was acting out some kind of self-imposed penance.

Another reason is the obsessive schedule he set for himself. For three decades—from about 1860 until his death in 1889—the Leatherman made a clockwise circuit of approximately 365 miles every 34 days, walking every step of the way, from Westchester County to Putnam, then crossing over into Connecticut at Ball's Pond. From there, he generally headed northeast to Harwinton, then southeast to the Connecticut River, which he followed down to

Saybrook. Turning west at Saybrook, he returned along the coastline to Westchester, only to commence the same journey all over again.

The Leatherman avoided large towns and main roads whenever he could and rarely conversed with people he met. And while he accepted food at the farmhouses where he stopped, he steadfastly refused invitations to stay overnight. Instead, after eating each day, with a polite but silent bow to his hostess, he would retire to a nearby cave or rockshelter—sometimes a hut he had built—and in the morning his never-ending trek would be resumed.

Over the years, as the regularity of his appearances was recognized, people realized that this solitary man with the mournful gray eyes was no ordinary tramp. In fact, when Connecticut enacted an anti-tramp law in 1884, it specifically exempted the Leatherman. Nor was he mentally deficient, despite his odd manner. He even exhibited a certain pride, accepting few handouts other than a meal each day, cast-off bits of leather to be used in repairing his outfit, and occasionally some tobacco.

One story that has been handed down tells of a farmer who, knowing the Leatherman was due, left some shiny pennies on a log where the wanderer usually rested. The next day the farmer found his pennies gone, but in their place was an equal amount of old and dull coins. Other reports tell of the Leatherman leaving money for eggs he occasionally took from some farmer's henhouse. But where he got those coins is a mystery, for he refused all monetary donations and was never known to take a job.

When he made his daily stop for food, it was not at just any farmhouse, but one he had selected and to which he would return every time he was in the vicinity. Such a distinction was enjoyed by rural housewives, and some of them even cooked special dishes on the day the Leatherman was expected. They could count on his arrival, too, for he was not usually delayed by bad weather or the rough terrain he traversed.

Stories began to gather in his wake, and in time children could be heard to chant a rhyme handed down from a seventeenth-century broadside:

> One misty, moisty morning
> When cloudy was the weather

> I chanced to meet an old man
> Clothed all in leather....

The rhyme followed him from one community to another, and mothers sometimes used his name as a bugaboo: "You better be good or the old Leatherman will get you!" But even though his weird appearance might occasionally frighten horses as he tramped down a country road in his creaking suit and clumping sabots, the Leatherman was never known to show unkindness to anyone. Indeed, he frequently was seen repairing holes in the road, possibly so that horses would not trip in one and break a leg.

On occasion, he would adjust his route, abandoning a farmhouse dinner stop if new owners had moved in or if other circumstances were not to his liking. For instance, when he was harassed one day by workmen building the second Croton Aqueduct, he never returned to that area. Another time, when trees were felled near a cave he used on the Ryder farm in Briarcliff, he gave up his overnight lodging there and built a hut on the nearby Dell farm.

Because of these changes, no exact route can be established for the Leatherman. However, it is still possible for modern-day travelers to approximate his circuit, seeing many of the places he frequented and perhaps joining the ranks of the hundreds of Leatherman buffs who have been captivated by the story of this strange but gentle man who became a folk hero in his own time.

His trail can be picked up at dozens of places in Westchester: from Chappaqua, where he reportedly read his Bible as he sat beside the old cemetery, to Whitehall Corners, where a resident once gave the wanderer a brand-new pair of boots. (The Leatherman promptly cut off the tops, which he stowed away in the huge bag he always carried on his back, then threw away the soles of the boots!) But perhaps the best place of all to start tracking down the Leatherman is at Ward Pound Ridge Reservation, in Cross River. Not only does the Trailside Museum there have a permanent Leatherman exhibit, featuring some of the wanderer's belongings, but park visitors can also see one of the caves he used near Honey Hollow Road.

Excavations of the Ward Pound Ridge Reservation cave have

produced little evidence of the Leatherman's occupancy, but another cave in Armonk (also called Helicker's Cave, on the hill overlooking the exit from Route 22 to Old Route 22) yielded a metal-stemmed pipe that may have belonged to him. Other overnight shelters of his that can still be seen in Westchester include one on the western slope of Bull's Hill (at Haines Road in Bedford Hills) and a small cave formed by fallen boulders on Hillcrest Drive, north of Briarcliff Manor.

From Briarcliff, the Leatherman usually headed toward Yorktown and then to Shrub Oak, where he surprised residents one day in 1885 by entering the Darrow grocery store at the invitation of the owner. Seeing this as an opportunity to learn something about the mysterious wanderer, Mr. Darrow handed the Leatherman a piece of paper and asked him to write down his age. The number given was 15342!

Was this the scrawl of a semiliterate, perhaps uncomprehending man, a man who simply did not wish to be bothered, or did it signify that the writer had been born on the fifteenth day of the third month in the year 1842? The latter would have meant the Leatherman was then forty-three years old—an age consistent with his appearance, as well as with an autopsy report made four years later, which described him as being "about fifty years." But nobody knows for certain, since the Leatherman never explained those cryptic figures— just as he never revealed what compelled him to continue his circuit.

Leaving Shrub Oak, the Leatherman would go through Jefferson Valley, Mahopac, and Brewster, eventually reaching the Connecticut border. From there, he sometimes headed southeast to Redding, for there are accounts of his stopping at the Platt homestead (now the headquarters of the Redding Historical Society), on Route 107. Usually, though, at the start of his trek into Connecticut, he followed a more northeasterly course through New Fairfield and New Milford and on to Woodbury.

It was at Woodbury that around 1885 a young man discovered some clues to the Leatherman's background. Finding the wanderer lying ill in a cave, the young man nursed him back to health, during which time he had occasion to examine the contents of the bag the Leatherman carried. Among various handmade utensils, there was a prayerbook printed in French and bearing the publication date 1844. The young man also reported that the Leatherman was wearing an Agnus Dei around his neck.

Obviously the Leatherman was a French Catholic—a conclusion further supported by his few vocal exchanges with others, wherein he was said to have spoken in halting English, or else French. The sabots he fashioned for his feet also hinted of a French origin. But it was still a mystery as to why he had left his homeland to pursue an apparently penitential existence in America.

If he was aware of the interest he aroused wherever he went, the Leatherman remained unconcerned, never varying from his travels, even when it was obvious he was ill and in need of medical care. By 1887, it was taking him longer to complete his circuit, and people began noticing an open sore on his lip that gradually spread. The pain must have been great even then, for he accepted medication from a Saybrook doctor at whose home he regularly stopped.

The sore worsened until, on December 2, 1888, concerned citizens of Middletown, Connecticut, literally arrested the leather-clad figure and took him to Hartford Hospital. But they could not legally detain him against his will, and after treatment he was released to continue his lonely and now painful journey.

Although newspapers throughout the area he traversed had been reporting on the Leatherman since 1885 (at which time a Connecticut man named Chauncey Hotchkiss had published an itinerary of his travels), it was not until after his arrest at Middletown that a number of stories appeared that claimed to solve the mystery of the Leatherman.

Individual accounts varied, but most agreed he had been born Jules Bourglay in Lyons, France, and as a young man he had fallen in love with the daughter of a wealthy leather merchant. The girl's father frowned on this romance, but he finally consented to give Jules a chance to prove himself worthy. Jules would go to work for him and if, within a year, the young man was successful, the merchant would allow the lovers to marry. On the other hand, if Jules did not do well in the leather business, he was to give up all claim to the girl and leave Lyons.

Details differ as to what caused Jules to fail, but his venture in the leather business was a financial disaster, followed shortly afterward by the death of the girl he loved. Some accounts say she died in a mysterious fire that destroyed her father's house.

Destitute and possibly demented by grief, Jules Bourglay emigrated to America, where he donned a leather suit as a symbol of his failure and became the derelict known as the Leatherman.

These stories about his background—widely circulated but never documented—brought forth even more offers of aid. One came from New York City's Globe Museum. The proprietors wanted the Leatherman to exhibit himself in exchange for financial gain. But the Leatherman silently turned his back on both friendship and freakdom, and followed his accustomed path.

Somehow the Leatherman survived the brutal winter of 1888-89, though the cancer he suffered from made it impossible for him to eat anything except bread soaked in coffee—and he only managed that by holding a leather shield over his ravaged lower jaw. His steps were slower now, almost stumbling at times, and he was forced to sit down and rest every few minutes. Yet he trudged on until March 1889, when he was found dead in the rude hut he had constructed on the Dell farm in Briarcliff.

Earlier that year, newspapers had reported the arrival of a Frenchman named Jules Martins, who was searching for the Leatherman in order to give him a fortune he had inherited. The newspaper accounts went on to relate that a meeting between the two men had been scheduled to take place in Bridgeport.

Whether the meeting ever occurred, or even if there was such a man as Jules Martins, has never been confirmed, but the idea of an inheritance was enough to touch off a flurry of fortune-hunting forays to all the Leatherman's known caves. There was even talk of the Leatherman having been murdered for his money, but this was ruled out at a coroner's inquest, which concluded he died of blood poisoning resulting from his illness.

Ironically, the body of the man who so zealously had protected his privacy was put on public view at White and Dorsey's funeral parlor in Ossining. Then, after his belongings were parceled out—his costume first going to the Globe Museum, then to the Eden Musée in New York City, and his shoes exhibited at a Danbury store—the Leatherman was buried in the pauper's section of the Sparta Cemetery in Ossining. For many years, the grave remained unmarked. Then, in 1953, the historical societies of Ossining and Westchester County erected a headstone with a bronze plaque that reads in part: "Final resting place of Jules Bourglay of Lyons, France—'The Leatherman.'"

His trail ends there, but not his legend. Those who had known the Leatherman passed on his story to succeeding generations, and poems, articles, and even books have been written about him. But none have solved the mystery. Attempts to locate some record of Jules Bourglay in France have failed, and a host of questions are still unanswered, including the purpose of a strange leather device resembling a dog's muzzle said to have been found in his pack, along with two handmade books "filled with hieroglyphics no one could decipher."

So in death the Leatherman has remained the enigmatic figure he was in life—and just as fascinating. For he represents different things to different people. Some see only the tragedy of a lost love. Others marvel at the superior woodsmanship that enabled him to survive three decades of living in the open with only the most primitive equipment. Still others see in him a kind of absolute freedom—a freedom seemingly unobtainable in our modern society. For many he is symbolic of utter loneliness, and there are those who are intrigued solely by the mystery he presents. But whatever his image and whatever his name, it cannot be denied that the Leatherman has taken a permanent place in the folklore of the Hudson Valley.

24 THE VENGEANCE OF TOM QUICK

TO SOME PEOPLE he was an avenging angel. Others called him a crazed cold-blooded killer. And even today—centuries after he stalked his human prey through the Shawangunks and the Catskills—mere mention of Tom Quick's name can spark controversy. But be he hero or hellion, it cannot be denied that this legendary loner was one of the most colorful characters ever to live in the region.

His life began back in 1734; the legend developed much later. Yet even during his boyhood years on a wilderness farm near what is now Milford, Pennsylvania, Tom Quick exhibited certain traits that—seen with hindsight—were unmistakable signs of what was to come.

He was bright and hardworking, with a deeply ingrained sense of duty and devotion to his parents. Young Tom's energies, however, were not expended in such pursuits as formal education and farming. These he left to his four younger brothers and sisters, steadfastly refusing to return to school after attending only a few sessions. The lessons Tom preferred were those taught him by the local Indians, and he readily learned their language, while becoming an expert hunter and trapper.

During the two decades prior to the outbreak of the French and Indian War, in 1754, peaceful relations existed between the native American population and the few white families that had settled in the area where the Neversink River meets the Delaware. It was therefore commonplace for Indians to show up at the Quick homestead, where Thomas Sr. befriended all and counted several as close friends. So did young Tom, who at an early age took over the job of supplying the family with meat and fish, while his siblings tended to more domestic tasks. That is not to say Tom shirked work; when an extra hand was needed at the family farm or lumber mill, he willingly wielded saw or scythe. It was just that Tom was happier as a hunter, and the large amount of meat needed for the family larder allowed him to follow in the footsteps of his Indian friends.

It was during this time that Tom learned all the Indian trails from Port Jervis to Ellenville and west to Callicoon. And as he traveled these trails, he memorized every major landmark, never realizing how often this knowledge would help save his life in later years, or that he was absorbing all-important survival tactics from trusted friends who were destined to become his mortal enemies.

The incident that triggered the blood feud that would rule the remainder of Tom Quick's life occurred at the start of the French and Indian War, when he was twenty years old. Convinced by his father that the woods were now too dangerous for a lone hunter, the six-foot, dark-haired Tom gave up his wilderness wandering and remained at home to help with the family business.

One winter day he accompanied his father and brother-in-law to the shore of the frozen Delaware in search of saplings for use as barrel hoops. Just as they rounded a bend in the river, a shot rang out from the ridge above them, and Thomas Quick Sr. crumpled to the ground. Shrill cries identified the ambushers as Indians, as well as revealing their exact location, but the three white men had neglected to bring rifles with them, and their only recourse was to retreat.

Dragging the injured man between them, Tom and his brother-in-law outdistanced the pursuing Indians for awhile. Then, as the Indians began closing the gap, Thomas Quick Sr. ordered the two younger men to leave him behind in order to save themselves. There was no hope for him anyway, the mortally wounded man insisted, and it was senseless for all three of them to die.

Tom and his brother-in-law reluctantly obeyed, risking a race across the open face of the frozen Delaware in order to reach safety on the opposite shore. As they ran, balls from the Indians' muskets whizzed past them. One ricocheted off the heel of Tom's boot, sending him sprawling. He was back on his feet in an instant, though, and shortly thereafter he and his brother-in-law had secreted themselves in the bushes on the opposite bank. From there, the two men were forced to listen to the death cries of Thomas Quick, Sr., as the Indians scalped and mutilated him.

It was a totally different Tom Quick who recovered his beloved father's body the following day. Never very talkative, he turned taciturn and humorless. In fact, after the death of his father, the only joke Tom Quick was ever heard to utter came years later when he killed an Indian carrying several deerskins. Upon bringing the booty to a settlement and being asked how he had managed to get so many deerskins, Tom smiled coldly as he explained, "I shot one buck on top of another." Indeed, shooting "bucks" had become his profession—a bloodthirsty path Tom Quick followed for more than three decades.

To return to the time of Thomas Quick, Sr.'s death: accounts differ as to the exact wording of his son's vow of vengeance. One tradition tells of Tom swearing to kill a hundred Indians, and that on his deathbed his sole regret was that the tally came to *only* ninety-nine. Another version has Tom vowing never to rest until no Indian could be found on the banks of the Delaware, while a third simply says Tom promised never to be at peace with the Indians. Whichever—if any—is the true version matters little, since the results were the same.

The French and Indian War provided a perfect medium for such a man with murder on his mind. And while Tom was too wildly independent to enlist as a soldier, it is said he acted as a guide, "rendering important services to the English in their excursions against the Indians." Nine years of war in no way vitiated his personal vendetta, though, and Tom was more than ready when a chance encounter put him in contact with one of his father's killers.

About two years after the French and Indian War ended, Tom had occasion to visit Decker's Tavern, near present-day Huguenot in western Orange County. Inside, an Indian named Muskwink, having had too much to drink, began boasting of his wartime activities, including the ambush of a settler down on the Delaware a decade earlier.

Tom listened only long enough to hear Muskwink mimic the cries of the torture victim. Then, as the befuddled brave displayed a set of silver buttons he had taken from the corpse—the same buttons that had been missing from the clothing of Thomas Quick, Sr.—Tom made his move. Grabbing a rifle from over the fireplace, Tom aimed it at Muskwink and motioned for the Indian to precede him out of the tavern. None of the other patrons interfered, nor did they question Tom Quick when he returned alone to the tavern later that day, replaced the rifle over the fireplace, downed a dram of rum, and once more departed.

What happened during those intervening hours was only guessed at until Peter Decker was plowing a field near the tavern a few years later and uncovered a skeleton. Tom Quick had shot Muskwink in the back, then buried the body in a shallow grave. One local legend says that Tom also hacked the head from the torso and impaled it on a post where the lane to Decker's Tavern met the Old Mine Road (Route 209), but that is unlikely, since subsequent events showed Tom to be quite cagey about his crimes—and shooting an unarmed Indian in the back was considered a crime even in those racially tense times of the late 1700s.

Shortly after he murdered Muskwink, Tom was hunting along the banks of the Delaware at Butler's Rift when he spotted a canoe containing an Indian family of five. Recognizing the man paddling as someone who used to visit his father's home, Tom ordered the Indian to come ashore. Then Tom shot the man, tomahawked the squaw and two children, but hesitated when he saw the Indian baby smiling up at him. It was a brief hiatus; hefting the innocent infant by the heels, Tom dashed out its brains on a nearby rock.

Tom never confessed to this bloodcurdling crime until the last days of his life when, no longer wary of possible prosecution, he gave a full accounting to his nephew, Jacob Quick, of Callicoon. As might be expected, Jacob questioned why Tom wreaked vengeance on a harmless baby. "Nits make lice," came the unrepentant reply.

Despite that oft-repeated tale, Tom rarely targeted children for his revenge, if only because they presented no challenge. For risk was something he relished, often taking chances he did not have to take, as if prompted by some deep-seated death wish—a motive suggested by one modern-day psychologist who saw in Tom Quick's outward anger a manifestation of inward guilt over leaving his father behind to die.

Whatever motivated Tom Quick, he was as cunning as he was cruel, often pretending a friendliness he did not feel in order to entice an intended victim. A vivid example of this ruse occurred in Sullivan County, where Tom met an Indian walking along a ridge trail one day. Fortunately for Tom, who was unarmed, the Indian did not recognize him. But the Indian had heard of Tom Quick, and when Tom companionably confided that he had seen the notorious "Avenger" walking in a field below the ridge, the Indian peered over the edge of the precipice, intent on getting a glimpse of his people's enemy—and perhaps getting off a shot as well. But the only thing he got was a hard shove from behind.

As is apparent in the preceding story, the Indians were not long in learning of Tom's vow of vengeance, and they were as determined to kill him as he was to kill them. Yet try as they might, Tom eluded death, and in time the Indians were convinced their adversary led a charmed life. It certainly seems as if he did.

For instance, there was the time Tom was in a toe-to-toe shootout with an Indian. Both fired at the same time. The Indian lost his life. Tom lost only the tip of his thumb.

Another time, Tom was captured by a war party who tied his hands with thongs and marched him toward their village, where they planned to torture him. Along the way, a rainstorm soaked the rawhide restraints, loosening them long enough for Tom to free his hands. Tom waited until the party was passing a hollow tree in which he had secreted a gun. (He habitually hid firearms along trails he frequented.) He then paused at the tree on the pretext of relieving himself and, with back turned to his captors, managed to load the gun. The unsuspecting Indians never knew what hit them.

Still another time, some Indians surrounded a cabin where Tom was staying. Rather than risk an open fight, they decided to lure him away from his weapons by taking his cow into the woods. When he came looking for the animal, they would ambush him. They hadn't counted on Tom's uncanny ability to sense danger, though. And while Tom's suspicions were not aroused by the untethered cow's straying into the woods, he did deem it odd when he heard the wild jangling of the bell around the neck of the agitated animal. Circling the sound, he surprised the Indians from behind, and the ambushers became the ambushed.

The best of the ambush tales, however, concerns a strange partnership Tom formed with an Indian called Cahoonzie. Supposedly a renegade Pequot whose people had perished at the hands of the Delawares, Cahoonzie is said to have joined forces with Tom at Lifting Rocks, a spectacular formation high above Hawk's Nest Drive (Route 97), a few miles west of Port Jervis.

The site was a perfect observation post, with a series of perched boulders set on a ledge overlooking the Delaware River, plus a nearby cave for shelter. It was there that the two men were staying when they spotted a large group of Delaware Indians setting up camp in the valley below.

Outnumbered but unwilling to lose an opportunity to kill more of their avowed enemies, Tom and Cahoonzie hit upon a daring plan that began with them smearing the Lifting Rocks with pitch. Then the two avengers stuffed dried wood inside the small cave and around the Lifting Rocks.

This done, Tom stealthily made his way down the mountain to a spot between the Indians and the river. There he waited until a plume of pitchy smoke rose from the fire Cahoonzie had ignited at Lifting Rocks. With the Delawares' attention fixed on the inferno above them, Tom set another fire, cutting the Indians off from the river. The Delawares had no choice but to head up the mountain. But just as they did so, a pitch-smeared flaming boulder came plummeting down the mountainside, setting fire to the underbrush as it rolled. Those Delawares not hit by the boulder were trapped between the two fires and the entire party perished, without Tom Quick or Cahoonzie firing a single shot.

A life lived constantly looking over his shoulder took its toll on Tom, who was gaunt and grizzled by the time he finished serving in the Revolutionary War—again, not as an enlisted soldier but as an independent agent in expeditions against the Indians. He had remained a bachelor and at war's end returned to his old haunts and habits, as is seen in an eyewitness account of an incident that took place at Brodhead's Tavern, on Sandburg Creek, around 1784.

The writer had gone into the tavern's taproom, where he found a "wild, rough-looking man.... His cheekbones were high like an Indian's and he was spare in flesh ... a very bony man. His eyes were gray, and such a fiery pair of gray eyes was never seen before nor since. They seemed to go right through you, and made you feel uneasy while he looked at you.... The landlord groaned... 'That's Tom Quick.'"

The writer went on to say how Tom followed three Indians out of the tavern and a little while later three shots were heard. Tom returned shortly thereafter carrying three extra rifles, but the "landlord charged all [the other patrons in the tavern] to say nothing of what had occurred, as it might bring the settlers into trouble with the Indians."

It certainly brought Tom trouble from the Indians, for he was captured by a group of them the following summer. Imprisoned in a cabin loft, he managed to escape with his life, but the loss of all his possessions, which had been stolen by his captors, rekindled his passion for revenge.

Tom, therefore, was more than ready when a man named Ben Haines summoned him to exterminate two Indians staying at his cabin near Handsome Eddy on the Delaware. When Tom arrived, the Indians, unaware of Haines's perfidy, were peacefully fishing from a large rock in the river.

Tom's first bullet struck the one called Canope, but did not kill him, so Ben Haines finished the Indian off by bashing him in the head with a pine knot. Meanwhile, the other Indian, Ben Shanks, escaped by feigning injury, then falling into the river, where the current swept him away from the blood-soaked boulder. Canope Rock, still a popular fishing site and named for the murdered Indian, is on the New York side of the Delaware, about 3 miles downriver from Barryville, in Sullivan County. Ironically, Barryville now hosts the annual powwow of the Indian League of the Americas, which owns 35 acres of the land Tom Quick once stalked.

The killing of Canope marked the end of Tom Quick's career as the "Avenger," possibly in part because of public disfavor—for Canope had been well regarded in the community of Cochecton, where he lived—as well as the fact that not many Indians remained in the area. But the main reason for the end of the murders was that Tom, though still in his fifties, had become an old and infirm man.

During his final years, Tom divided his time between a hut near Hagen Pond, in Lumberland, a friend's cabin by the Mongaup River, and the Rosencrantz home, a few miles down the Delaware from Port Jervis. It was in the Rosencrantz home that he died, during 1796, and he was buried in the Rose family cemetery.

According to one tradition, when the Indians heard of Tom's demise, they exhumed the body of their old enemy, cut it up, and sent pieces of it to outlying villages of their people as a symbolic ritual. They were unaware that Tom had died of smallpox—and the decimating disease was thus distributed among the Indians.

This tale of Tom Quick's final revenge is more fanciful than factual. For Tom's remains are known to have been removed (assumedly intact) from the Rose family cemetery in 1889 and reinterred under a monument on Sarah Street in Milford, where they remain until this day. As for the rest of the legend and the man himself: take Tom Quick in the context of his times; take some of the stories about him with a grain of salt.

25 RAMAPO COWBOY

ON A FRIGID January day in 1779, a tall, handsome man was unshackled from a dungeon in the Orange County Jail at Goshen, and escorted outside to a waiting gallows tree. The condemned man was garbed in black broadcloth on which silver buttons reflected the bleak winter sunlight. He carefully kicked off the shoes he wore, causing a shocked murmur to riffle through the assembled crowd.

A brief nod was accorded several onlookers standing below him. An even briefer glance was cast over their heads, as if in search of a rescue party he knew would never come. Then the noose was tightened around the neck of the prisoner. Where the shoeless feet had been unflinchingly standing was suddenly empty space. The body plummeted down, then swung crazily for a few minutes, finally slowing down to a sway.

It was over. The "Scourge of the Ramapos" was ended. Claudius Smith was dead.

Yet there is no way to kill a legend, and Claudius Smith had become a legend long before his life ended that winter day in Goshen's public square. The legend has grown even more colorful and controversial as the intervening years help smother the flames of old hatreds, and historians take a cooler look at what was, in fact, America's first civil war.

Had it not been for that war—the Revolution—Claudius Smith might be remembered today only as a member of the family that gave its name to Smith's Clove, in the Orange County town of Monroe. As it was, the Revolution did break out, pitting brother against brother and making enemies of friends.

For Claudius Smith, then in his fortieth year, King George was still the legal ruler of the British colonies in America. Therefore, though his son Samuel sided with the Patriots, Claudius fought for the Loyalist cause. Wars are not necessarily won on the battlefield, though, and Claudius used the tactics best suited for the mountain-ous terrain in which he lived: quick guerrilla-type raids on outlying Patriot farms and the solitary supply wagons of Washington's army. It was a career that lasted less than three years but would result in a mystery that the passage of more than two centuries has not seen solved.

Part of the mystery is the location of the loot Claudius Smith buried somewhere in the Ramapos—a treasure that has been sought many times but apparently never found. Equally intriguing is the mystery of the man variously referred to as the "Scourge of the Ramapos" and the "Ramapo Cowboy." For there are those who insist Claudius Smith was loyal to no one but himself; that supplying the British with cattle and horses stolen from the Patriots was done only to enrich his own purse and not because of any fealty to George III. Others believe he was a true partisan of the Crown, possibly even holding some sort of secret commission in the British Army, and thereby does not deserve the outlaw brand burned onto his name. There are even those who maintain he was a latter-day Robin Hood, giving to the poor what he stole from the rich and bent on aiding the helpless.

Strangely enough, there is evidence to support—if not prove— each of the three claims. And while the myth may never be separated from the man, the story of Claudius Smith makes for an exciting excursion into the history of the Hudson Valley. For there are numerous sites still in existence that may be visited by anyone following the trail of the Ramapo Cowboy.

That trail begins and ends in Monroe, where Claudius' father David settled prior to the Revolution. Not much is known about those early years, except that when he married and began raising his own family, Claudius lived just north of where his father's house still stands, on the southeast corner of Route 17M and Stage Road. It may have been there that Claudius' stepmother predicted he would "die like a trooper's horse"—with his shoes on. Her harsh words apparently bit into him deeply, for it was in defiance to her prediction that he kicked off his shoes moments before he was hanged.

Yet during the early years of the Revolution there seemed little if any chance of ever catching the wily Claudius and his gang of "cowboys" (a name given to those Tories or Loyalists who stole cattle and horses to sell to the British). It is true that he was apprehended once, in July 1777, for "stealing oxen belonging to the Continent," but he promptly broke out of jail and returned to the rugged Ramapo Mountains he knew so well. From there, using carefully selected caves as hideouts, he led a series of raids that terrorized inhabitants throughout the Ramapos and beyond.

The largest and best known of his hideouts is in Harriman State Park, along the Tuxedo-Mount Ivy Trail atop Huckleberry Hill—a cave that provides dramatic insight into why it was impossible to capture the Ramapo Cowboy in his mountain stronghold (though militiamen tried often enough). For a natural tunnel through the rocks leads up from the main chamber of the cave to the top of the hill, offering a protected escape route. In addition, a sentry stationed above would have ample time to warn of an impending attack, since there is an unobscured view for miles around.

A few hundred feet downhill to the east, there is another cave called Horse Stable Rock Shelter, since it was used to harbor the gang's four-footed loot, while a third rocky refuge is on Horsestable Mountain, just opposite Wesley Chapel—reachable by hiking northwest on the Sherwood Trail from Route 202.

These sites have long been popular with history buffs and hikers attracted by the legend of the enigmatic cowboy who could be as compassionate to his enemies as he was to his friends. As an illustration, the story is told of a meeting one morning in October 1777 between Claudius Smith and a man he knew called William

Bodle. The latter was returning home after his regiment had been defeated by the British at Fort Montgomery, so he understandably feared for his life when Claudius accosted him on the lonely road.

The fact that they were enemies seems not to have crossed the dark-haired cowboy's mind, however. Nor did he take advantage of what would have been easy pickings from the battle-weary Patriot soldier. Instead, Claudius sympathetically offered Bodle rest and breakfast at his nearby house—an invitation the startled Bodle accepted, although he then fled as soon as the Ramapo Cowboy was out of sight.

Defenseless women were not fair game to Claudius either, as he demonstrated one night a year later when he and his gang broke down the door of the Woodhull house, in Oxford. As they were doing so, the quick-witted Mrs. Woodhull, knowing the raiders were surely after the family silver, hid these possessions beneath her baby daughter lying in a cradle. With her husband away from home on duty with the army, the unprotected Mrs. Woodhull could easily have been forced to reveal the hiding place of the silver. Yet Claudius refrained from doing so, even after a thorough search of the house proved unsuccessful. And without harming Mrs. Woodhull or her child, he and his gang rode off, taking only a horse they found hobbled in the meadow outside.

This is not to say that Claudius could not be cruel. He could be—and cunningly so—especially when he felt he was avenging some wrong. The best example of this is his midnight raid on the home of Abimal Youngs, in Oxford Depot.

Prior to this, in October 1777, when the British overran Fort Montgomery, a Colonel McClaughry was captured and incarcerated in one of the infamous British prisons in New York City where so many American soldiers died before the Revolution ended in 1783. Only those prisoners with money to buy food and other necessities stood a chance of leaving those pestholes alive—a fact that was soon made apparent to Colonel McClaughry's wife.

Since Abimal Youngs was perhaps the only man in the farming community who had enough hard cash on hand to meet her needs, Mrs. McClaughry applied to him for a loan. After all, she reasoned,

Youngs was a professed supporter of the American cause. Surely he would help her husband, who had so courageously fought for that cause and was now being punished for doing so. But Mrs. McClaughry was wrong. Abimal Youngs would not lend her a penny, and she was forced to sell or pawn everything of value she owned—even her shoe buckles—in order to save her husband.

When Claudius Smith heard about this, he became enraged. It mattered not to him that he and the McClaughrys were on opposite sides of the Revolutionary fence. Youngs's heartless refusal was inexcusable in the opinion of the angry cowboy, and he vowed vengeance on the miserly man.

Not long after that, Claudius and his gang came calling on Abimal Youngs, demanding that he turn over all his money to them. Secure in the knowledge that his cash box was well hidden, Youngs stalwartly refused to reveal his secret, even when Claudius threatened to hang him.

As good as his word, Claudius had Youngs brought outside, where he was strung up on the well pole. But Claudius' cruelty did not extend to premeditated murder, and so he ordered Youngs to be brought down after only a few moments on the well pole. Again Claudius demanded that Youngs turn over his money. Again Youngs refused. And again Youngs was dangled from the well pole. But the miserly man remained adamant, and rather than kill him, Claudius released him, contenting himself with looting the house of all Youngs' valuable papers, including mortgages and bonds.

A little more than a year later, when Claudius stood waiting for his own hanging, Abimal Youngs called to him from the crowd gathered in Goshen Square, begging the condemned man to tell him where the papers were. Claudius nodded as the frantic Youngs went on to say that the papers were useless to anyone else but of great value to him. Then with the hint of a smile on his handsome face, the Ramapo Cowboy boldly replied, "Mr. Youngs, this is no time to talk about papers. Meet me in the next world, and I will tell you all about them!"

Since the souls of executed criminals were believed to lodge in hell, Abimal Youngs was effectively silenced by this invitation, and

Claudius Smith went to his death satisfied that he had extracted the last drop of vengeance.

It was not his crime against Abimal Youngs that brought Claudius to the gallows tree, however. It was not even the alleged murder of Major Nathaniel Strong, which occurred in October 1778, and which Claudius was believed (but never proven) to have committed. But Strong's death did prompt New York Governor Clinton to offer a reward of $1,200 for the capture of the cowboy leader, and that was when Claudius' luck began running out.

By eighteenth-century standards, $1,200 constituted a small fortune, so it is not surprising that Claudius fled to British-held New York City rather than risk betrayal by a member of his gang or by one of the mountain people he had befriended and who in turn had sheltered him during his cowboy career. As it turned out, Claudius probably would have been safer with the impoverished but proud mountain folk, many of whom regarded him as a hero. For despite his partisan activities, the British in New York City did little to make him welcome, and Claudius soon decided to head for Long Island, where he had been born.

At that time, the British also controlled Long Island, though it was easy enough for Patriots to row across the Sound from Connecticut and conduct whatever business they had pending. It was just such an infiltrating patriot, Major John Brush—arriving to inspect his Long Island farm, which at the outbreak of the war had been left in the care of tenants—who spotted Claudius in Smithtown. Returning to the mainland, Brush enlisted the aid of several other men, and they set back out across Long Island Sound, bent on capturing Claudius Smith.

It was late at night when they reached the house of the widow who had rented an upstairs bedroom to the cowboy from Orange County. A few minutes of conversation with the landlady, perhaps the tinkle of a few coins in her palm, and the four bounty hunters broke into the room where Claudius was sleeping. He reached for the pistols under his pillow, but his captors were too quick. The "Scourge of the Ramapos" was securely bound, then hastily conveyed to the waiting whaleboat.

Once across Long Island Sound, the party continued west through southern Connecticut and thence to Fishkill landing on the Hudson. From there, Orange County Sheriff Isaac Nicholl escorted Claudius to Goshen, where he was chained to the floor in the basement of the Orange County jail. Fearing that the cowboy gang might attack the log-and-stone structure to rescue their leader, Sheriff Nicholl made a public announcement that the guards had orders to shoot Claudius if the jail was stormed. It was not.

Capital punishment was meted out more freely two centuries ago, and on January 13, 1779, when Claudius was found guilty of "burglary at the house of John Earle," "robbery in the dwelling house of Ebenezer Woodhull," and "robbery of the dwelling...and...still house of William Bell," he was sentenced to die. Nine days later he was hanged in Goshen Square, and his body was buried nearby in an unmarked grave in the southwest section of what is now the greensward of the First Presbyterian Church.

But that is not the end of the Claudius Smith story. Many years later, when Goshen's 1841 courthouse was being built, workmen uncovered a cache of human bones in the area where Claudius had been interred. Some accounts say the bones were discovered by a gentleman who happened to notice a depression in the ground and began probing the spot with his walking stick.

Whatever the manner of discovery, the nearly forgotten grave yielded a number of bones, including a skull whose larger-than-normal dimensions identified it as belonging to Claudius Smith (for it was remembered that he had been an exceedingly large man with a leonine head). Tradition holds that, as a warning to all would-be criminals, the skull was immured over the doorway of the courthouse then being built, and that it remains there to this day. As for the other bones recovered, some were made into knife handles for fanciers of such "morbidiana," and supposedly one shinbone was placed in a specially built glass case which still rests in some private collection.

It is believed that whatever was left of Claudius Smith's skeleton after the collectors got finished with it was secretly buried in an unmarked grave in the western section of the Monroe Cemetery, on Route 17M. It is there one can find the red sandstone marker (with self-composed epitaph) of Claudius' father David, with his brother Hophni buried alongside. Between the two tombstones there is a spot of bare ground large enough to bury a few bones but unmarked by any tablet. And so it is that the last resting place of the Ramapo Cowboy remains something of a mystery, as has the man.

26 THE CANNIBAL OF COLUMBIA COUNTY

SOMEWHERE IN THE Columbia County town of Austerlitz, high atop one of the cloud-capped cones of the Taconics, lies an abandoned gold mine. The mine was never commercially profitable—the yellow-streaked white quartz yielded little more than enough gold for a single vest button. But that button was enough to precipitate one of the most macabre murders ever committed.

It was on a snowy January day in 1882 that the grisly remains of a hacked-up human torso were found in a secluded mountain cabin near the New York/Massachusetts border. Despite the condition of the corpse—its charred skull inside a wood stove, bits of its liver cooked in a frying pan, and other parts apparently prepared for pickling in a brine barrel—the victim was readily identified, as was the perpetrator of the ghastly crime. Yet it took more than six years for the case to be settled, and there are still those who question whether justice was really done.

Certainly there was little sympathy for Oscar Beckwith when, at the age of sixty-seven, he returned from the Far West to live in Austerlitz, where he had been born in 1810. People still remembered Beckwith's wild ways as a youth and the fact that thirty-five years earlier he had escaped from a Poughkeepsie jail after being charged with counterfeiting. Old rumors were also repeated of his purported association with a gang of horse thieves at Boston Corner, just south of Austerlitz. But Beckwith had grown old and stooped during the many years he had been absent from Austerlitz, and when he repaired to a mountain cabin on the small parcel of land he owned, residents of the rural community seemed content to let sleeping dogs lie.

Hungry dogs do not sleep, however—and Beckwith was hungry. In the past, he had come across traces of gold on his property, and since he still retained mining rights, he sought financial backing to develop what he claimed was a rich vein of the precious metal.

Beckwith eventually convinced a man named Simon Vandercook, an ex-miner then boarding at the home of Harrison Calkins, not far from where Beckwith lived. For $600, Vandercook bought a two-thirds share of the gold prospect, and said he could raise even more money as soon as the ore was assayed. Beckwith complied by bringing his new partner additional ore samples, which reportedly assayed at about $20 per ton—no bonanza, to be sure, but Vandercook did not tell Beckwith this, and the old man retained his dream of riches.

The gold extracted from the assayed ore was returned in the form of a small disk. Vandercook promptly drilled holes in it and had it sewn on his work clothes like a vest button—for safekeeping, he said. Beckwith did not object to the appropriation of the button, though it may have made him suspect that Vandercook was not entirely on the up and up.

Shortly thereafter, Vandercook's motives became even more suspect, when he and two other men formed the Austerlitz Mining Company. Although Beckwith owned a one-third interest, the corporation was set up so that he had no say in how the business was run. He could only wait and hope that mining operations would soon begin. But Vandercook kept delaying, giving Beckwith one excuse after another, possibly in the hope that the impoverished old man eventually would be forced to sell his remaining shares in the mine. But if this was Vandercook's plan, he was wrong—dead wrong.

January 10, 1882, dawned gray and blustery, with an ominous sky thick with snow-laden clouds. Harrison Calkins, whose house was located just over the state border, in Alford, Massachusetts, was not looking forward to the long ride to Pittsfield, where he was to serve on a grand jury. But at least he would not have to make the return journey later that day, for his wife would accompany him to Pittsfield, where they planned to stay with relatives until Calkins had fulfilled his jury duties. While they were gone, their boarder, Simon Vandercook, would take care of the chores.

Vandercook was already preparing to chop some wood when Calkins hitched his horse to the wagon. Assuring Calkins that he would be around, since all he planned to do that day was to visit Oscar Beckwith and then return home, Vandercook bade his landlord goodbye. Calkins never saw Vandercook again—at least not alive.

Had Harrison Calkins been absent for the time originally anticipated, Oscar Beckwith might never have been accused of the murder of Simon Vandercook. But upon his arrival in Pittsfield later that day, Calkins was excused from jury duty. Then, when his wife suffered a shoulder injury, the couple hastened back to Alford, hoping to reach home before the threatened snowstorm made the roads impassable.

It was well after dark when the Calkins' adopted daughter Isabelle greeted them at the door. (Isabelle had stayed home to prepare Vandercook's meals while her parents were away.) While Harrison Calkins was in the barn tending to his tired horse, Oscar Beckwith arrived at the house, bearing a bundle of clothes. Seemingly surprised to find Mrs. Calkins there, Beckwith said something about wanting the older woman to make him some shirts. Pointing to her obviously injured shoulder, Mrs. Calkins explained she would be unable to sew for awhile, and with that Beckwith left before Harrison Calkins came in from the barn.

The report of Beckwith's brief visit bothered Calkins, for who would come trudging through a snowstorm after dark just to inquire about some new shirts? And why had Beckwith burdened himself with a bundle of clothes? Another thing that bothered Calkins was the absence of Vandercook. None of the chores had been done, and when Isabelle said she had not been Vandercook all day, Calkins became worried. Calkins remembered not only Vandercook's stated intention of visiting Beckwith that day, but also that the two men recently had argued violently over their gold mine, at which time Beckwith had threatened to kill his partner.

Despite the snow, the late hour, and his own weariness, Calkins set out for Beckwith's cabin. The storm had abated by the time he arrived, and in the moonlight Calkins could see great billows of black smoke coming from the chimney. This was explained by Beckwith, when he opened the door, as coming from some old bones and pork rinds he was burning. This, Beckwith added, also accounted for the sickening smell pervading the cabin—a smell like burnt flesh.

Already suspecting the worst, Calkins stayed only long enough to inquire about Vandercook. Beckwith admitted to having seen his partner that day, but said some man had come looking for Vandercook and the two of them had gone to Green River, a village in the town of Hillsdale, south of Austerlitz. Vandercook, Beckwith further explained, would not be back until spring.

Calkins was positive Beckwith was lying, for he knew Vandercook was not the type to renege on his promise to look after the house and young Isabelle while Calkins was away in Pittsfield.

Alone and unarmed, Calkins dared not challenge Beckwith's statement. Nor did he dare to look at what was in the barrel beside Beckwith as he said goodbye. But the bloodied ax handle protruding from that barrel hinted at a butchery that sickened Calkins as he stumbled home through the snow. Once there, Calkins went to Vandercook's room. The missing man's dress clothes were still in the closet, along with other possessions Vandercook would surely have taken with him had he really gone off to Green River for a three-month stay.

As soon as he could round up some neighbors, Calkins returned to Beckwith's cabin, only to find it dark and deserted. The smell of burning flesh still hung in the night air. A constable was called, the locked cabin door forced open, and a grisly search got under way.

Calkins had not been mistaken. It had been Vandercook—at least parts of the murdered man—that Beckwith had been burning. A thumbless hand, found along with the charred skull in the firebox of the wood stove, identified the victim as Vandercook, who had lost a thumb in a mine explosion years before. There was other evidence as well: there were two blood-smeared axes found in the cabin, and one was known to have belonged to Vandercook. The work clothes Vandercook had been wearing when Calkins last saw him were also there, but the gold button was missing from the vest. The corpse itself was beyond recognition, having been methodically dismembered and disemboweled, much like a deer carcass being prepared for winter preservation. An old overshoe, it was later reported, had been used to catch the blood.

No longer able to bear the sight or the stench of the cabin-turned-abattoir, the constable and his posse took off after the missing Beckwith, whose horse had left easily followed tracks in the freshly fallen snow. They had not gone far when they encountered Beckwith's horse returning riderless along the trail. That Beckwith was now on foot encouraged the posse to think the suspected murderer of Simon Vandercook would be quickly and easily apprehended. But they were woefully wrong.

The tracks made by Beckwith's horse led to Fog Hill in northern Austerlitz. There the trail suddenly stopped at the rim of a limestone ledge overlooking No Bottom Pond—a body of water that sometimes disappeared abruptly, as if the plug had been pulled from a bathtub filled with water.

Those posse members familiar with the area suggested that Beckwith might be hiding in one of the small caves lining the limestone ledge. Along with a larger opening in the bed of the pond, these caves gave way to a network of tortuous subterranean tunnels through which the water periodically drained into an underground stream. But no one relished the idea of an encounter with a maddened murderer in such close confines, nor the thought of crawling along a wet passageway in the January cold. In any event, the posse had no jurisdiction, for they had come from Alford, on the Massachusetts side of the border, and No Bottom Pond was in New York. The decision was therefore made to return to Beckwith's cabin, gather up the evidence, and report Vandercook's death to the authorities in Green River, New York.

The sensational crime immediately became a cause célèbre in the small border community of Green River. Rewards were offered and reporters flocked in. Some of the incidents that occurred might be considered comic if they were not so macabre. For instance, there was the advertisement in a local paper touting an "Electro-Therapeutic Institute"; had Beckwith taken their treatments, the ad proclaimed, "the Austerlitz Cannibal would not be in such a peck of trouble."

Then there was the tragic case of a former mental patient who had been well for many years but, upon viewing the gory remains, had a relapse and was institutionalized for the rest of his life.

As for newspapers, their accounts were graphic, to say the least—especially those written by two young reporters from Pittsfield, Hiram Oatman and James Harding. When they asked about the evidence, they were taken into a barn where a barrel containing Vandercook's remains was kept. The barrel was then upended, its bloody contents spilled on the floor, and the shocked reporters instructed to "put them back when you are through."

The effect this had on Oatman and Harding was obvious in the stories they filed with their respective papers, the *Pittsfield Morning Call* and the *Sun*. And if anything positive can be said about the bucket incident, it is that the dramatic accounts by Oatman and Harding also had an effect on a deputy sheriff in Great Barrington, the Massachusetts town adjoining Alford, where Harrison Calkins lived. His interest aroused by the newspaper stories, Sheriff Edwin Humphrey interviewed Calkins, and after learning the details of the night Vandercook had been murdered, Humphrey theorized that the crime must have been premeditated.

Beckwith's appearance at the Calkins home late in the evening, when he thought Mr. and Mrs. Calkins were absent, indicated—at least to Sheriff Humphrey—that Beckwith also had intended to murder young Isabelle Calkins and blame it on Vandercook. This would explain the bundle of clothes Beckwith had under his arm on the night he came to the Calkins house. They were the clothes Vandercook had been wearing when Beckwith killed him—bloodstained clothes that, if left at the scene of Isabelle Calkins's murder, would make it look as if Vandercook had killed her and then run away. Having thus provided a reason for Vandercook's sudden disappearance, Beckwith could dispose of his partner's body. No suspicion would be leveled at him, and he would remain free to enjoy the profits of his gold mine.

Sheriff Humphrey further speculated that the unexpected early arrival of Mr. and Mrs. Calkins had prevented Beckwith from carrying out the second murder. Then when Calkins showed up at his cabin, Beckwith chose to flee, knowing it would be only a matter of time until Calkins figured out what had been burning in the stove.

This theory made the crime even more reprehensible to Sheriff Humphrey, and as days passed with no word of Oscar Beckwith's being seen, let alone apprehended, the lawman mounted his own manhunt. It was a manhunt that lasted more than three years, for Beckwith had headed for Canada on the night of the murder.

The flight of Oscar Beckwith, then in his seventies, who traveled alone and on foot over 600 miles to northern Ontario during the dead of winter, is an example of endurance rivaled only by his pursuer's pertinacity and patience.

Sheriff Humphrey started out by questioning anyone who had the slightest association with Beckwith, and he eventually learned that the fugitive had relatives in Ontario. Figuring this was where Beckwith must have gone, but unable to pinpoint the exact location, Humphrey alerted local postmasters to be on the lookout for a letter from Canada addressed to any member of Beckwith's family living in the Austerlitz area.

Months passed by, then years, but eventually such a letter arrived. It bore the signature of "C. White," but Humphrey—who had convinced the recipient to allow him to read it—knew that the writer was none other than Oscar Beckwith.

Apparently Humphrey distrusted the local authorities, for he appealed directly to President Chester A. Arthur for extradition papers. At his own expense, and aware that as a lawman he would be ineligible for any of the rewards being offered for Beckwith's apprehension, Humphrey first traveled to Washington to see President Arthur, then went on to Ontario, where Beckwith was arrested. In Beckwith's possession was the gold button from Simon Vandercook's vest.

Exactly three years and ten months after the murder of Simon Vandercook, Beckwith was jailed at Hudson, New York. But it was to take another two years and three months before the "Cannibal of Austerlitz" was punished for his crime.

In all, Beckwith was tried six different times, because of the many petitions and appeals filed on his behalf. One of these contended Beckwith could not be tried in New York because there was no proof the crime had been committed in that state. During the time it took surveyors to prove Beckwith's cabin was, indeed, on the New York side of the border, the wily septuagenarian almost escaped from the Hudson jail. Reportedly, Beckwith used part of a Jew's harp to file through his shackles and was at work on the cell wall when his escape plan was discovered.

There was also a hearing before a lunacy commission, and not just because of the alleged cannibalism involved in the death of Simon Vandercook, whose liver had been found in a frying pan on Beckwith's stove. Beckwith also was obsessed with the idea that he was being persecuted by members of the Masonic order, and he blamed most of his troubles on what he called "those Jack Mason skulls." Despite this, Beckwith was deemed sane and answerable for his actions, so the trials went on.

At his first three trials, Beckwith maintained he was innocent, but at the latter three he admitted to second-degree murder, saying he had killed Simon Vandercook in self-defense. The jury didn't believe him the first time or the last, and the sixth trial ended with a verdict of guilty of murder in the first degree. The jury did, however, recommend clemency.

Given the opportunity to speak in his own behalf, Beckwith entreated the judge to heed the jury's recommendation. While doing so, the condemned man shocked the courtroom by describing not only how he had killed Simon Vandercook—by bludgeoning, stabbing, and even tearing out his victim's tongue—but also that he had planned to dispose of the body by eating parts of it. Perhaps because of this, the judge adhered to the strictest limits of the law and sentenced Beckwith to be executed by hanging.

Despite Beckwith's confession of intended—if not actual—cannibalism, there was a groundswell of sympathy for the old man people had begun calling "Uncle Oscar." There were constant visitors to his cell, many of whom gave him money while they listened to his claims of having discovered a vein of gold even richer than the one that had turned him into a killer. Beckwith would not reveal the location of his new find—if, indeed, there was one—for he hoped the governor of New York would commute his sentence.

That hope died with Beckwith on a March morning in 1888, when he was hanged in the courtyard of the jail at Hudson. Even during those last moments, there was present the same macabre mood that had mantled his life. It is said the hanging rope was too long, allowing Beckwith's feet to drag on the ground, thus prolonging the fatal torture for a full eighteen minutes.

Shortly after his execution, and as if to eliminate any sign of the "Cannibal of Columbia County," the infamous blizzard of '88 swept across the Taconics, destroying Beckwith's cabin and obliterating his gold mine. But the memory of the murder lives on, as do the questions regarding its perpetrator. Was Beckwith a monster or madman? Victim or avenger? Callous killer or self-defender? Only Oscar Beckwith knew the answer, just as he was the only one who knew the location of the second, richer vein of gold. Both lie buried somewhere in the Columbia County town of Austerlitz, where they have remained untouched for a century.

V

THE
LITERATI

27 WASHINGTON IRVING:

MASTER WEAVER
OF VALLEY TALES

IT WAS EARLY spring 1783. At his Hudson-shore headquarters in Newburgh, George Washington was awaiting word from the Continental Congress that the Revolutionary War had ended. Meanwhile, 60 miles downriver, at a house on William Street, New York City merchant William Irving and his wife Sarah were just as anxiously awaiting another imminent, though more personal, event: the birth of their eleventh child.

The baby, born on April 3, preceded the peace announcement by two weeks. But for the Irvings, who had been ardent supporters of the Revolution, the two events were auspiciously aligned. Therefore, they named their newborn son Washington, in honor of the general who had successfully led the country's fight for independence. It proved to be a prophetic choice, for Washington Irving also was destined to serve his country, as an ambassador as well as an author, and his life would end, as it had begun, entwined with that of his namesake.

There was no hint of this, however, during that April of 1783, nor for many years thereafter. Irving was of delicate health and decidedly less than brilliant as a student, and he grew up dreaming of becoming a sailor. But in a well-to-do family such as his, the wayfaring life of a mariner was unthinkable, and at the age of fourteen, Irving began to study law. He remained more interested in travel than in torts, however, and slaked his thirst for adventure by taking long walks into Westchester County. Shorter excursions were made to the wharves near his Lower Manhattan home, where he could watch the tall sailing ships and hear the stories their crewmen told. Irving also sneaked out to the theater at night, usually by way of his bedroom window and the rooftop. For his father—a dour disciplinarian and devout Scotch Presbyterian—disapproved of his youngest son's choice of amusement over academics.

Then, in 1800, when Irving was seventeen, he took his first long voyage on a Hudson River sloop bound for Albany, where he visited his older sisters Catharine and Ann. Irving was ever an avid listener, and he absorbed every sight and sound along the way, relishing the rich folklore of the region, which he was to use to great effect in his first book, the *History of New York*, as well as subsequent volumes throughout his long career.

Yet when Irving originally picked up his pen for publication at the age of nineteen, it was not legends but contemporary life that concerned him. A staunch follower of Aaron Burr, Irving began contributing political and satirical pieces to his brother Peter's newspaper, the *Morning Chronicle*, meanwhile continuing his law studies. Poor health soon curtailed both activities, though, and in 1804, he set sail for Europe, where he traveled for the next two years.

His absence in no way dimmed his devotion to writing, and upon his return to America, Irving joined his brother William and James Kirke Paulding in producing a series of papers called the *Salmagundi*. Like the flavorful salad for which they were named, the *Salmagundi* offered readers a spicy mixture of essays satirizing New York society. And though only twenty of these irregularly issued papers appeared, that was enough to establish Irving as a writer (albeit pseudonymously), and his success convinced him to broaden his authorial horizons.

Encouraged by his fiancée, Matilda Hoffman (daughter of Judge Josiah Hoffman, under whom Irving had studied law), the twenty-five-year-old author set to work on a humorous history of New York during the days of the Dutch. Using the penname Diedrich Knickerbocker, Irving was to combine seventeenth-century folklore and fact with some not-so-subtle allusions to his own era. The latter element, along with Irving's comic treatment of the Dutch, caused the ire to rise in many an old Hudson Valley family when the *History of New York* was published in December 1809. Reportedly, one angry Albany woman threatened to horsewhip the author! And while not enough to affect the popularity of the book, this rumpled-feather reaction wounded Irving, who was at that time recovering from an even deeper hurt—the loss of his beloved Matilda.

Following the death of his fiancée on April 26, 1809, the grieving author had accepted the invitation of William Van Ness to spend the summer at his country estate in the Columbia County community of Kinderhook, now a National Historic Site open to the public. Buoyed by the breathtaking scenery and the sympathetic hospitality of his host, Irving had divided his time between completing his *History of New York* and going about the neighborhood, meeting the local folk. One of those he met was a schoolteacher named Jesse Merwin—and therein lies a tangent tale of regional rivalry that persists to this day.

Understandably, any community would enjoy being the setting for a literary classic, and in the case of Irving's ever-popular tale of Ichabod Crane's encounter with a headless horseman, both Westchester and Columbia County claim "The Legend of Sleepy Hollow."

Irving, of course, was familiar with Westchester County's Sleepy Hollow, a wooded vale through which the Pocantico River runs, north of Tarrytown. As a boy, he had gone hunting there and had surely heard of the Headless Horseman—the ghost of a Hessian soldier said to haunt Sleepy Hollow and the nearby graveyard of the Old Dutch Church. In addition, it has been suggested that Tarrytown was Irving's source for Katrina Van Tassel (the maiden Ichabod Crane was wont to woo), since the Van Tassel family once owned the house Irving later transformed into his famed Sunnyside mansion.

On the other hand, a Columbia County tradition has Katrina—or at least the model for her—living in the old Van Alen farmhouse, a short distance north of the Van Ness home, where Irving was a guest in 1809. (The Van Alen House and adjacent Ichabod Crane School-house, maintained by the Columbia County Historical Society, are open during the summer.) The farmhouse itself is similar to the Van

Tassel home described in "The Legend of Sleepy Hollow," and it was close to the school where Irving's friend, Jesse Merwin, taught.

The schoolteacher and the author had spent long hours together discussing local lore, according to a letter Irving wrote to Merwin many years later, and it is possible Merwin had told him of a spectral headless horseman that supposedly had been seen in Kinderhook. Merwin may also have told Irving of a prank played on him when he was courting his wife. According to family tradition, a rival suitor, Abram Van Alstyne—whose nickname was "Brom"—tried to frighten Merwin one dark night by dressing up as a ghostly Hessian soldier, as did Ichabod Crane's rival, Brom Bones.

Whether such anecdotes are actual or apocryphal may never be ascertained, but Columbia County's case is strengthened by a statement of President Martin Van Buren, who bought the Van Ness home—Lindenwald—in 1839, that Jesse Merwin was definitely the model for Ichabod Crane. There is also a letter addressed to the author by Jesse Merwin, on which Irving wrote: "the original of Ichabod Crane."

As to which county "owns" Irving's tale, perhaps the best answer is neither—and both. For "The Legend of Sleepy Hollow" is a marvelous amalgam of personalities and places, originating in the Hudson Valley, of course, but universal in appeal, and that is why it has been an enduring favorite.

An equally popular Irving tale is "Rip Van Winkle," and while it unquestionably has a Catskill setting, no one can say exactly where in the Catskills, since its author had only seen these mountains from afar at the time he composed the story. Irving had written that his first far-off view of the Catskills—from the deck of a Hudson River sloop in 1800—"had the most witching effect on my boyish imagination," but an even more spectacular view was the one he beheld from the eastern shore of the Hudson in Columbia County, when he visited Kinderhook in 1809.

Three years later and thirty miles to the south, Irving was treated to still another vista of the distant Catskills, when he was a guest at the Barrytown home of John Robert Livingston in Dutchess County. While there, Irving also dined at Clermont (now a New York State Historic Park open to the public, and the northernmost of the line of

Livingston mansions that once marched down the eastern shore of the Hudson to Staatsburg).

At the time of Irving's visit to Clermont, the fields stretching eastward from the mansion were still being tilled by tenants who retained many seventeenth-century customs. Since it was August when Irving was there, he surely observed the farmers at work, and years afterward he may have called on these pastoral scenes when, at his sister Sarah's house in Birmingham, England, he was to create "Rip Van Winkle."

That tale may well have been an exercise in escapism for Irving, who was then at a low point in his life. After spending several years as an editor, plus serving as a colonel in the New York militia and as aide-de-camp to Governor Daniel Tompkins, in 1815 Irving had gone to England to help with a faltering family-owned business in Liverpool.

Irving was burdened by financial woes, and he remained in Europe until 1832, writing plays with John Howard Payne and turning out five more books, in addition to serving as a diplomat in London and Spain. But while he was in Europe, his heart was at home in the Hudson Valley, and when he embarked on a book of European sketches, he couldn't resist including some stories set in America. Thus it was that in 1820, when his *Sketch Book* was published in England under the pseudonym Geoffrey Crayon, it contained the now classic tales of "Rip Van Winkle" and "The Legend of Sleepy Hollow," as well as two chapters about the American Indians. In addition, his sketch entitled "Little Britain" ostensibly describes an area in London by that name. Hudson Valley readers, however, may well find parallels to Orange County's Little Britain, home of DeWitt Clinton, whom Irving had satirized as "Linkum Fidelius" in the *Salmagundi* papers.

Two years after the *Sketch Book* appeared, Irving published *Bracebridge Hall*, another collection of European tales counterpointed by the purely American portrait of "Dolph Heyliger." Poor Dolph never did approach the fame of old Rip or Ichabod Crane, but it remains a favorite of Hudson Valley folklore fans. For in this marvelous tale within a tale, Irving takes his readers on an eerie voyage up the Hudson, utilizing the supernatural lore he heard as a boy—from haunted houses, psychic dreams, and a devilish doctor to Highland imps, spectral ships, and hidden treasure—all set in readily recognizable surroundings, such as Albany's Vanderheyden Palace.

That "palace," by the way, was to figure prominently in Irving's later life when he was remodeling the Van Tassel farmhouse at Tarrytown into his beloved Sunnyside. The southern gable of Sunnyside is said to be a replica of one on the Vanderheyden Palace while the gable's "galloping horse" weathervane originally graced the Albany mansion.

But getting back to Irving's European stay: *Bracebridge Hall* was followed two years later (1824) by *Tales of a Traveler,* and in it Irving once again included a section with an American setting. This collection of colorful stories, called "The Money Diggers," is introduced by a sketch titled "Hell-Gate"—which is the name of that area east of Manhattan Island not far from Irving's childhood home. And it is here the reader glimpses a bit of autobiography, if not a hint of Irving's homesickness, when he describes the Hell-Gate as being "a place of great awe and perilous enterprise for me in my boyhood." It was then "a region of fable and romance," abounding with tales of pirates and buried treasure.

Nor was Irving likely to have forgotten the other Hell-Gate, a narrow channel in the river between Upper and Lower Shodack Islands, just south of Albany, which he had seen on his teenage sail up the Hudson—a dangerous passage that superstitious sloop captains were apt to imbue with all sorts of evil spirits.

But it is the last tale in "The Money Diggers" that best reflects Irving's lifelong love of the legends he absorbed in his youth. Called "Wolfert Weber, or Golden Dreams," it is the granddaddy of treasure tales, ranging from Manhattan's Corlears Hook to Orange County's Danskammer, and one which was to spark several spinoffs by other authors, including the even more famous "Gold-Bug," by Edgar Allan Poe.

Indeed, Irving's influence on Poe extended past a single tale. For instance, compare Irving's "Westminster Abbey" with the opening of Poe's "Fall of the House of Usher," or legends contained in *Knickerbocker's History of New York* with "The Devil in the Belfry." As for the influence of "An Unwritten Drama of Lord Byron" on "William Wilson," this was acknowledged by Poe in a letter he wrote to Irving in 1839, seven years after the master weaver of Hudson Valley tales had returned in triumph to his homeland.

Before he came back to America, however, Irving had undergone a "Spanish period," engendered in part perhaps by the less than warm reception accorded his *Tales of a Traveler* by both British and American critics. Smarting from the negative reaction to that book (which is actually quite good), Irving devoted his energies to the Spanish language and Spanish history, and his studies resulted in such works as *The Life and Voyages of Christopher Columbus* (1828), *Voyages and Discoveries of the Companions of Christopher Columbus* (1831), and his still popular collection of tales *The Alhambra*, published in 1832.

It was in May of 1832, following critical acclaim, that Irving returned to New York, his long European exile finally ended. During his absence, America's frontiers had expanded, and Irving joyfully set out to see these changes, which he later recorded in a trio of travel books. He also toured the Hudson Valley, and this time he got a closer look at the Catskills, as well as meeting the locally famous witch doctor Jacob Brink, of Saugerties.

Irving, however, had by now quenched his thirst for travel, and in 1835 he purchased Sunnyside, his 24-acre, Hudson-shore estate. (Sunnyside is now owned and operated by Historic Hudson Valley and is open to the public.) Remodeling the simple farm cottage then standing on the property took up much of his time during the next few years, for Irving had his own ideas of what would best suit him, and he personally supervised the work. And despite the fact that some architects were aghast at his combination of Spanish, Dutch, English, and Hudson River Gothic styles, none could deny that Irving's "snuggery" turned out to be as picturesque as it was unique—"a little old-fashioned stone mansion, all made up of gable ends, and as full of angles and corners as an old cocked hat" was the way the delighted author described it.

Except for a period during the early 1840s when he served as U.S. Ambassador to Spain, Irving made Sunnyside his home for the rest of his life, surrounded by family members and an unending parade of close friends, fellow writers, and influential folk. It should be noted, however, that the well-known painting of "Washington Irving and His

Literary Friends at Sunnyside," depicting over a dozen famous writers grouped around the author, is a bit of a fraud. While most of those writers did visit Sunnyside, they were never all there at the same time.

Various female members of Irving's family hosted these events, since the author had never married. There is evidence of several romantic interests following the death of his fiancée, but none matured into matrimony, possibly because his abiding love was Matilda Hoffman—at least it was her portrait in miniature that Irving kept beside his bed until the day he died.

When he was not writing or entertaining, Irving would roam the grounds of Sunnyside, interested in even the smallest details of daily life. The doings of his pig, Fanny, the duck pond he called "The Little Mediterranean," his geese that had driven off an invading gaggle, constructing an ice pond—all were observed and later recorded in letters or the notebooks he carefully kept through the years.

The master weaver of Hudson Valley tales also enjoyed an occasional jaunt into New York City, where he took boyish delight in staying at the opulent Irving House—named for him, of course. At last his contribution to American literature was being recognized. And well it might be, for as Kenneth S. Lynn pointed out in a 1983 article in *Smithsonian*, not only was Washington Irving "the first American writer to be accepted as quality by English critics, he was also the first to give his countrymen a literary sense of their own past, both rural and urban." What's more, he and his fellow Knickerbockers (a group of romantic writers and artists who took their name from Irving's fictitious narrator of the *History of New York*) were at the forefront of the movement to preserve New York's historic sites, especially those in the Hudson Valley.

The depth of Irving's regard for the region is perhaps best revealed in his introduction to *A Book of the Hudson*, "collected from the various works of Diedrich Knickerbocker," which begins: "I thank God that I was born on the banks of the Hudson. I fancy I can trace much of what is good and pleasant in my own heterogeneous compound to my early companionship with this glorious river." And it is in this volume, reprinted many times since it first appeared in 1849, that readers can find the most representative sampling of

Irving's Hudson Valley stories, although *Wolfert's Roost*, another selection of his Knickerbocker sketches, runs a close second.

Wolfert's Roost—Irving's nickname for Sunnyside—appeared in 1855, and marked the end of Irving's involvement with Hudson Valley lore. The remaining five years of his life were spent in completing his five-volume *Life of George Washington*. While working on the biography of his namesake, Irving frequently visited the Orange County home of his nephew Irving Van Wart. There in the small community of Craigville, Irving was only a short distance away from the place where George Washington spent the final days of the Revolution. Sitting on the long porch—a porch that prompted Irving to call his nephew's home "Bandbox Hall"—the aging author could contemplate the historic countryside and perhaps his own involvement with the man whose name he bore.

Shortly before his death on November 28, 1859, Irving finished his *Life of Washington*, and then made his last visit to Bandbox Hall. Had he written it himself, Irving couldn't have come up with a more fitting finale to that memorable association between two memorable men: one the father of his country, the other the father of Hudson Valley literature.

28 POE'S HUDSON

LITTLE POPULAR ATTENTION has been accorded Edgar Allan Poe's association with the Hudson Valley—he is commonly thought of as a Southerner. While it is true that his early years were spent mainly below the Mason-Dixon Line, Poe was a Northerner by birth (Boston) and a New Yorker during some of the most productive periods of his life.

Edgar Poe first came to New York as an infant barely six months old, when his actor parents, David and Elizabeth Poe, obtained bookings at several Manhattan theaters in July 1809. Although Poe's mother was a talented thespian, his father was not, and David Poe's propensity for appearing on stage while "in his cups" soon brought the curtain down on his acting career. Elizabeth Poe continued to be in demand as a leading lady, however, and the family remained in New York City until the summer of 1810, when Mrs. Poe was offered acting jobs in such Southern cities as Norfolk, Charleston, and Richmond. It was in Richmond, a little more than a year later, that Elizabeth Poe succumbed to tuberculosis. David Poe, suffering from the same disease, survived his wife by only a few days.

At the time of the parents' death in December 1811, Poe's older brother William was already living with their paternal grandfather in Baltimore, but the two other orphans (Edgar, just under three years old, and his baby sister Rosalie) were not accorded such familial hospitality. Instead, each was taken in by a different nonrelated family, Edgar going to the home of a prosperous Richmond merchant named John Allan, who had the child baptized Edgar Allan Poe.

Except for a seven-week stay in New York City when he was eleven years old, Poe did not return to the Hudson Valley until June 1830, when he entered West Point as a cadet. Along with his fellow plebes, Poe spent the summer months in a tent camp at old Fort Clinton, on the heights overlooking the river near present-day Cullum Road. It may well have been there that Poe was introduced to some of the legends about Captain Kidd's treasure being buried in the Hudson Highlands, for Kidd's Plug Cliff, as well as Captain Kidd's Cave on Crow's Nest, were less than two miles north of the cadet encampment. In addition, Kidd's Point was a short distance to the south at the foot of Dunderberg Mountain, and there was still another reputed booty site at what is now Hook Mountain State Park.

There is no way of proving that any of these legends were in Poe's mind with he later wrote about Captain Kidd's treasure in his world-famous tale "The Gold-Bug," but it seems likely that he had heard them, since such stories were then—as now—traditional campfire fare. The advent of Halloween would also have sparked an exchange of Hudson Valley folklore, even though the new cadets were expected to devote most of their waking hours to scholastic and military matters.

By this time—October 1830—the cadets had moved into regular quarters, with Poe assigned to #28 South Barracks. Older than most of his classmates, the twenty-one-year-old Poe was regarded as something of a hero, having served in the regular army prior to his appointment to the military academy, and already a published author (his first book of poems had appeared in 1827). He also had a better education than most of his classmates, if only because of age superiority, and he placed third in his French class at the end of the first semester.

But it wasn't Poe's scholastic achievements that the other cadets found so remarkable. It was the fanciful tales he told and the even wilder escapades in which he engaged. None of the former was true, including his claim to being the grandson of Benedict Arnold, or having voyaged to South America as a sailor. Yet each of these stories contained a grain of fact. Arnold was the maiden name of Poe's mother, and his older brother William actually did travel to South America. Like the proverbial oyster, Poe covered these factual grains with coats of pure fancy, until he came up with pearls of prevarication—a less-than-exemplary though harmless trait he exhibited from time to time throughout his life.

As for his escapades at West Point, some are a matter of record, while others are surely myth. The wildest of Poe's purported pranks falls into the latter category: as the story goes, one day, when the cadets were ordered into formation wearing crossed belt and sword, Poe showed up wearing *only* those two items—nothing else. The story is always good for a laugh, but it is far from credible, considering Poe's upbringing and documented descriptions of his behavior. He was capable of bare-faced fibs, certainly; but bare-bottom exhibitionism, hardly.

More in keeping with Poe's character is the tradition that he named a goose for one of his superiors, and when the bird had been roasted, he proceeded to "eat the officer in effigy." He is also known to have penned verses lampooning various officers, much to the amusement of his classmates. Unsigned, the squibs would be posted in some public place for all to see, including the officers, who never did catch the culprit.

Thoroughly believable, too, is a story that Poe patronized the nearby tavern of Benny Havens, a man the poet is said to have called "the only congenial soul in this godforsaken wilderness." But those visits to Benny Havens' tavern were probably less frequent than has been supposed, since Poe had very little money during the eight months he remained at West Point. It was this impoverishment—at least that is how Poe regarded his financial condition—which brought about the end of his military career. Unable or unwilling to sustain himself on his 93-cent-a-day cadet pay, Poe appealed to his foster father for help. When John Allan refused, the disappointed Poe neglected his duties to the point that in January 1831 he was court-martialed and subsequently dismissed from the academy.

After leaving West Point, Poe spent several months in New York City, then headed south, where he lived for the next six years, working off and on as a magazine editor, as well as writing poems and prose. During that time, he published one of his finest tales, "MS. Found in a Bottle," which has as its theme the ancient legend of the Flying Dutchman, though the story of another supernatural vessel—the Storm Ship said to ply the Hudson during the days of Dutch rule—may have contributed something to Poe's creation.

By February 1837, Poe was back in New York City, living on Carmine Street with his bride Virginia and her mother. Contrary to myth, Poe's marriage to his thirteen-year-old cousin was not prompted by pedophilial lust. Encouraged by Virginia's mother, the poet proposed in order to save the girl from being taken into the home of a man whose motives he did not trust. The two cousins did love each other, however, and their union was a congenial one, though beset by poverty and the poor health of both partners.

In April, Poe attended a banquet given for writers at the City Hotel on lower Broadway. There he met Washington Irving, whose influence is apparent in a number of Poe's tales. Being invited to that writers' banquet indicates Poe was regarded as an established author whose poems and prose were being published with regularity. But payment was paltry, his work was often pirated for reprinting without recompense, and Poe was hard-pressed to make ends meet.

In the hope of securing a permanent position, Poe moved to Philadelphia in 1838, and for the next six years he made only occasional visits to the Hudson Valley. Absent though he was, the region was still very much in his mind, as is evidenced in his tale of 1842, "The Mystery of Marie Roget." It was also in 1842 that Poe penned "The Landscape Garden," inspired in part by the ideas of Hudson Valley horticulturist Andrew Jackson Downing. And though Downing's home on Newburgh's Liberty Street was built in 1838, it is doubtful that Poe ever saw it; instead, he relied on an 1841 review he read of Downing's work on American landscape gardening.

Poe was still a resident of Philadelphia during the summer of 1843, when he visited Barhyte's Trout Pond on the outskirts of Saratoga Springs. One of the owner's grandsons later reminisced that he had been fishing in the trout pond one day in 1843 when he spotted Poe pacing the shore and "speaking a piece." The "piece," according to Barhyte, was the first draft of "The Raven." But it was not until 1844 that Poe completed his poem, and by that time he had moved his family back to New York.

The spring of 1844 found Poe and his wife residing in Lower Manhattan, first on Greenwich Street and then on Ann Street, as the poet struggled to make a living by writing the kind of stories that were so popular in that era. Indeed, Poe's preoccupation with the macabre was not so much a personal choice as it was a practicality: that was the type of tale that sold.

Though Poe has often been referred to as a man out of step with his own world, he actually was very much a part of his surroundings, especially during this time when contemporary events formed the basis for many of his tales. Among those he wrote in 1844 is "The Oblong Box," inspired by the gruesome 1841 murder of Samuel Adams by John C. Colt, brother of Samuel, the gunmaker. Colt killed Adams in an apartment at Chambers Street and Broadway, then attempted to dispose of the body by packing it in salt and shipping it out of the city on a boat docked at Maiden Lane pier. The corpse was discovered, Colt was apprehended, tried, and sentenced to death, but he killed himself on the day set for his execution: November 18, 1842.

Another chilling tale written during 1844 was "The Premature Burial." Poe had long been fascinated by stories concerning interment of living people, but his tale must be regarded in the context of its time. The subject was of popular interest—so much so that in 1843 a "life-preserving coffin" (with a lid designed to pop open at the "least stir of the occupant") had been displayed at the annual fair held at the American Institute in New York City. If Poe did not see it himself, he must have read about it in newspaper accounts of the exhibit.

Gloom and doom were not the only things to come from Poe's pen during this period, for in October he wrote "The Literary Life of Thingum Bob," a witty satire on the world of publishing—something he had experienced from "both sides of the desk" and which certainly was on his mind, since during that month he had joined the staff of the *Evening Mirror*.

Around this time, Poe moved uptown, to the farmhouse of Patrick Brennan, located near what is now Eighty-fourth Street and Broadway.

Nearby, on the shore of the Hudson, was a large rock called Mt. Tom, where he and Virginia liked to sit and watch the river. It was at the Brennan farm that Poe completed "The Raven," which was published in January 1845, a year in which Poe was to realize a long-held dream of owning a literary periodical. Admittedly, the weekly *Broadway Journal* was not the magazine he had envisioned himself as establishing, but it was his, as the issue of October 25, 1845, proudly proclaimed: "Edgar A. Poe, Editor and Proprietor." Poe was no businessman, however, and the *Broadway Journal* steadily lost money until January 1846, when the last issue was printed.

Worried about his wife Virginia's declining health, Poe moved north to the village of Fordham (then in Westchester County but now part of the Bronx). The small house they rented from John Valentine was later to be described by Poe in "Landor's Cottage," but first he would compose another scenic sketch, "The Domain of Arnheim."

"The Domain of Arnheim" was written late in 1846, not long after Poe had completed "The Cask of Amontillado" (which also contains hints of the Hudson Valley). It is an expanded version of his earlier "Landscape Garden" but with significant additions. Among these is a comparison of Arnheim's domain to a place called Fonthill. Although Poe was familiar with Fonthill Abbey in England, it seems more likely that he had in mind Fonthill Castle, which was then being built on a hill overlooking the Hudson, not far from his own Fordham cottage. Originally the home of actor Edwin Forrest, Fonthill Castle now serves as the Elizabeth Seton Library of Mount St. Vincent College, located in the Riverdale section of the Bronx.

Another inspiration for "The Domain of Arnheim" could have been a series of paintings by the founder of the Hudson River School, Thomas Cole, who also wrote explanatory notes to accompany each of his landscapes. Cole's paintings, collectively called *The Voyage of Life*, had been exhibited during 1841 in New York City, where Poe may have seen them.

The serenity of mood expressed by Poe in "The Domain of Arnheim" was soon to be shattered. Less than two weeks after he celebrated his thirty-eighth birthday, Poe was plunged into grief by the death of his wife. Like his parents, she was a victim of tuberculosis. Following Virginia's funeral on February 2, 1847, Poe became seriously ill, though not from alcoholism or drug addiction, as might be inferred from the myths that shadow his memory.

To set the record straight, Poe was not a daily drinker, though he experienced periodic bouts of alcoholism. He could go for long stretches without touching a drop, but at other times one drink might trigger a drunken episode. As for his supposed dependence on drugs, he occasionally took laudanum—obtainable at any apothecary shop in those days—to ease the symptoms of a worsening heart condition and perhaps, as was then common, as a remedy for the intestinal dysfunction following a drunken debauch. Nor are the references to opium in his tales necessarily autobiographical; an opium "high" was a handy writer's device for explaining weird situations to skeptical readers. Madness has also been attributed to Poe, who certainly displayed manic-depressive tendencies; he may have been suffering from a brain lesion, as was suggested by the eminent New York doctor Valentine Mott at the time Virginia Poe died.

Nursed back to health by his faithful mother-in-law, the depressed Poe paid a brief visit to a lady friend in Albany and spent part of the summer of 1847 in the South, but he was back in New York by October. During that month, he took a walk to Mamaroneck, where he chanced upon a private cemetery overlooking Guion Creek. Local tradition says that while he sat upon a rock gazing at the hillside tomb of Thomas Guion, Poe was inspired to write his strange yet lyrically beautiful poem "Ulalume."

Except for "The Bells," which was prompted by the ringing of church bells one day in 1848 when he was visiting someone in Lower Manhattan, "Ulalume" was the last of Poe's poems to be linked with the Hudson Valley, though two more of his tales were to have such an association.

By January 1848, Poe had completed "Mellonta Tauta," a satiric look at the future, in which he credits the "Poughkeepsie Seer" with translating the story from a manuscript contained in a jug found floating in the Atlantic Ocean. This is pure fiction, of course, except for one small fact: the "Poughkeepsie Seer" was a very real man.

Andrew Jackson Davis—not to be confused with the Newburgh horticulturist Andrew Jackson Downing, or the New York architect

Alexander Jackson Davis—was born in the Orange County town of Blooming Grove. He was a spiritualist who practiced mesmerism and clairvoyant healing in Poughkeepsie. Poe probably had heard Davis lecture during the numerous times the "Poughkeepsie Seer" appeared in Manhattan during 1845 and 1846, and the two men met at least once, for Davis reported that Poe visited him on January 19, 1846, at which time they discussed Poe's story of "Mesmeric Revelation." (Although the tale was purely imaginary, Davis found "the main ideas...were strictly and philosophically true.") But there is no record of any other meeting, despite speculation that Poe may have seen Davis during the summer of 1848, when he took a walking tour of Westchester and Putnam and then went on into Dutchess County.

That walking tour had other more definite results. Late in 1848, Poe wrote what was to be one of his last tales—the serenely lovely "Landor's Cottage," which is a sequel to "The Domain of Arnheim." Both these pastoral word-pictures reveal Poe's appreciation of the Hudson Valley, but it is in "Landor's Cottage" that the reader is treated to an idealized view of Poe's own Fordham cottage, which is now owned by the Bronx Historical Society and open to the public. Within this simply worded description of a scene Poe loved so well can be found an even more meaningful revelation: that the tormented poet had found solace, if only briefly, in the beautiful Hudson Valley.

Edgar Allan Poe died less than one year after writing "Landor's Cottage." A trip South was punctuated by periods of heavy drinking, and on October 3, 1849, Poe was taken to Baltimore's Washington Hospital. There he lingered, unconscious or delirious most of the time, until he died in the early morning of October 7, from what one newspaper called "congestion of the brain."

He was forty years old.

Slightly askew—from its foundation being banged into by barges and ice blocks—the Esopus Meadows Lighthouse guards a river shoal where cows once grazed.

Above, it is said that if you look closely enough around the Dutch Garden in New City, you can find fifty different brick trademarks, commemorating the companies which once made nearby Haverstraw a leading producer of this building material. Of the two bricks shown on the corner of the teahouse piazza, "JJJ" represents the Jova Brick Company of Roseton, just north of Newburgh, while "MBCO" stands for the Morrissey Brick Company of Haverstraw.

Left, taking the Indian Ladder Trail at John Boyd Thacher State Park is much like walking around the inner side of a huge bowl, although this isn't immediately apparent to first-timers awed by the rugged rock wall looming high above them. As can be seen in the photograph, numerous water-carved caves—some with unusual names and almost all with interesting histories—occur in the layered limestone.

Reminiscent of prehistoric monoliths found in Europe, uncut spires of local stone mark the graves of early settlers in Hurley's old burying ground. Time has obliterated many of the inscriptions, with the earliest decipherable date being 1715.

Beautiful old houses are not the only historic features of Hurley. Preserved on the front lawn of the bank is a rutted section of the bluestone road over which heavy quarry carts hauled the huge slabs to the Hudson for ferrying downriver. In the background (on the other side of the street) can be seen one of the outdoor fairs that are part of the hamlet's annual Stone House Day celebration.

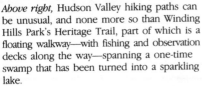

Above right, Hudson Valley hiking paths can be unusual, and none more so than Winding Hills Park's Heritage Trail, part of which is a floating walkway—with fishing and observation decks along the way—spanning a one-time swamp that has been turned into a sparkling lake.

Above left, sight-seers amble along the D&H towpath at Lock #16 in High Falls, following a trail that leads past several more locks which the local Canal Historical Society is trying to preserve. In the foreground is the keystone from the original bridge—later replaced by an aqueduct by John Roebling—that carried the canal across the nearby Rondout Creek. When the bridge was demolished, the keystone was found to contain a copper box filled with coins and specially stamped metal plates commemorating the bridge's construction in 1826.

Right, the mansion of Edward G. Cornish in what is now Hudson Highlands State Park. Gutted by fire several decades ago, it is a silent reminder of the days when opulent estates predominated the east shore of the Hudson. Though constructed of rough-hewn rock from nearby Breakneck Mountain to give it the look of a rustic retreat, the mansion was as modern as early twentieth-century technology would allow, including the then-luxury of indoor plumbing.

Who carved the stone steps in the amphitheater-like area at Rockland County's Monsey Glen? Theories range from Archaic Indians to nineteenth-century quarrymen, but the origin of the steps remains a mystery. *Below,* one of the most recent of the dozens of prehistoric mastodons recovered from Orange County black dirt, "Sugar" (named for the hamlet of Sugar Loaf, near which it was found) is now on display at Orange County Community College in Middletown. Featuring an unusual third tusk in its lower jaw, this adult male mastodon weighed between five and six tons when, around 10,000 years ago, it became enmired and died in what was then a swamp.

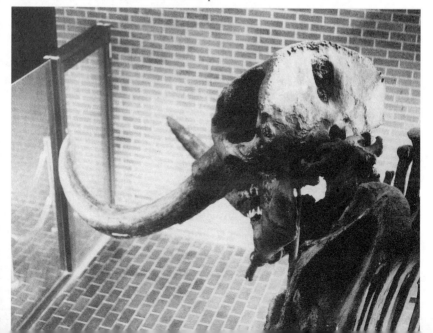

Called by a variety of names—from witch hovels to root cellars—slab-roof chambers like this one in Putnam County are part of the ongoing controversy as to whether America was visited by Old World explorers prior to the time of Columbus.

Below, once part of a large ironmaking complex, the Southfield furnace (at right) lies in ruins along Orange Turnpike in the town of Tuxedo. Built in 1804, it is unusual for its double-arched bridge over which ore was carted to be dumped into the top of the furnace.

Some scientists insist that North Salem's Great Boulder is simply a glacial erratic deposited there at the end of the Ice Age. Others argue that more than happenstance is responsible for the sixty-ton chunk of granite being perfectly balanced atop seven limestone legs. But no one can deny that this landmark along Route 121 resembles prehistoric dolmens found in Europe.

Left, in any season, but particularly in winter, the wide roof of Blauvelt's easternmost tunnel serves as a convenient walkway through the woods. In the background is the observation tower of the old rifle range, with connecting rooms and wall built at a right angle to the tunnel.

29 THE GIRL WHO WOULD NOT WEEP

WHEN CHURCH CHOIRS and congregations across the country lift their voices in song, quite often the hymns they choose have a Hudson Valley origin. For it was on March 24, 1820, that Fanny Crosby was born in the Putnam County town of Southeast—a child touched by tragedy who overcame almost impossible odds to become a beloved teacher and one of the world's most prolific hymn writers.

There was no indication of such future fame, however, when their first and only child was born to Mercy and John Crosby at their hardscrabble farm on what is now Foggintown Road. If anything, the reverse was true, for shortly after she was christened Frances Jane Crosby in the nearby Southeast Church in Doansburg, Fanny (as she was called throughout her life) developed a severe eye infection. The only physician then practicing in the area was unavailable, and in desperation John Crosby sought the services of a stranger who professed medical knowhow. But the man turned out to be a charlatan, whose "cure" was to place searing-hot compresses on the month-old baby's eyes. By the time the competent care could be secured, scar tissue had formed. Fanny was blind.

Nor was that the only tragedy the impoverished Crosby family suffered that year. Within six months, Fanny's father John was laid to rest in the Doansburg Cemetery, having worked too long and too hard in fields drenched by chill November rains. There was nothing Mercy Crosby could do except take a job as a domestic in the home of some well-to-do neighbors, while her mother Eunice cared for Fanny during the day.

Though she earned barely enough money to meet their needs, Mercy never gave up hope that someday, in some way, she would be able to afford the services of a specialist who might restore the sight of her baby daughter. Years passed—hard, scrimping years during which Fanny grew into a lovely and much-loved child. And finally Mercy Crosby was ready. Aided by contributions from concerned neighbors, Mercy made an appointment for five-year-old Fanny to be examined by the famous New York City surgeon Valentine Mott, and an equally renowned ophthalmologist, Dr. Delafield.

It was a long tiring trip in those days—overland by wagon from Southeast to the sloop landing at Sing Sing (Ossining), then an overnight sail down the Hudson to the city. But it was a joyful journey, since hope accompanied the young widow and her sightless child. That companion was absent on the return trip, though. The doctors' diagnosis had been as definite as it was disappointing: there was absolutely nothing medical science could do for Fanny.

Whatever dejection Mercy Crosby may have felt when she heard the news was soon overcome by her determination to have her daughter live as normal a life as possible. Fanny's grandmother Eunice was equally determined. And in an era when methods for teaching the blind had not yet been developed, Eunice intuitively guided Fanny into learning about a world she would never see.

Fanny herself was not disillusioned by the doctors' grim words. Allowed—in fact, encouraged—to act as a sighted person, Fanny grew up climbing trees and stone fences, playing tag and hide-and-seek, and even riding a horse as capably as any of her playmates. There were countless cuts and bruises, but Mercy and Eunice Crosby never regretted their decision, especially when they heard one of the first of Fanny's poems, which the child composed a few years later:

> Oh, what a happy soul I am,
> Although I cannot see,

I am resolved that in this world
Contented I will be.

How many blessings I enjoy
That other people don't.
To weep and sigh because I'm blind
I cannot, nor I won't!

At this time, Fanny and her mother were living in the Westchester County community of North Salem, where Mercy was employed as a housekeeper. It was not far from Southeast, and Fanny's grandmother Eunice was often with her, teaching her to substitute other senses for sight, as well as developing her memory by reciting Bible verses. Later, when Mercy and Fanny moved to Ridgefield, Connecticut, the child's lessons were augmented by a kindly landlady named Mrs. Hawley, but it was only too obvious that Fanny thirsted for a more formal education.

Though she desperately wished she could go to school like other children, Fanny did not become depressed. Her ebullient nature, along with her deep faith in God—seasoned with more than a dash of mischievousness—easily overpowered any feelings of self-pity that might have assailed her. And it was that mischievousness, as much as her innate sense of fair play, that caused Fanny to compose what became her first published verse. She had heard people complain about a neighborhood miller who mixed his flour with cheaper cornmeal, and she became so incensed over this dishonest practice that she made up a poem beginning:

There is a miller in our town,
How dreadful is his case;
I fear unless he does repent
He'll meet with sad disgrace.

A friend who read the verse sent it—unbeknown to Fanny—to P. T. Barnum, who was then publishing a weekly paper called the *Herald of Freedom*. Much to Fanny's embarrassment, the sensation-loving Barnum printed her poem. There were no more verses about the miller, but a continuous flow of poems, even obituaries, came from Fanny's agile mind—a mind that still longed for regular schooling. And eventually that, too, became a reality.

In November 1834, someone sent Mercy Crosby a brochure describing the New York Institute for the Blind. Mercy immediately sought more information, and on March 3, 1835, fourteen-year-old Fanny and her mother took the stagecoach to Norwalk, Connecticut, where they boarded a steamboat for New York City.

The two decades she spent at the institute—first as a student, and later as a teacher—were joyous ones for Fanny. She was to meet many of the famous people of her day, including President James K. Polk, Horace Greeley, Jenny Lind, William Cullen Bryant, and Grover Cleveland (the latter when he was teaching at the institute). Encouraged by Cleveland and others who thought her poems deserved wider attention, Fanny began submitting verses to periodicals like the *Saturday Evening Post*, and in 1844, her first book appeared, *The Blind Girl and Other Poems*. A year before that, she had addressed a joint session of Congress when a group of students from the institute were invited to Washington to tell of the work being accomplished in educating the blind.

Then, in 1851, a chance conversation started Fanny on the career she would pursue for the rest of her life. One day at the institute, music instructor George F. Root was playing an original composition. Since he already was a well-known composer, Fanny asked why he did not publish the piece. When he explained he had no words to go with the music, Fanny wrote "Fare Thee Well, Kitty Dear." It was the first of more than fifty songs she would write with Root.

After her marriage in 1858 to fellow teacher Alexander Van Alstyne, Fanny left the New York Institute for the Blind. Van Alstyne was himself an accomplished musician and composed the music to several of her hymns during their more than forty years of married life, much of it spent in Manhattan and Brooklyn. Only one thing marred their happiness: the death of their only child in infancy.

At the start of the Civil War, Fanny met composer-publisher William B. Bradbury, who asked her to write "There Is a Sound Among the Forest Trees." This patriotic song was used during the war years, and afterwards Fanny asked Bradbury if perhaps they could change the words to make it a missionary hymn. The result was "There's a Cry from Macedonia," and Fanny's career as a hymn writer was assured.

Through the succeeding years, she would compose more than five thousand hymns, at the same time lecturing for such organizations as the YMCA, New York's Bowery Mission, and the Drew Seminary, in her native Putnam County, and at evangelical meetings throughout the Northeast. Of her thousands of hymns, perhaps "Blessed Assurance," "Safe in the Arms of Jesus," and "Rescue the Perishing" are the most familiar. And it was the last that was responsible for an oft-repeated anecdote concerning its composer.

One hot summer evening when Fanny was addressing a meeting at the Bowery Mission in Lower Manhattan, a sudden intuition prompted her to invite any boy who had "wandered away from his mother's teaching" to come forward.

At the end of the service, an eighteen-year-old approached Fanny. "Did you mean me?" he inquired. Then he confessed he had promised his mother on her deathbed that he would meet her in heaven. The life he had been leading, however, was far from upright, and he feared he would never be able to keep his promise.

Although the hour was late and Fanny was exhausted, she devoted the remainder of the evening to the young man, talking and praying with him. Finally she sensed he had been helped, and she was confident he would change his life for the better.

When she reached home that night, Fanny composed:

> Rescue the perishing,
> Care for the dying,
> Snatch them in pity from sin and the grave;
> Weep o'er the erring one,
> Lift up the fallen,
> Tell them of Jesus, the mighty to save.

It was one of her finest hymns, destined to receive world recognition and be translated into many languages. But that is not the end of the story. Nearly four decades later, in November 1903, at a YMCA gathering in Lynn, Massachusetts, Fanny related how she had come to write "Rescue the Perishing." At the conclusion of her talk, a man came up to her and said, "I am the boy you rescued so many years ago. And I want you to know I am now certain I will keep my promise to my mother." Then before the amazed Fanny could say anything, the well-dressed man disappeared into the crowd.

Another of Fanny's hymns was inspired by a dying harbor pilot, who kept murmuring something about seeing a light. Considering his profession, the people attending him were certain he meant a shipping beacon or lighthouse. But the pilot shook his head. His final words were: "I see the light of Glory. Now let the anchor go." This story so impressed Fanny that she wrote "I See the Light," a hymn still popular today.

One might think that such a prolific hymn writer would have accumulated a fortune during a lifetime spanning more than nine decades, but Fanny Crosby (or "Aunt Fanny," as she was referred to in later years) was paid only about $5 for each hymn, plus royalties. It is true that she received much more for her secular songs, but her generosity and charity were ever at the fore. And so the treasure she amassed was not in dollars and cents but in the love and inspiration she engendered in the hearts of countless people.

Today her name lives on not only in her books, songs, and hymns, but also in such organizations as the Fanny Crosby Circle of King's Daughters and the Fanny Crosby Memorial Home in Bridgeport. Fanny moved to that Connecticut town in 1900, when relatives became fearful for the safety of the fragile eighty-year-old widow then living alone on Brooklyn's Lafayette Avenue.

When Fanny Crosby died in 1915, hers was one of the largest funerals ever seen in Bridgeport, where her grave initially was marked by a small headstone bearing the simple inscription: "Aunt Fanny—she hath done what she could." Then, in 1955, a larger headstone was erected by a host of caring folk whose lives had been enriched by the tiny woman in dark glasses who had given so much happiness and hope to so many, yet asked so little for herself.

Time has not dimmed the memory of Fanny Crosby in the Hudson Valley, either. A movie about her life is still shown to church groups around the region, and commemorative services are conducted from time to time. Most meaningful, perhaps, are those held in the beautiful old Southeast Church (near the junction of Routes 22 and

65, north of Brewster), where Fanny was christened in 1820. This 1794 church, lovingly restored by the Landmarks Preservation Society of Southeast, is a registered national historic landmark—and deservedly so.

Overlooking the church, on nearby Foggintown Road, is the privately owned, pre-Revolutionary farmhouse where Fanny Crosby was born. It is easily identifiable by a plaque embedded in the retaining wall bordering the road and, like the church, is well worth viewing by architectural aficionados as well as history buffs. Those who do pass by the places associated with Fanny Crosby's Putnam County childhood might like to keep in mind an autobiographical verse she composed:

> Her home was near an ancient wood,
> Where many an oak gigantic stood;
> And fragrant flowers of every hue
> In that sequestered valley grew.

The scene is still the same. So is the inspiring example set by the girl who would not weep.

30 MAXWELL ANDERSON'S MOUNTAIN

IT WAS ON A late spring morning in 1936 that a Rockland County man stood looking out an upstairs window in his South Mountain Road home. The panorama of the Hudson Highlands provided an eye-pleasing scene, but the man's stare remained fixed on a single cone—that of the northernmost point of the Palisades, the peak known as High Tor.

From this distance, and with its heavily forested flanks already in full foliage, High Tor gave the appearance of peaceful perpetuity. But the watching man knew otherwise, and it was with a determined step that he descended to the first floor. Once outside the door of his renovated farmhouse, he did not pause as he usually did to enjoy the sound of the waterfall plunging into the gorge by the patio. Instead, he hastened along a footpath through the woods, emerging several minutes later at a small and secluded cabin.

The man entered and seated himself at a table set with the simple tools of his trade: pencils, blank paper, and the notebooks in which he jotted down ideas for the plays that had made him famous. It was time for him to start a new play. It was time for him to try to save a mountain. And it was then that Maxwell Anderson—author of such theater classics as *Key Largo*, *Winterset*, and *What Price Glory*—boldly stroked two words at the top of a fresh page. *High Tor* was the title he chose.

Maxwell Anderson's first conscious thought of writing a play about High Tor had occurred earlier that year, while taking a mid-March hike with his son along the oak-canopied trails leading to the summit. However, it is likely that subconscious seeds had been sown as far back as 1921, when the Pennsylvania-born dramatist was working as a journalist in New York City.

Acting upon the suggestion of Rockland resident Mary Mowbray-Clarke, whose Sunwise Turn bookstore in Manhattan was a haven to upcoming artists and authors alike, Anderson went on a walking tour of New City. The then still-rural community enchanted Anderson, who longed for a home in the country. And when he strolled down the quiet lane curving around South Mountain, with High Tor dominating the skyline, he knew he had found what he wanted.

Anderson and his family moved to New City the following year, after purchasing a farmhouse he dubbed "Seven Fields" for the way the property was divided by centuries-old stone walls. This link with the past pleased the playwright, for whom history had always been a favorite theme, and it is fairly certain that his ever-attuned ear soon picked up some of the strange stories local residents recounted about High Tor.

The most ancient of these tales originated with the long-gone Indians, who believed evil spirits had been buried beneath High Tor at the time the world was created. Many millennia later, a stranger—some say it was one of the Magi—arrived and began building a stone altar atop High Tor for the purpose of converting the Indians to Christianity. The natives wanted none of the newfangled religion and rallied their warriors for a rush up the mountain. Before the war party reached the top, however, High Tor's side split open, swallowing the would-be attackers and creating a chasm through which a torrent of water flowed. Thus was formed the mighty Hudson—at least according to one of several legends concerning the river's creation.

While High Tor may share river-birthing honors with other Hudson Highland locations, it also boasts some colorful folklore all its own, including a complicated sequel to the tale of the mountain-top altar. Supposedly, sometime in the eighteenth century a German immigrant named Hugo was employed at one of the iron forges then flourishing in the Ramapos. A Rosicrucian as well as an ironworker, Hugo listened to the legends about High Tor and decided he could convert the entombed evil spirits by building a forge where the ancient altar once stood.

Meanwhile, the evil spirits conspired to corrupt Hugo, who was promised great power if he would release them by reading aloud the words inscribed on the back of a giant salamander living within his forge. (Fire-living salamanders, myth lovers will recall, date back to the days of Ancient Greece.) When Hugo balked at the bribe, the supernatural salamander supposedly rose from the flames, killing the ironworker's son and wife. This caused poor Hugo to lose his sanity, and he aimlessly roamed the forest trails of High Tor until the time his daughter reached maturity.

One day the young woman met a strange man on the mountain who offered his help as well as his heart. Love also prompted him to reveal he was not mortal but a spirit first turned into a salamander, then later into that of a man sent by the evil forces to seduce Hugo's daughter. As myth would have it, the demented Hugo wandered by just as the confession occurred. The words shocked Hugo back to reality—and rage. He flung the offender into the fire, which released the enchanted one to return to wherever such spirits come from, and the now-sane Hugo and his daughter were reunited.

If folklore like that was not enough to inspire Maxwell Anderson to pen a play about High Tor, there were other stories, too—ones about a ghostly "storm ship" seen on Haverstraw Bay at the foot of the mountain. The sighting of this specter supposedly presaged the kind of storms that wrecked river vessels, while the thunder that often seemed to emanate from High Tor's interior was interpreted by some to be the sound of Henry Hudson's long-dead crew playing ninepins.

Oddly enough, the one supernatural story that would have been the most obvious candidate for inclusion in his play seemed not to have been known by Anderson at the time he was writing *High Tor*. It involves the ghost of a girl seen by a modern-day dweller in one of the houses along South Mountain Road. According to local lore, the girl had been the fiancée of Elmer Van Orden, the last individual to

own the top of High Tor and the man on whom Anderson patterned
his play's protagonist, Van Van Dorn.

Anderson knew and liked Elmer Van Orden, whom he met
shortly after he moved to New City when he needed someone to
rebuild the chimney of his house. Van Orden did the work, though
his main occupation was farming a parcel of land on the southern
slope of High Tor, which had been in his family since Colonial times.
Self-sufficient and fiercely independent, Van Orden steadfastly resisted
all attempts by traprock developers to buy him out so they could
quarry away the backbone of his beloved mountain. It was a stand
Anderson admired, for the "rock robbers" already had left ugly scars
on the Palisades and other areas of the Hudson Highlands.

Nor was Anderson himself averse to taking a stand in the battle of
industry versus nature. As reported by Alfred S. Shivers in his 1983
biography of the playwright, Anderson and a neighbor had waged
their own private war in the early 1920s when a utility company tried
to construct a power line over the scenic waterfall next to Anderson's
house. By day, the company set out its survey stakes; by night,
Anderson and his friend pulled them up, delaying the project until
more legitimate means were found to stop it.

These, then, were some of the diverse threads of folklore and fact
that Anderson wove into the fabric of *High Tor*, a richly poetic play
that won the New York Drama Critics Award for 1937 and launched
a successful movement to save the mountain. Needless to say,
Anderson was in the forefront of the campaign, which began with a
fund-raising committee of celebrities, including the cast of *High Tor*.

By 1942, when the elderly bachelor Elmer Van Orden died,
enough money had been collected for his property to be purchased
by the Rockland County Conservation Association and the Hudson
River Conservation Society. The land was then deeded over to the
Palisades Interstate Park Commission in 1943. During the same year,
Little Tor—the prominence to the west of High Tor—was also given
to the PIPC, and the 492-acre High Tor State Park was established.

Unfortunately, some would-be hikers shy away from the park,
thinking the only access to High Tor is the steep trail leading up the
eastern slope from the trailhead just off Route 9W, about a half mile
south of the Haverstraw Railroad Station. Taking that trail is the

shortest way to reach the summit, but those who prefer their hiking more horizontal would do better to approach High Tor from the west. This route, well marked by blue blazes, follows the Long Path and can be picked up at the parking lot on the eastern side of Central Highway, about one mile from its intersection with Route 202, in West Haverstraw.

The distance from the parking lot to High Tor is about two miles, and along the way hikers can take advantage of a side trip to Little Tor, with its northern perimeter of step-like basalt offering breathtaking views of Haverstraw 710 feet below. In addition, there is a massive boulder crowning the rocks on the western rim which shouldn't be missed. Grayish-white and studded with broken garnets, this "erratic" is totally different from the basalt on which it rests, having been brought there eons ago by a glacier. Look for the north-south scratches on the bald bedrock—evidence of the glacier's path.

On the way to High Tor, hikers also pass the foundation of an airplane beacon, a modern-day version of the signal fires that once burned there during the Revolution. At night, the beacon was visible from Maxwell Anderson's home three miles away, and the playwright used it to great effect in *High Tor*, having a group of ghostly Dutchmen knock down the beacon with their bowling balls. Actually, the tower was still standing at the time *High Tor* was written; park officials later removed it when it was extensively damaged by vandals.

Despite all the other points of interest, High Tor remains the treat of any trek along this section of the Long Path. It is aptly named, too, for at 827 feet it is the highest point in the Palisades and offers wide-ranging views of the Hudson Valley. *Tor*, by the way, comes from the Anglo-Saxon *torr*, meaning "tower" or "rock."

Three miles to the north, Stony Point juts out into the Hudson, with Grassy Point just south of it. Directly below, Haverstraw looks like a toy village embracing the west shore of the Hudson. The small ponds seen from this height are actually the remains of old clay pits that once supplied Haverstraw's vast brickmaking industry, while a look south toward Hook Mountain reveals some of the traprock excavations that so aroused Maxwell Anderson's ire.

Anger, however, was not the main emotion the vista evoked in

Anderson on that March day in 1936 when he and his son climbed to the top of High Tor. Reportedly, the playwright was struck by the history represented in the panorama spread out before him, and "the evanescence of civilization." Could he capture it all in a play? He could and did, and in the process preserved a legendary landmark.

Many thanks, Mr. Anderson; no mountain ever had a better friend.

31 MARK TWAIN'S LIFE ON THE HUDSON

MOST AMERICANS ASSOCIATE Mark Twain with the Mississippi, and rightly so. For Samuel Langhorne Clemens adopted that pen name in memory of his early days as a riverboat pilot, when a depth of two fathoms (the "twain" mark on a sounding line) meant safe passage for the huge paddle-wheelers then plying the mighty waterway. But while the Mississippi may have given Twain his name and much material for his long literary career, it is the Hudson that is more closely associated with his later life—and the friendship he formed with a Tuxedo Park teenager that endured until his death in 1910.

That friendship was still many years in the future when Twain arrived in New York City during January 1867. Fresh from the Far West, where he had earned a modicum of fame as a journalist—and full measure as a carouser—the thirty-one-year-old bachelor carried with him a commission from a California newspaper to write a series of travel articles during a sea voyage he was planning. His ship would not sail until spring, however, so Twain settled in to life along the Hudson. He found it to his liking, too, for many of his California friends had drifted East, and he soon had offers of newspaper assignments, plus a proposal to collect some of his Far West sketches in book form—his first.

Another first was his appearance at Cooper Union Institute on

May 6, scheduled to coincide with the publication of *The Celebrated Jumping Frog of Calaveras County and Other Sketches*. Although Twain had done some public speaking before, he had never lectured in the East, and the huge hall on Seventh Street in Lower Manhattan filled him with trepidation, particularly when he found out that on the same night as his program, several popular performers would be appearing elsewhere in the city.

The promoter of the Cooper Union program likewise envisioned a scant audience for his little-known lecturer, and rather than have a half-filled house, he sent out scads of complimentary tickets to schoolteachers throughout the metropolitan area. The result was a rousing success—maybe not financially, but the teachers found Twain enchanting, and he became the talk of the town. This public acclaim generated other invitations to lecture, but Twain was forced to refuse, since his ship was scheduled to set sail for the Mediterranean on June 8.

Five months later, Twain returned to New York a celebrity. More than sixty of his travel articles from abroad had been printed in newspapers across the country, and a publisher soon contacted him about writing a book concerning his tour. (This was to be *The Innocents Abroad*, published in 1869.) Yet it was an affair of the heart, more than the finding of fame, that ever endeared New York City to Twain.

Following a tradition of the time, on New Year's Day, 1868, Twain set out to call at the homes of close friends, but he got no farther than the first house. For there he encountered Olivia ("Livy") Langdon, a fragile dark-haired beauty who had been on his mind—and in his heart—since late November, when he had seen her at the St. Nicholas Hotel on lower Broadway. From that time on, no other woman turned Twain's head, and despite initial opposition by the Langdon family, the two were married at Livy's home in Elmira on February 2, 1870.

The couple lived first in Buffalo, then in Hartford, Connecticut, and during the next three decades Twain returned to the Hudson River region only for brief visits. Some of those short stints were quite colorful, however, including an 1885 visit to Albany, when he called on President-elect Grover Cleveland.

Cleveland, who was still serving as governor of New York, received the author in his office at the State Capitol and began to twit Twain about never having visited him when they both were living in Buffalo. Twain retorted that in Buffalo Cleveland had held the office of sheriff, and he always avoided sheriffs. Then content with his comeback to Cleveland (whom he had staunchly supported for the presidency), Twain sat down on the edge of the governor's desk. Within seconds, a passel of men appeared, much like a posse, to surround the startled author. Cleveland savored the situation for a moment, then dismissed his staff by saying that his guest was resting his rump on the call bells!

There was a touch of typical Twain humor, too, in a visit he made to West Point during January 1890. He had addressed the cadets on previous occasions, but this time Twain read them passages from his just-published social satire, *A Connecticut Yankee in King Arthur's Court*. And of course the passages Twain picked were those in which the narrator of the novel organizes his own West Point—complete with cadets—in medieval England.

Later that year, Twain spent some time at Onteora Park, the summer colony founded in 1883 by Francis B. Thurber just north of Tannersville in Greene County. Reportedly, the relaxed atmosphere wasn't conducive to much creative writing on Twain's part, but his skills as a raconteur were applauded by the seasonal residents who gathered around his cabin on many an evening. Nor did he confine his Catskill Mountain sojourns to Onteora—Twain was equally appreciated whenever he accepted an invitation to stay at Twilight Park, another of the private communities that sprang up in the 1880s, located between Haines Falls and Palenville in the town of Hunter.

It was not until the turn of the century that Twain and his family took up permanent residence along the Hudson's shores: first in a house on West Tenth Street in Manhattan, then at a handsome mansion called Holbrook Hall at West 249th Street and Independence Avenue in the Riverdale section of the Bronx.

Present-day visitors to Holbrook Hall (now known as the Wave Hill Environmental Center) will marvel, as did Twain, at the magnificent river view from the hilltop site. But what "sold" it to Twain was the 30-foot-long dining room, boasting two enormous fireplaces, where he and his beloved Livy could entertain their many friends. In October 1901, they decided to rent the house for a year or so, during which time they would decide whether or not to buy it—a purchase that never came to pass, despite their love of the place.

Reluctantly, Twain had to concede that the house was too costly. Yet he loved the beauty of the lower Hudson Valley, with its easy access to the city, so he and Livy searched for and found another, more affordable home. This one, called Hillcrest, was farther upriver, in Tarrytown, close to Washington Irving's Sunnyside and overlooking the Tappan Zee. (Hillcrest was torn down in 1916, and another building soon took its place, but Mark Twain's presence there is still recalled on a historical marker near the junction of Benedict and Highland Avenues.)

Permanent residence at Tarrytown was to remain another unrealized dream for Twain. Poor investments and a writing career that had long ago peaked were part of the problem, but mainly it was Livy's chronic ill health. And after Twain had spent the winter of 1902–3 tending to his bedbound wife, doctors told him to take Livy to Italy, where the climate might aid her recuperation.

On October 24, 1903, they sailed for Europe. The following June, Livy was dead. The grief-stricken Twain brought her body back to America to be buried in Elmira, beside the son and daughter they had lost years earlier. Then with his two remaining children—Jean and Clara—he moved to a house in Manhattan, at the corner of Ninth Street and Fifth Avenue.

It was around this time that Twain began visiting Tuxedo Park, that exclusive Orange County enclave where he was much in demand as a guest. In *The World with a Fence Around It*, George Rushmore recalls that when his father met Twain at a crowded wedding reception in Tuxedo Park, he immediately invited the author to "rest his feet" at the nearby Rushmore home. Twain accepted gratefully and wound up staying with the Rushmores for several days, entertaining visitors all morning while still in bed and puffing away at the pungent black cigars that had become his trademark. However, Twain steadfastly refused all suggestions that he sample some of the elder Rushmore's expensive smokes, explaining that as a young man, the only ones he had been able to afford were cheap cigars, and he still preferred them.

Twain's services as a storyteller were also sought at Tuxedo, and although his sharp delivery was somewhat dulled by age (he was then past seventy), he always drew a crowd. So it was a blow when, in 1906, he was asked to address a Tuxedo school group and only a few people attended. Nor was the incensed author much mollified by an explanation that the lack of audience merely reflected the social schism of the community: Tuxedo Parkites simply didn't mingle with the rest of the townsfolk, and vice versa. Because each group thought the other was going, neither showed up.

Children, however, tend to be less class-conscious, and a year later when Twain agreed to read passages from *Tom Sawyer* and *Huckleberry Finn* from the front steps of the Tuxedo Park Library, he was surrounded by youthful fans.

It is not known whether Margery Clinton was among the audience at the library that day, but when the book-loving Tuxedo Park teenager found out the famous author was renting a house there for the summer, she decided to call on him. According to Margery's niece, Margaret C. Burt, Twain himself answered the young lady's knock at the door. Surprised to find the bespectacled Margery standing there, he blurted out, "Oh, I was expecting the plumber. Do you know how to fix this radiator?"

Undaunted, Margery cheerfully replied, "Well, I'll try." Doubtless she didn't know a valve from a gasket, but her spunk delighted Twain, and the two immediately became fast friends despite the disparity in age.

For the few years remaining in Twain's life, this friendship never faltered; if anything, the author—beset by a worsening heart condition, plus family and financial woes—came to rely on the lively young lady he called "The Plumber" in memory of their first meeting.

Twain had moved, by then, to Redding, Connecticut, and he issued an open invitation for Margery to visit him there anytime she chose. This she did on several occasions during 1908 and 1909, and guest book entries for some of those visits bear Twain's jocular notations about her being the "Official Plumber" of the house. As for

Margery, she always addressed him as "Mr. Clemens" in her letters, though their correspondence was otherwise informal and covered all kinds of topics, from Twain's belief in Francis Bacon's authorship of Shakespeare's plays to his love of smoking.

Yet no matter what other topic he might temporarily take up in his letters, Twain consistently returned to one theme: an appeal for Margery to visit him. Usually his plea was worded humorously: his billiard table was askew and needed leveling by the "plumber (who doesn't know how to plumb)," or that she should not forget to bring along "a change of soldering irons." But underlying the humor was an unmistakable urgency. For Margery—described by George Rushmore as "one of the wittiest and most entertaining persons that I have had the good fortune to meet"—was a refreshing breath in the stale atmosphere of Twain's declining days.

Margery saved Twain's letters in a leather-bound album, along with other memorabilia pertaining to him. For the next seven decades, that album remained in the hands of Margery and her family, so the existence of the letters was not widely known. Then, in 1982, Margery's niece Margaret Burt decided this small treasure of Twainiana belonged in a place where researchers might have access to it. The place Mrs. Burt chose was Vassar College—in Poughkeepsie—which first opened its doors to students around the time Mark Twain came East to begin his own life on the Hudson.

Surely he would have approved.

32 THE THREE BURROUGHS OF RIVERBY

SOME MAY HAVE loved it as much, but it is doubtful that anyone has loved the Hudson Valley more than did John Burroughs, the world-renowned naturalist, who left a rich legacy of outdoor lore and whose literary talent happily was handed down to two other members of his family.

Burroughs' first love, however, was the Catskill region where he was born on April 3, 1837, the seventh in a family of ten children. His childhood, on an isolated farm at the foot of Clump Mountain in the Delaware County town of Roxbury, was far from carefree. Hard work was expected of him by his Old School Baptist parents, whose cash income came mainly from the butter they made with a dog-tread churn. It was a boyhood of never-ending chores, and although it did not embitter him—indeed, he reveled in physical labor throughout his fourscore-plus lifespan—young John yearned for something more.

Whenever he had the time, Burroughs would climb atop a huge rock in a nearby pasture, there to sit dreaming of the future and taking in the scenic countryside. The seeds of the longing that possessed him were probably first sown when he joined his older siblings as they trekked down the dirt lane near Hardscrabble Creek, on their way to the Westfield Settlement School. Though only a one-room structure, which the children jokingly called the "little stone jug," it offered young John a glimpse of the world outside the Roxbury hills.

Books soon became his passion—a passion not shared by other members of his family, who felt that a basic grounding in the three R's was all that farm folk really required. Even though she did not understand her son's bibliophilia, and never read very much herself, Amy Burroughs made sure John had the books he craved, sometimes lingering long over her mending of an evening, so that the boy could read by the light of the hand-dipped candle attached to the back of her chair.

Nor did his desire for knowledge ever diminish, and there was at least one instance when Burroughs sacrificed personal comfort in order to purchase some books. That occurred in 1855 when he had gone job-seeking and stopped off at a secondhand bookstore in New York City. Buying the volumes he wanted left him without any money to eat and only partial fare for his return journey, and he wound up walking the last twelve miles to his home. Those very books were to occupy a place of honor in the study he built at his Hudson-shore home many years later.

Despite his family's lack of enthusiasm concerning education, Burroughs was determined to go further than the Westfield Settlement School, and in April 1854 (when only seventeen years old), he obtained a six-month teaching assignment at the Ulster County village of Tongore (now Olive Bridge). This allowed him to earn enough money for tuition at the Ashland Collegiate Institute in Greene County, where he studied for three months. The school is no longer standing, but in back of its site, just off Route 23, is a rock where Burroughs supposedly sat while composing his first essay.

In September 1855, Burroughs returned to Tongore, where he taught school until April of the following year, and in the meantime met Ursula ("Sulie") North, the young woman who was to become his wife. First, though, he wanted to continue his education. With money saved up from his Tongore teaching stint, he enrolled at the Cooperstown Seminary for a three-month course—all he was able to afford. But it was sufficient to convince him that literature was as important to him as life itself; not only reading but writing, too, for it was during this time that his first article to appear in print was published by a Delaware County newspaper.

Recognition did not mean riches, however, and Burroughs was forced to return to teaching, one assignment taking him as far away as Buffalo Grove, Illinois. Teachers were not paid much either, and for two years following his 1857 marriage to Sulie, he frequently was so financially strapped that he had to live in a boardinghouse while she stayed with her parents in the town of Olive. Eventually, a better-paying position at an East Orange, New Jersey, school allowed them to set up housekeeping on their own, and he started publishing articles in New York newspapers.

By the fall of 1860, Burroughs and his wife were living at Marlboro-on-Hudson, where he had secured a teaching post. They were happy to be closer to their families, and usually spent part of the summer at Roxbury or Olive. But the highlight of that year—at least for John—was the publication of his essay "Expression" in the *Atlantic Monthly*. The essay was so Emersonian in style that the editor, James Russell Lowell, at first doubted that Burroughs had written it, and only published it after checking through all of Ralph Waldo Emerson's known writings. This was more of a boon than a blight to Burroughs, for it convinced the young essayist that he must develop his own distinctive style—something that he began showing in a series of nature essays, "From the Back Country," which appeared in the *New York Leader*.

Although he had told Sulie early in their marriage, "If I live, I shall be an author," Burroughs well knew that he could not make a living writing. Nor did he receive any encouragement from his wife or family, who could not understand why he wasted his time at such "scribbling." In addition, he was still unsettled as to the focus and form his writing should take, though he had always known that fiction was not for him; indeed, he rarely even read any. Poetry did interest him, and it was around this time that he wrote the pensive and oft-reprinted ode "Waiting" (a portion of which appears on the plaque where he is buried, by his "Boyhood Rock" at what is now the Burroughs Memorial Park in Roxbury). But time would tell that versification was only an accessory vehicle for his literary talent: of the more than twenty volumes in the Burroughs canon, only one is a collection of his poetry (*Bird and Bough*, 1906), although his *Birds and Poets* (1877) does have a chapter concerning it.

A move to the Orange County village of Highland Falls (where he had been hired as a teacher late in 1862) proved to be an important milestone in Burroughs' life. He had decided to study medicine while there, but by the spring of 1863 he gave it up in favor of wildflowers—a decision influenced in part by a botanist friend of his. Following close on the heels of this decision was his discovery, in the nearby West Point Library, of John J. Audubon's monumental study *The Birds of America*, and for weeks afterward, Burroughs thought and talked of nothing but birds. He had found his focus.

That summer, Burroughs also came to the sad conclusion that a teacher's salary would never be sufficient to meet his and Sulie's needs. Motivated by this, plus the fact that the Civil War was then raging and he wanted to get closer to the conflict, in October 1863 he headed for Washington, D.C. It was a move as momentous as the one to Highland Falls. His new job in the Currency Branch of the Treasury Department meant that he and Sulie could afford their own home (a comfortable cottage on V Street, complete with a garden). He would also have time to pursue his writing, but perhaps most momentous, it was there he met Walt Whitman and their lifelong friendship was forged.

The "Good Gray Poet" was to have a profound influence on Burroughs, whose first published book was not about nature, as one might suppose, but *Notes on Walt Whitman as Poet and Person* (1867). In fact, it was another four years before his *Wake-Robin* appeared—a small volume of eight nature essays that received critical acclaim and is still popular today. (Incidentally, "wake-robin" is another name for trillium, a wildflower that blooms in the early spring and heralds the arrival of the birds.)

Buoyed by the book's success and the subsequent publication of several more magazine articles, in 1872 Burroughs resigned his job in Washington and went looking for a home in the Hudson Valley. He had been hired as a bank receiver in Orange County's Middletown, and also was appointed a national examiner of regional institutions, so he needed a place midway between Albany and New York City, convenient to both Poughkeepsie and Middletown, as well as one within a day's traveling distance of his parents' home in Roxbury. The west side of the river would be ideal in more ways than one, as it offered him the opportunity to follow a fresh dream: that of being a fruit farmer. He figured that by supplementing his income in this way, he would be able to afford the kind of home he had always wanted, while continuing his career as a writer.

Burroughs looked at land in Nyack, Milton, and Marlboro, but settled on a 9-acre apple farm in West Park, with terraced orchards and a sweeping view of the Hudson. There was also an old cottage that he and Sulie could use until he built a permanent home, and there was plenty of stone nearby that would provide him with free building material.

Nowadays, paying $5,400 for 9 acres of Hudson-shore property might seem an unbeatable bargain, but for a man then earning only $3,000 a year it represented a considerable risk. So Burroughs delayed his decision for nearly a year, finally purchasing the farm in September 1873. It was to be his home for the rest of his life and the source of much of the material in the books he produced thereafter at the rate of one every two or three years until his death, at age eighty-three, in 1921.

With the help of local hired men, Burroughs immediately began building the house of his dreams—a three-and-a-half-story structure overlooking the Hudson, which be called "Riverby" (pronounced "Riverbee"). Whenever he was not doing bank work or writing, he was trekking through the West Park forests, inspecting rock ledges for the stone walls of his house and selecting trees for the various woods he wanted. He preferred the richness of natural wood over painted surfaces, calling the latter "blank" and "meaningless" in "Rooftree," an essay he wrote about the building of Riverby.

That first winter was a hard one; river traffic had ceased as soon as the Hudson froze over, the west-shore railroad had not yet been built, and the road going past Riverby (present-day Route 9W) was only a dirt track frequently drifted over by snow. The nearest store was a half mile away, but its stock was limited, and if Burroughs needed something more, he would have to trudge another couple of miles to Elmore's Corners (now the village of Esopus). He had always been an outdoor man, however, and welcomed these trips as opportunities to observe such things as the "embroidery" of bird tracks in the snow. (In subsequent years, he and Sulie often spent the coldest months at a boardinghouse in Poughkeepsie and later in their life would winter at a friend's house in the South.)

As for the river that winter, Burroughs enjoyed watching the ice-harvesting activities of the Knickerbocker Ice Company, which operated just south of the Riverby dock. At this period in his life, he didn't even own a horse, but if he needed to travel very far, he could always hike across the frozen Hudson—about a mile wide at this point—and take the train at Hyde Park.

By the autumn of 1874, Burroughs and his wife were settled in their new home and he was looking forward to the publication of his third book, *Winter Sunshine*, due out the following year. When it appeared, he was lauded as the "Prophet of Outdoordom"—a title "no one has held so well since Thoreau's death." Indeed, some critics thought Burroughs to be a better writer than Henry Thoreau, and his place among America's literati was assured. Magazine editors were now actively soliciting his articles, but Burroughs could not— nor did he wish to—devote all his time to writing.

Aside from his banking commitments, he was struggling to develop the fruit farm, with row upon row of apples, berries, and grapes requiring countless hours of cultivation, picking, and shipping. He also had beehives and a vegetable garden to tend, plus a flock of chickens to feed, and he always helped with harvesting and maple-sugaring at Roxbury. But most of all, he needed time to walk in the woods west of Riverby. One of his favorite spots was Black Creek, a small waterway with lovely rock-ribbed cascades, where he would sit for hours, sometimes reading a book but more often simply contemplating the wonders of nature.

Although one of the selling points of Riverby had been its riparian setting, and Burroughs did enjoy boating as well as ice skating, the Hudson was too awesome—too impersonal—for him. As he explained in an essay entitled "A River View" (included in his 1886 book, *Signs and Seasons*), a big river like the Hudson "does not flow through the affections like a lesser stream." Yet he appreciated that "long arm of the sea" and penned a paean to the Hudson which has long been a favorite with his readers.

Speaking of favorites, Burroughs liked his birth month of April most, for that was the time all nature came alive and his beloved arbutus bloomed. Then, in 1878, the month was made even more meaningful when, on April 15—after more than twenty years of marriage—Sulie gave birth to their first and only child, Julian. The forty-one-year-old author was ecstatic, and before the baby was a year old, Burroughs had written to a friend, "I think I see a future poet in him." His prediction was not far off the mark: Julian Burroughs did become an accomplished journalist, photographer, and painter, though he never pursued these talents to the fullest, because of family responsibilities.

As he grew to boyhood, Julian proved to be an amiable compan-ion who shared his father's love of the outdoors, and as soon as the child was old enough, Burroughs took him camping. One of those earliest trips was to Ulster County's Woodland Valley, not far from two of Burroughs' best-loved mountains, Wittenberg and Slide. Named for an 1820 landslide that scarred its northwestern slope, Slide Moun-tain is the highest point in the Catskills; one that Burroughs often climbed and wrote much about. (A plaque has since been placed at the summit that reads, in part, "John Burroughs...introduced Slide Mountain to the world...and slept several nights beneath this rock.")

Also like his father, Julian enjoyed the many people who visited them over the years—Walt Whitman, Oscar Wilde, John Muir, Harvey Firestone, Henry Ford, and Thomas Edison, to name only some of the more famous folk. These, however, were far outnumbered by the host of family, neighbors, friends, and sometimes utter strangers who showed up at Riverby.

In order to accommodate his growing number of visitors, as well as to take some of the pressure off Sulie and have more work space nearer to nature, in 1881 Burroughs constructed a separate cabin (called the Bark Study) a short distance east of the stone house. But even this was not entirely satisfactory, and in 1895, Burroughs purchased some land in the woods west of Riverby and began building a rustic retreat he called "Slabsides." (Now a National Historic Landmark owned by the John Burroughs Memorial Associa-tion, Slabsides is open to the public two days a year—usually a Saturday in May and October. In the 1960s and '70s, additional land was purchased surrounding the original Slabsides plot to make what is now the 174-acre John Burroughs Wildlife Sanctuary. As for Riverby, it is privately owned and not open to the public.)

Burroughs had more time now, for he was no longer employed as a bank examiner, and on his fruit farm he had completed the transition from apples as the prime product to grapes. There was still the hectic time of the harvest—what Burroughs referred to as the "grape war"—which was made even more exhausting by the fact that he grew table (or eating) grapes, and they required more delicate handling than the kind used for wine. But all the work was worth it, since the Riverby label on the crates Burroughs hammered together was now recognized as a symbol of quality, and he could consider his fruit farm a financial success (except, of course, in years when the weather wreaked havoc on the crop).

Yet his farmer's eye was ever on the lookout for productive places, and in choosing the site for Slabsides, Burroughs also had plans for growing celery and other vegetables. Hence, before he commenced building his retreat, the fifty-eight-year-old author first cleared and drained a nearby swamp, and the rich bottomland had already produced a crop by the time Slabsides was completed in 1896. The name, incidentally, refers to the exterior of the story-and-a-half cabin, which is covered by several kinds of wood varying in texture and tone.

It is in this setting that Burroughs is perhaps best remembered. He did much of his post-1896 writing here, and many of the people who came to see him at Slabsides published reminiscences of their visits. He was also being thought of more as a philosopher and prophet than just a nature writer (his works include scientific treatises and literary criticism as well as comments on world affairs), and the title "Sage of Slabsides" soon became a familiar one. Despite all this, he retained his simple and hospitable ways, equally at home with an industrial baron, an incumbent president, or a group of students.

Although he wasn't fond of giving talks at schools—"Nature cannot be taught," he said, "and I cannot bring the country with me"—he delighted in welcoming classes to Slabsides, where he could show them the natural world he knew so well. Such visits usually included a trip to his "icebox"—a small cave in the rock outcropping beside his cabin, where he kept perishables cool and where he could point out glacial striations in the stone. Cattail penholders were sometimes made as souvenirs for his young visitors, and always he bade them farewell by waving a stick he kept on the mantel of his cobblestone fireplace, saying it was his magic wand that would ensure their return to Slabsides.

For smaller groups and family picnics at Slabsides, Burroughs would cook his favorite "brigand steak"—skewered beef cubes, bacon, and onions broiled over a bed of hot coals in a rock cleft near the cabin, with adjacent boulders serving as seats and tables. Even when Theodore Roosevelt came to Slabsides in July 1903, the menu was simple: peas cooked on a small kerosene stove in the cabin, while the white-bearded Burroughs broiled chicken over an outdoor fire, with potatoes and onions baked in the ashes. Burroughs' only concession to the presidential presence was having a neighbor provide an apple pie for dessert. Reportedly, Roosevelt relished not being treated as royalty, and when the presidential yacht left the Riverby dock, he called out an affectionate goodbye to "Oom John." ("Oom" is an endearment used by old Dutch families like the Roosevelts, as well as their word for "uncle.")

Burroughs did not always play host, however. As his writings gained worldwide recognition, he was besieged by people inviting him places, and he traveled extensively—from Hawaii and Canada to the Caribbean and Europe, as well as throughout the continental United States. Books resulted from these travels too: for instance, *Far and Near* (1904) concerns his cruise with the Harriman Expedition to Alaska, while *Camping and Tramping...* (1907) details a trip to Yellowstone Park with Theodore Roosevelt.

Closer to home, Burroughs often visited Twilight and Onteora Parks, and in 1894 he was a guest at the dedication of Artist's Rock on nearby North Mountain, where Thomas Cole painted some of his spectacular Catskill scenes. Burroughs also loved going to Yama Farms, the famous Japanese-style retreat in the Ulster County town of Wawarsing that Frank Seaman began developing in 1906. Burroughs' first visit was in 1908, and he returned many times thereafter, saying, "I come here to find myself; it is so easy to get lost in the world."

And in a lighter vein one day, he composed a couplet about the retreat's trout-filled waterway: "I lost my heart to Jenny Brook / I think she took it with a hook."

In the same year that he first visited Yama Farms, Burroughs decided to refurbish a farmhouse built by one of his brothers in Roxbury, for he wanted a summer home near the scenes of his childhood. He named the place Woodchuck Lodge (now a National Historic Landmark) and for the rest of his life spent at least part of each summer there, though Riverby remained his primary residence. Nor did he absent himself from civic responsibilities; he served as West Park's first postmaster, as a school trustee, and for a time was the official historian of the community.

Earlier in his life, Burroughs had turned down honorary degrees from several universities, but when Yale repeated its offer in 1910, he accepted the degree of Doctor of Letters. This was followed by two more honorary degrees: Colgate (1911) and the University of Georgia (1915). But perhaps the degree that meant the most to him was the one Julian earned from Harvard. During the four years that his son was an undergraduate there, Burroughs frequently journeyed to Cambridge, enjoying the academic ambience he had longed for—and been denied—when he was Julian's age. And when his son began publishing articles in periodicals, Burroughs was his staunchest supporter, saying in one letter, "It is becoming very plain to me that you are cut out for a man of letters. This is as I would have it." Yet Burroughs also expected his son to run the Riverby fruit farm after he graduated college—a task that would eventually curtail the young man's creative output.

By that time, Julian had fallen in love with Emily Mackay, whom the elder Burroughs had met when he was giving a talk on birds at Harvard Memorial Hall and afterwards introduced to his son. The couple was married on September 25, 1902, and moved to Riverby, where Julian built a home just down the hill from his parents' house. A year later, their daughter Elizabeth was born, followed in 1905 by Ursula (named for Sulie), and then Burroughs' namesake, John II, in 1909.

Burroughs took great pride in these three grandchildren, whose presence helped him through the pain-filled days following Sulie's death in 1917. And it was young Ursula who was beside him four years later, when Burroughs died on a train returning East after a California vacation. His last words were to ask how far they were from New York, for he had wanted to be back home by his birthday.

The body of America's beloved naturalist was brought first to Riverby, where mourners gathered around the simple gray casket in Julian's living room, while Burroughs' favorite melody—Brahms' "Cradle Song"—was played. Then on April 3, 1921, the funeral cortège wended its way west to Roxbury. It was John Burroughs' eighty-fourth birthday. He had made it home.

At the time of his death, Burroughs had been working on his autobiography, and in the months that followed Julian completed the manuscript, with a concluding chapter called "My Father." The book, *My Boyhood*, appeared in 1922, and thereafter Julian's writings consisted mostly of articles that were published in outdoor magazines. Had he not been John Burroughs' son, Julian's name might be better known today. But as so often happens with offspring of the famous, Julian was destined to remain in his father's shadow. And as Elizabeth Burroughs Kelley points out in her book *John Burroughs: Naturalist*, "to many people...he was his father's living representative." Julian even looked like him: the same erect stance and spare build, though his beard was trimmer than the long spade of white whiskers that readers associate with the elder Burroughs. (Indeed, that single feature was once so well known that a postcard, containing just the sketch of a beard for an address, was promptly sent by the New York City post office to Burroughs at West Park.)

Being his late father's "living representative" didn't seem to bother Julian, whose creativity was often channeled into architectural projects (including a gracefully arched stone bridge over Black Creek, near Riverby), and when the John Burroughs Memorial Association was formed, he accepted the vice presidency. Julian always spoke at the group's annual meetings and gave numerous slide shows and lectures, in addition to the articles he continued to turn out. Yet when pressured to write his own autobiography, Julian always demurred, putting it off until the final year of his life.

The project was still in the form of manuscript pages and tape-recorded reminiscences when Julian Burroughs died in December 1954. Fortunately, there was a third literary Burroughs at Riverby: Julian's oldest daughter Elizabeth, who edited and published her father's *Hudson River Memories*, meanwhile writing several of her own books and working to preserve the voluminous papers left by her grandfather.

Elizabeth Burroughs had not set out to be an author, editor, and archivist, nor had she followed her grandfather's wish that she become his "Vassar girl." (Burroughs had held the Poughkeepsie-based school in high regard, and even had Elizabeth register there.) She chose Bryn Mawr instead, and after graduating magna cum laude, embarked on a career of teaching in private girls' schools, with art as an avocation.

Following her late-in-life marriage to Hugh Kelley, and the building of their home on the Riverby grounds east of Julian's house, Elizabeth devoted more of her time to her grandfather's journals, aware that his popularity had waned at a time when an appreciation of nature—and the conservation consciousness it fosters—was needed more than ever. Then came her father's death, and she realized there was no one else to carry on this work, since other family members had different pursuits. So aided by her husband, she devoted herself to keeping the name of John Burroughs alive.

At the time of this writing, Elizabeth Burroughs Kelley, now widowed and in her eighties, is still hard at work collating what must sometimes seem a bottomless accumulation of old letters, photographs, diaries, and documents. But it is a labor of love, and one made even more satisfying by the recent resurgence of interest in the work of her grandfather. This renewed popularity has developed, in part, from the increased awareness of modern-day dangers to our natural environment, but without doubt some debt is owed to the third member of Riverby's literary trio—and future generations are certain to profit from her dedication.

VI

LEGENDS
AND
SUPERNATURAL
LORE

33 SPIRITS OF '76:
THE GHOSTS OF
THE REVOLUTION

COULD ANYTHING BE DULLER THAN DIGGING A DITCH? The Irish laborer didn't think so, despite the fact that he was spading up some of the most historic ground in the whole Hudson Valley. Pausing to swab his sweat-streaked face, the man stared across the sloping lawn at the handsome fieldstone building on Forge Hill Road. The house was built in 1754 by a merchant miller named Thomas Ellison and served as headquarters for Major General Henry Knox during the Revolutionary War. At this time (the early 1920s), it was being rented by John Wilkie, who had decided the old house needed a new water supply.

Remembering that this was the reason he had been hired, the laborer resumed his ditch digging, only to halt a few minutes later when his spade uncovered the collapsed roof of a subterranean tunnel. Amid the heaps of dirt-caked stones, something shone brightly yellow in the afternoon sun. It was hair—human hair, long and blond.

Just as the ditch digger made the macabre discovery, John Wilkie walked over to him. The workman scooped up the scalp to show his employer, jokingly flopped the golden tresses on his head, and proceeded to dance a jig.

There is no record of John Wilkie's reaction to this burlesque, but years later he was to recall how the Irish laborer suddenly began to feel sick—so sick that Wilkie had to send him home. The previously healthy laborer died that same evening, which prompted speculation that he had been the victim of a vengeful ghost. For it was thought that the hair belonged to Kitty Wint, a blond maiden who had disappeared while a guest at the Ellison house more than a century and a half earlier.

It seems young Kitty had made the mistake of falling in love with a British officer, and her disapproving father had shipped her off to stay with the staunchly American Ellisons, in the hopes that separation would smother the romance. But Kitty's lover followed her to the fieldstone house in Vails Gate, and one night Kitty sneaked off to meet him.

The escape route she reportedly chose was an underground tunnel leading to Ellison's mill on the banks of nearby Moodna Creek. This might account for the blond hair later found by the laborer, but the manner of Kitty Wint's death remains a mystery. Some say the door of the tunnel slammed shut behind her, and when she found the other end of the tunnel also blocked, she perished in the inky blackness, her screams for help unheard or unheeded.

Did someone purposely lock that door? Was a murderer waiting for her in the tunnel? Or did the unmortared stones—perhaps loosened by a backwash of the creek—accidentally cave in on Kitty? These and other questions remain unanswered, though long before the hapless Irishman did his "dance macabre" in the 1920s, there had been rumors of Kitty's restless spirit roaming the Ellison estate.

And hers is not the only Revolutionary War ghost to be found on the estate. In an upstairs bedroom of the house, the supernatural footsteps of Henry Knox have been heard occasionally. In life, the outwardly jovial general, when worrying over some wartime problem, was said to have paced the floor in the privacy of his bedchamber during the several times he was headquartered at the Ellison house.

Adjoining that chamber, and once accessible from what is now a closet in the Knox bedroom, is a strange and steep flight of steps known as the Witch's Staircase. These may have been the steps down which a servant girl—some say a mistress—was pushed or fell to her death. Other accounts maintain the young woman was a daughter of the resident family and that her demise came when she plunged down a dumbwaiter leading to the stone-slab floor of the basement kitchen. Whichever account—if either—is correct, the victim's screams supposedly have been heard on the anniversary of her death, while her ghost stalks the halls of this historic old house. Now known as Knox's Headquarters State Historic Site, the Ellison house and grounds are open to the public.

The Revolution was also responsible for numerous Westchester County haunts, including one at Watch Hill in the town of Cortlandt, where a British soldier supposedly emerges from a crevice in a rock on nights when the moon is full. One version of the story is that a local miller's daughter had fallen in love with the soldier, much to the disapproval of her brothers, who murdered the Redcoat behind a rock outcropping near Route 9A and Furnace Dock Road.

Violent or untimely death seems to generate ghostly doings, and no roundup of the region's Revolutionary wraiths would be complete without mentioning the meaningless murder of four British soldiers taken captive at the Battle of Stony Point in 1779. Following the fight, some of the British prisoners of war were marched west, across what is now Rockland County, to Fort Sidman, in the Ramapo Pass. Darkness fell before the fort was reached, so the American guards stopped for the night at Coe's Tavern in New Hempstead, locking their British captives in an adjacent barn.

At some time during the hot summer night, an argument erupted in the overcrowded outbuilding. Thinking the ruckus to be an escape attempt, the guards outside fired blindly into the barn. Four British prisoners died in the fusillade and were quickly buried in unmarked graves nearby. But the murderous mistake was not so easily covered over, for the Redcoat quartet haunted the spot thereafter.

Back across the Hudson in Westchester County, a Peekskill farmer was supposedly haunted into an early grave by the ghost of a British spy he had hanged. But the Revolution's best-remembered British spy—Major John André, who abetted Benedict Arnold's treason—apparently left his executioner alone. Instead, André returned after death to the Tarrytown tree where he had been apprehended; he continued to appear there in sad repose, bothering no one.

On the other side of the county, in the old Saw Pit section of Rye, the daughter of a Captain Flood allegedly was killed in retaliation for her father's part in the death of a Tory named William Lounsbury. The murdered girl's presence was felt so strongly in the neighborhood that for more than a century few but the most fearless folk ventured near the Flood house after dark.

Yet by no means is the captain's daughter the most famous of Westchester County's Revolutionary revenants. That distinction unequivocally belongs to the Hessian haunt of Sleepy Hollow, thanks to Washington Irving, who wrote so chillingly of the German mercenary leaving his grave at night to go looking for his missing head. The Hessian, who was buried in Sleepy Hollow Cemetery following his decapitation by a cannonball, is only one of several legendary headless horsemen in the Hudson Valley. A similar soldier was said to gallop around Kinderhook in Columbia County, and stories are told of a headless man appearing on the Albany Post Road near the border of Dutchess and Putnam Counties, though whether he is of Revolutionary origin is only speculation.

Nor can it be said with any surety that this period produced the specters spotted in an upstairs window when the Dutch Colonial homestead of Mount Gulian was being destroyed by fire in 1931. However, this Beacon landmark (now rebuilt and open to the public) was headquarters for General Friedrich Von Steuben during the closing days of the Revolution. So it well may be that the phantom couple in Colonial clothes—observed only once during the conflagration and never again—were Revolutionary War–related specters.

A more definite date of origin can be set for the ghost at the Old Drover's Inn in the western Dutchess County town of Dover, where it is said a young doctor hanged himself rather than go to war. And an exact day—August 30, 1778—can be pinpointed as the time an open field, 60 miles to the south, became haunted. For it was on that day Chief Nimham and his small band of Stockbridge Indians were annihilated by the forces of British Colonel Banastre Tarleton (known as "Bloody Tarleton"). Near what is now called the Indian Bridge, across Tibbett's Brook in southern Yonkers, Nimham lost his life and was buried with his men in a field not far away. This field, located on the northeastern edge of Van Cortlandt Park (in the Bronx, but originally part of Westchester County), is still haunted by Nimham's ghost. At least that is who is blamed for the eerie war whoops sometimes heard coming from the empty field at night.

Another Indian ghost of the Revolution is said to be seen descending the hill in back of the Chester Cemetery, in Orange County. Supposedly the Indian had been assigned as the bodyguard of a Continental Army officer then billeted in a small house at the base of the hill. But the Indian fell asleep on duty one hot August night, and was killed when Redcoat raiders stealthily entered the house. Whether or not the officer also died is not known—all that is sure is that the repentant Indian returns to haunt the scene of his disgrace on the anniversary of his death.

A few miles to the east, on the road leading to Blooming Grove's Bull Mine, an old farmhouse has been the scene of spectral visitations by the "Ramapo Cowboy" Claudius Smith, who was befriended by British sympathizers in the area. It is thought that Claudius must have been given overnight accommodations in an upstairs bedroom of the once-isolated farmhouse, for that is where the manifestations occurred.

Revolutionary phenomena can take the form of music, too, as is the case with the Senate House in Kingston, where a visit by Aaron Burr is recalled by the sad strains of a lone violin. Like most oft-repeated tales, several versions of Burr's visit have been handed down over the years, including one that places him there as a young officer in the Continental Army, when the Senate House was still being operated as an inn. The owner's daughter fell under the spell of the dashing bachelor, and would play her violin for him—something she continued to do even after Burr had departed Kingston. In an effort to end his daughter's hopeless infatuation, the innkeeper is said to have taken her violin and walled it up in some nook that has never been discovered to this day. The unhappy girl then pined away, and upon her death the sounds of the violin began.

Interestingly enough, though he slept in many a Hudson Valley house, there seems to be no tradition of an after-death visitation by George Washington. The only supernatural story stemming from his stay in the region concerns a pocket watch Washington is said to have lost in a rock crevice atop the Ramapo Torne, in Rockland County. Anyone caring to affix an ear to the fissure can hear that timeless timepiece still ticking—or so legend lovers allow. More practical-minded people say the sound is simply the dripping of water deep within the crevice.

Nor do most modern-day residents pay heed to a local legend concerning General Anthony Wayne, the daredevil who led the successful assault on the British-held fort at Stony Point. But according to the late newspaper columnist Danton Walker, General Wayne was witnessed galloping a ghostly steed along the Storm King Highway (Route 218) as late as the 1950s.

Prior to the time he wrote about the Wayne legend, Danton Walker had hosted a ghost in his own home on Camp Hill, near Mount Ivy. Strange footsteps on the stairs, the thud of an invisible body falling to the floor, and knuckles rapping on the front door when no caller was there—such were some of the multiple manifestations of a supernatural presence that eventually convinced the newsman to seek the aid of a psychic. Following a traditional séance (during which the psychic revealed the poltergeist to be a Polish mercenary brutally beaten by British soldiers and left to die inside the house), the ghostly guest in Danton Walker's home was heard no more. The séance, apparently, had brought it peace.

Many more tales could be told of the numerous Revolutionary War wraiths that have appeared in the region, but it is perhaps best to conclude with an old tradition that says Patriot soldiers grow restless in their graves whenever America is in danger. According to H. A. von Behr (writing in *Ghosts in Residence*), that apparently was what happened in the early days of World War II, when the shade of a Revolutionary soldier resolutely marched across the mantel of a Columbia County mansion, as if coming to the aid of his country.

Of course, not everyone believes in ghosts, and historians tend to scorn such supernatural sightings. But others may find some assurance that the patriotic Spirits of '76 live on in the lore of the Hudson Valley.

34 LOST TREASURES OF THE HUDSON VALLEY

FEW PHRASES IN THE English language can match the kind of instant interest created by the mere mention of lost treasure, yet many inhabitants of the Hudson Valley are unaware that numerous hoards of gold and silver supposedly lie hidden in the time-rounded hills that bracket the mighty river. The passing years seem to have buried these treasures even more deeply, for most of them date back to the distant past—to the days of the Indians, the Dutch, and of course that infamous seventeenth-century sea captain William Kidd.

While there is some disagreement as to whether Captain Kidd was actually a pirate, there is no doubt that he buried his booty in true buccaneer fashion, and stories of his hidden treasure have popped up in dozens of places from Maine to Madagascar. New York seems to be one of the likelier locations, however, for Kidd's home port was New York City, where he owned a mansion on what was then Crown (now Liberty) Street. In addition, following his execution on a London gibbet in May 1701, some of his treasure—worth about £14,000—was recovered on Gardiner's Island in Long Island Sound.

Since his privateering (or piratical) ventures had surely netted him much more than that, and because there was a vague report of Kidd having once eluded an enemy man-of-war by sailing up the

Hudson, local treasure seekers have concentrated on the area of the Highlands near Cornwall.

One high bluff on the Hudson's western shore is known as Kidd's Plug Cliff, where a projecting rock gives the appearance of a giant stopper closing off a hole in the cliff face. The more credulous treasure hunters of yesteryear actually believed there was a cave behind the Plug, while others maintained it was only a landmark easily sighted from the river below, and that Kidd had secreted his booty in a nearby cave on Crow's Nest (just north of West Point). Oddly enough, a treasure of sorts was found in the Crow's Nest cave, but it was not Captain Kidd's. In the fall of 1870, a group of explorers found several old coins, none dated earlier than 1782. This would eliminate Kidd by almost a century, even though the locality came to be known as "Kidd's Pocket-book."

Magdalene Island, in Tivoli Bay, also became pockmarked by successive—if unsuccessful—generations of money diggers. But while searching the Hudson Highlands for Kidd's treasure was a Sunday pastime for most, there was a time in the late 1840s when a full-fledged recovery operation was undertaken. The search was predicated on the belief that when Kidd had been chased up the Hudson, rather than give up his booty to the pursuing man-of-war, he had sunk his ship at the foot of Dunderberg Mountain. On just such "evidence," the Kidd Salvage Company was formed, a coffer dam constructed, and an attempt made to raise the sunken ship—or at least the treasure it reportedly contained. In truth, more money was dumped into the project than was taken out of the Hudson (though a Revolutionary War cannon was recovered), and this section of the river shore just above Jones Point was soon named Kidd's Humbug (or Kidd's Point).

Nor was the eastern shore of the Hudson ignored by those seeking the gold of William Kidd. Not long after the failure of the Kidd Salvage Company, a Dutchess County woman claimed she had seen, in a dream, Captain Kidd bury his gold at the foot of an oak tree in the vicinity of Hughsonville. The lady must have been very persuasive, for not only were the men in her family convinced to search for the treasure, but subsequent diggers were, too—only to be frightened away, they were to report, by the ghost of Captain Kidd!

Another ghost-guarded pirate treasure purportedly is secreted somewhere along Annsville Creek, north of Peekskill. And a ghost also was blamed for a Westchester County farmer's failure to find the treasure of a mysterious wanderer called the Leatherman. Following the death of the Leatherman, in 1889, Clematis Sorrel went alone one night to search a cave the Leatherman had been known to frequent in the Saw Mill Woods near Shrub Oak. But Sorrel's search was cut short by the appearance of the Leatherman's ghost, who angrily gestured for the farmer to leave. The frightened man did just that and never returned to the cave. Nor did anyone else ever find the treasure of the Leatherman, if, indeed, such a treasure ever existed.

Better substantiated, but equally elusive to all who have hunted for it, is the lost silver mine of a counterfeiter named Jubar, whose bogus coins contained enough of the precious metal to make them look like the real thing. When Jubar was apprehended in 1765 and later hanged at Poughkeepsie, his accomplice—a man named Taylor—fled the area. Following the Revolution, Taylor returned to search for Jubar's silver mine in what is now Clarence Fahnestock State Park. But either the intervening years had dulled his memory or the landscape had changed so much that Taylor was unsuccessful, and he died a pauper.

A later counterfeiter named Henry Holmes conducted his illegal operations in a cave off Indian Brook Road in Putnam County, and for many years this "Money Hole" was searched for the treasure Holmes was believed to have buried shortly before he was caught. But the only thing the cave gave up was a few tools of Holmes's trade. No money, real or counterfeit, has ever been found there, not even any ore.

It should be pointed out that it is not likely for gold or silver in their natural state to be discovered in any appreciable amounts in the Hudson Valley. For while parts of the valley are rich in other minerals, such as iron, the geological makeup of the area is not that in which large deposits of those two precious metals are usually found. Yet stories persist of rich lodes discovered then lost, such as a gold mine near the Columbia County community of Austerlitz. The only sure thing produced by this mine was one of the most horrendous crimes ever recorded in the region—the grisly story of "The Cannibal of Columbia County"—so maybe it is best the mine remains lost.

Probably the most thoroughly documented lost gold mine in the region is also the oldest, for it dates back to the early 1640s when William Kieft was governor of what was then called New Netherland. Having seen gold worn by some Indians, Kieft sent a party of men to explore the Catskills. The men returned with ore that yielded a fair amount of gold, and samples were dispatched to Holland—all of which was duly recorded by the historian Adrian Van der Donck. It is unfortunate that Van der Donck was not privy to the exact location of the gold, for the ship carrying the ore samples never reached Holland. Also lost at sea was Governor Kieft, who sailed for Holland on a later ship, carrying with him the secret of the Catskill mine.

Not long after William Kieft was replaced by Peter Stuyvesant as governor of New Netherland, a Dutch farm girl reportedly discovered silver in the Catskills. But when an agent of the Patroon of Rensselaerswyck (on whose lands the silver was found) went to investigate the site, a torrential storm produced a flood that washed away all evidence of the find, including the home of the unlucky farm girl. Perhaps one day some wandering backpacker will come across that ancient vein of silver, but it is much more likely that such a find would occur in the Shawangunk Mountains, where tales of lost silver and lead mines abound.

While lead mines are not unknown in the area—the most familiar being the old Wurtsboro mine in Sullivan County and Ulster's famous Ellenville diggings—stories have been handed down of even richer deposits, including one that supposedly was shown to a farmer by a friendly Indian in the days preceding the Revolution. The two men worked the mine in secret, closing it up with a huge boulder when both went off to war. Only one came back—the farmer—to find that a forest fire had destroyed the trees used to mark the mine site, which was never located again.

An Indian was also responsible for leading a young boy to a large vein of silver elsewhere in the Shawangunk Mountains. But the Indian had no intention of sharing the wealth—only in showing the boy the silver—and kept his companion blindfolded during the journey to and from the rich vein. Many times after that the boy attempted to find his way back, but without success. Others have tried, too, for supposedly every seven years, at midnight, a bright light shines for a few minutes directly over the vein, then disappears.

Even more fabulous than the mysterious Shawangunk light is the treasure cave supposedly hidden somewhere on the mountain's flanks. Here again, it was an Indian who led a blindfolded white friend into a cave containing chests of precious jewels and other costly items such as oriental rugs and works of art. Where the treasure came from or how it got there the Indian would not divulge, though there are tales of shipwrecked Spaniards or Spanish explorers reaching the area. (One account even places Captain Kidd's treasure this far inland.) The only information the Indian would give was a warning that there would be dire results if his friend ever returned to the cave.

While superstitious fear kept that man away from the treasure site, there is a report that someone else came across it in later years. By then the expensive rugs had rotted and the precious paintings were cracked, but the jewels were still in perfect condition. So the newcomer set off down the mountain with the intention of procuring some conveyance to haul the treasure out. Whether he returned to the cave is not known, for he was never seen again. But anyone who has ever trekked through the dense forests of the Shawangunks, or gazed down into the fissures that scar their rocky brows, cannot help but feel that the Shawangunks could hide anything forever—be it treasure or treasure seeker.

So, too, can the Ramapo Mountains, which lie to the east of the Shawangunks. At least, they supposedly still hide the treasure of the notorious "Ramapo Cowboy" Claudius Smith, whose daring raids during the Revolutionary War terrorized the people living in Orange and Rockland counties. That there ever was such a treasure has been disputed by some historians, but judging from what happened in the years following the death of Claudius Smith, it seems likely that he did secrete at least some of his loot in the Ramapos. For it is known that when his gang was finally broken up, some of its members (including one or more of his sons) escaped to Canada. Around

1820, two sons of these fugitives showed up in Orange County carrying maps or other written instructions as to where the loot was buried. Their search uncovered a hoard of muskets said to have been stolen from a supply wagon of Washington's army, but that was all they found, and eventually they returned to Canada.

A generation later, some other Canadians arrived in Monroe, intent on recovering a valuable silver stand supposedly hidden in a mountain spring, as well as other items, such as pewter plates. They, too, had instructions on where to look—instructions given them by elderly relatives who had ridden with Claudius Smith. But their search was unsuccessful, and after a few days they went home.

Since then, others have sought the treasure of Claudius Smith, but so far as is known it has never been recovered. Nor have there been any reports of unearthing the treasure chest that Depression-era gangster Dutch Schultz is said to have buried by the Esopus Creek, west of Kingston. There was a witness to that 1930s deposit in the creek bank, and even a treasure map was sketched. But all individuals involved, including Schultz, were "rubbed out" by rival gangsters not long afterward. So $5 million, stuffed into tobacco sacks, supposedly still sits in a steel trunk somewhere between Route 28 and the Esopus.

Treasure hunters in that area might also be interested in the fact that the Modena neighborhood was once called Money Stump, because of family valuables placed in hollow trees by shore-dwelling settlers fleeing the threat of British warships that sailed up the Hudson in October 1777. But keep in mind that Money Stump can have a double meaning. For not only were some of those tree troves never retrieved, but most of the other lost treasures of the Hudson Valley have stumped all seekers.

35 THE LURE AND LORE OF THE HIGHLANDS

MOST MAJOR WATERWAYS are awash with colorful tales of the past, but no river—not even the mighty Mississippi—surpasses the legend-laden Hudson, whose Highlands section is literally flooded with folklore dating from the dawn of time right down to the present day.

Indeed, the very creation of the river is described in an ancient Indian tale that tells of a time when Storm King Mountain was joined to Breakneck Ridge. Impounded behind this natural dam was a huge lake where plentiful fish provided food for the local Indian population.

Life was good, but the Indians grew greedy. And soon enough, a tribe living south of the dam began killing more wildlife than they needed. This indiscriminate waste was repugnant to their god Mani-tou, who vented his wrath by breaking the dam with one blow of a supernatural bludgeon. The torrent of water thus released took with it the offending Indians, who were drowned as the newly formed Hudson River rushed south to meet the sea.

Apparently the surviving Indians never forgot that early lesson in conservation, since many of their legends reflect a deep respect for nature, with an animistic philosophy common to all tribes living along the Highland shores. Animism—the belief that all things, inanimate as well as animate, are imbued with a spirit—is exempli-fied by the shad legend of an Algonkian group known as the Noch

Peems, who lived near what is now the Putnam County community of Cold Spring.

Each spring, when the silver-finned shad swam up the Hudson to spawn, the Noch Peems would "marry" a young girl to the fishing net. They did this, they said, because one long-ago springtime they had been unable to catch a single shad, due to the loneliness of the net spirit, who demanded they give him a wife. The Indians complied, and shortly thereafter they were rewarded with a full net of fish. So the mock marriage became an annual event among the Noch Peems.

In those pre-PCB days, the unpolluted Hudson hosted not only the yearly shad runs but also great schools of other fish, including sturgeon of stupendous size. One such piscatorial prize was partly responsible for the naming of Anthony's Nose (that rocky prominence at the east end of Bear Mountain Bridge)—or so wrote the founding father of Hudson River folklore, Washington Irving. According to Irving, the dubbing dates back to the early seventeenth century, when Dutch Governor Peter Stuyvesant sailed up the river to survey his domain. Accompanying Stuyvesant was Antony Van Corlear, a man whose most memorable feature was his unbelievably bulbous nose.

One morning Antony was washing his face at the ship's rail when the sun broke through the clouds and beamed down directly on his beak. Bouncing off Antony's freshly shined proboscis, the sunbeam struck a sturgeon in the river below—killing the fish and cooking it, too. Hefted aboard the vessel, the sunbeam-broiled sturgeon was sampled by the hungry Hollanders, who pronounced it a delectable dish. Then in honor of what might be termed New York's first fast-food enterprise, as well as the man whose rhinal reflector brought it all about, Peter Stuyvesant named a nearby (and equally prominent) headland "Anthony's Nose"—and so it is called to this very day.

Nearly two centuries later, while on a similar sail up the Hudson, seventeen-year-old Washington Irving heard such legends told by a sloop captain who took pleasure in entertaining his passengers with river lore. Other crewmen contributed to the storytelling, so that landmarks along both shores were fancifully captioned for that imaginative teenager, who would one day use them in the books that brought him—and the Hudson—worldwide renown.

As the sloop passed Stony Point on its way to Albany, it is possible that Irving heard about the imp-inhabited mountain looming ominously over the western shore. The Dutch had called it Dunderberg, or Thunder Mountain, believing it to be the birthplace of the sudden storms that sometimes struck just as sailors were negotiating the narrow bend in the river where Jones Point (at the foot of Dunderberg) pokes out toward Peekskill. If Irving doubted that evil imps brewed up these storms, "proof" was offered in the form of a story about one bedeviled ship captain who found a little sugarloaf-shaped hat set atop his mast during the Dunderberg downpour. Now, everyone knew imps wore such headgear, just as it was common knowledge that the numerous fireflies along this stretch of river were actually the spirits of ugly old women—at least that was the explanation given by the early Dutch for the troubles their vessels encountered near Dunderberg.

Nor were ships safe until they passed Pollepel's Island, opposite Cornwall, for this was the northernmost boundary of the imps' empire. (It is also the place where the river widens, making sailing a lot simpler and safer—but why focus on dry facts, when folklore is such fun?) Relieved Dutch ship captains developed the habit of "dipping their peaks" whenever they breasted Pollepel on upriver runs, and first-time sailors through the narrow channel were ceremoniously dunked (à la crossing the equator) as soon as the island was sighted.

As for Pollepel, it is perhaps the most legendary of all Hudson River islands. One tradition holds that the Indians regarded it as haunted and refused to stay there at night. Modern archeological excavations, however, have revealed that prehistoric Indians inhabited the place. So the haunted tradition, if true, could only have come about at a later date—mayhap the Indians were scared off by spooky tales of the Dutch.

The name of the island itself is lodged in legend. Some say Pollepel comes from a Dutch word for ladle, and that ship passengers who had ladled in too much grog were dumped off at the island to regain their sobriety, then picked up on the vessel's return run.

Another story says the name originates with Polly Pell, an eighteenth-century damsel in distress who was romantically rescued from the icebound river and brought to the island. Whatever the etymology, Pollepel became Bannerman's Island when a nineteenth-century munitions merchant by that name bought it and built a castle that stands in ruins today—ruins in which strange lights are reportedly seen from time to time, true to the island's supernatural traditions.

Practically every other island and peninsula in the Hudson harbors some intriguing Indian tradition, including the ancient council site of Esopus Island, near where a mysterious carved boulder in the river is still known as Indian Rock. Wildercliff, too, was named for a primitive petroglyph depicting "wild men" that was found along the shore a couple of miles south of Rhinecliff.

Then there is the large ceremonial rock near Newburgh known as the Danskammer, or the Devil's Dance Chamber. Dutch sailors named it that when they mistook Indians dancing around a bonfire to be evil spirits, and from there on the legend grew like Topsy. One particularly sanguine story tells of a young couple who erroneously rowed over to the rock and were tortured to death by the so-called savage celebrants. True or not, this seventeenth-century tragedy evoked such fear that even warning rhymes were written about the Danskammer (as is recorded by Harold W. Thompson in his classic compendium of New York folklore, *Body, Boots and Britches*):

> For none that visit the Indian's den
> Return again to the haunts of men.
> The knife is their doom; oh sad is their lot;
> Beware! Beware of the blood-stained spot.

Of course, Indians warred with Indians, too. Cruger Island, off Annandale in Dutchess County, is the reputed arena for a great battle fought between the Tuscaroras and the Mohawks, while conflict on a lesser scale supposedly resulted in the naming of Poughkeepsie. It seems that when enemy warriors chased an Indian couple in a canoe along the eastern edge of the Hudson, the fleeing brave spotted a secluded cove near present-day Call Rock. He secreted his sweetheart there and then paddled back to face his pursuers. Somehow the outnumbered Indian was victorious, and the cove thereafter was called "Safe Harbor," or Apo-keep-sink, which some folks say is the origin of the strange-sounding name, Poughkeepsie.

It was also a chase that spawned the legend of Table Rock, which overlooks the Hudson from Mount Taurus, just north of Nelsonville. Before the European settlers arrived, an Indian spy from another tribe was tracked down and trapped at Table Rock by Wappinger warriors. Rather than surrender and endure slow torture from the Wappingers, the spy leaped to his death.

As is so often the case in folklore, the legend of the suicidal spy overlaps with another death-leap tale of Mount Taurus. More familiarly called Bull Hill, Mount Taurus was the purported province of a wild bull who, when chased to the brink by colonial farmers, chose death to captivity. And, it is interesting to note, the ridge just north of Mount Taurus is called Breakneck. Still another tale of Mount Taurus can be traced back to Washington Irving, who observed that Bull Hill "bellowed back the storms" generated downriver on Dunderberg Mountain, thus contributing to the eerie echoes for which the Highlands are famous.

One set of such eerie echoes is said to emanate from Rogers Island, located just north of where Catskill Creek empties into the Hudson, between Greene and Columbia counties. For it was there in the late 1620s that a ragged remnant of Mohawk Indians retreated from a fierce battle with the Mohicans. Knowing the Mohicans would follow them for a final kill, the desperate Mohawks made camp in the center of the thickly forested island. Only instead of gathering around the fire, they set up bundles of branches wrapped in blankets to resemble sleeping warriors. Then they hid in the surrounding trees, waiting to ambush their enemies. The ruse worked, and the small island ran red with the blood of the slaughtered Mohicans, whose death cries continued to be heard there on nights when the moon was low and the wind moaned in the trees.

About five miles northwest of Rogers Island and five generations later, the sound of hoofbeats recalled a wrongful death on a lonely road in Leeds. Versions vary as to exactly what took place, but it is certain that a servant girl lost her life when she sneaked away from Salisbury Manor (on present-day Route 23B) to attend a party at a neighboring farm. Upon discovering her absence, the master of Salisbury Manor supposedly rode after the servant and ordered her to follow him home. To ensure that she did, he tied a rope around her waist and attached the other end to the pommel of his saddle. Whether by accident or deliberate action on the part of the rider, the horse began to gallop, dragging the helpless servant to her death against a roadside boulder.

William Salisbury was charged with murder, but a grand jury refused to indict him, possibly because of his prominent place in society, and he remained unpunished—except for a noose he reportedly wore around his neck for the rest of his life in memory of the servant girl.

There were other reminders too.

Nighttime travelers along the Leeds road began reporting the presence of a riderless gray horse dragging something behind it. Year after year the spectral stallion galloped along that road, until 1801, when William Salisbury died. Thereafter, the ghost horse was still seen—only now it had a rider.

As for the boulder where the servant had died, it was renamed Spook Rock because the ghost of the girl was said to sit there at night, a lighted candle on the tip of each finger of her hands upraised in a mute plea for mercy.

There are other Spook Rocks in the Hudson Highlands, too. One so-named stone in Claverack (Columbia County) supposedly harbored the ghosts of an Indian maiden and her lover, who were buried beneath the boulder when it became dislodged during a thunderstorm. That legend is likely as fanciful as the one told about Rockland County's Spook Rock near Tallman, where an early settler's daughter supposedly was sacrificed by the "savages" and the child's screams occasionally could be heard coming from the cracks in the boulder. Actually, it is doubtful that the Lenni-Lenape Indians who lived in that part of the Hudson Valley ever indulged in human sacrifice. The boulder is, however, a distinctive landmark located on what was once a major Indian trail—now the junction of Airmont and Spook Rock roads—and it perhaps did serve as a council rock or ceremonial center for those long-ago native Americans.

Not far from there, Spook Hollow Road in Upper Nyack recalls still another supernatural story associated with the region's native Americans. Legend says that an elderly Indian named Camboan lived here at peace with the white settlers until the French and Indian War broke out in 1754. Fearful of a possible French-inspired massacre by the Indians, the once friendly settlers decided that the innocent Camboan was their enemy, and they banished him from his ancestral homeland.

No one knows what happened to Camboan or where he went, but it is said his spirit still haunts the area he was forced to leave. From time to time, tendrils of woodsmoke reportedly have been seen coming from the ravine where Camboan camped. But while the smoke has been seen, no campfire was ever found. What was found—or so the story goes—were footprints in the mud of the bank of the creek that runs along the bottom of the ravine. The prints were those of Indian moccasins, just like Camboan had worn. But here again, no one ever saw the person who made those footprints.

Most of the Hudson Highlands legends recounted so far have dealt with the outdoors, but its legacy of indoor lore is just as rich, especially when it comes to haunted houses. In addition to the residences mentioned elsewhere in this book, some of the region's religious houses have been subjected to supernatural doings. Kingston's Old Dutch Church—the one burned by the British during the Revolutionary War—once sported a phantom-inhabited steeple. Another reportedly haunted fane—or, more properly, its rectory—is Poughkeepsie's Christ Church, where a departed pastor apparently did not agree with the practices of his successor, and manifested his malcontent in a variety of poltergeistic maneuvers.

It was also along the east shore of the Hudson that Abraham Lincoln's funeral train chugged its slow way north in 1865, and for many years afterward workmen along the line reported the passage of a crape-covered cortège each April. Despite the powerful locomotive pulling it, this ghostly train made no noise, for a black shadow would engulf the tracks like a carpet being rolled out in advance of the oncoming apparition. Witnesses reported that the air would suddenly grow chill, and clocks would stop at the exact instant the flatcar carrying the coffin passed by—which is why the tradition has been handed down that every train on the Hudson line was always late on that fateful April anniversary.

And if that story is not scary enough, there is the tale of General Israel Putnam's wife, who died during the Revolution while he was headquartered at Mandeville House near Garrison. Interred not far from the dwelling, Mrs. Putnam's body was later exhumed for burial elsewhere, at which time it was discovered that her hair had continued to grow so that it filled the coffin. Needless to say, this finding led to speculation that Mrs. Putnam might not have been dead when laid to rest. But eventually such answerless questions stopped being asked, and the story took its place among other local legends.

The most poignant of these is also the one that best rounds out any discussion of Hudson Highlands lore. For the legend of Indian Brook Falls (now a part of Hudson Highlands State Park) concerns an Indian maiden who saved the life of a Dutch sailor and subsequently fell in love with him. The sailor reciprocated only until he saw another Dutch ship in the river; then without a backward glance, he swam out to the vessel, which took him aboard and soon sailed out of sight.

The abandoned maiden wept as she wandered along the bank of the brook. Each tear she shed—or so it is said—became one of the exquisite white flowers that are found only in the vicinity of Indian Brook. And thus is symbolized what is the greatest and truest tradition of the Hudson Highlands—their legendary beauty.

36 ELLENVILLE'S GHOSTLY TELEGRAPHER AND KINDRED TALES

TUCKED AWAY IN the northeastern corner of the Ulster County village of Ellenville, Berme Road gives little hint of the history and mystery it harbors. Through the trees along one side of this quiet country lane lies the once busy but now dormant D&H Canal; while on the other side of the road a mysterious tunnel and an old lead mine pierce the slope of Shawangunk Mountain. All three excavations, along with the restored D&H Canal office building, figure prominently in a little-known Ellenville legend of ghostly messages and a ghastly murder that had "never been more than whispered" before Charles Gilbert Hine recorded it in his 1909 book *The Old Mine Road*.

It was the disappearance of a man named David M. Smith that precipitated the macabre events. Smith was employed as a telegrapher in the Ellenville office of the D&H Canal, but he did not show up for work one Monday morning in February 1866. At first this aroused no suspicion, since there was no barge traffic on the icebound canal during the winter months, and it was assumed that Smith had taken advantage of the business lull to extend a weekend visit to his mother in Port Jackson (present-day Accord).

Several days passed before it was learned that the young telegrapher never reached his mother's home. A search was then mounted, but the only thing that could be determined was that Smith apparently had not planned his disappearance, since he had not taken any of his belongings with him.

The question of what happened to David Smith was not answered for thirteen years. Then in March 1879, a grisly discovery was made by workers reopening an entrance to one of the old Ellenville lead mines on Shawangunk Mountain. The bones of David Smith lay at the bottom of the mine shaft.

Foul play? Suicide? Accident? None of these appeared likely, for Smith had been a well-liked, well-adjusted fellow who would have had no reason to be poking around a dangerous mine shaft on a frigid February day. If there were those who recalled that Smith had once argued with another man over the attentions of a certain young lady, apparently no one thought such a minor matter could have had anything to do with the tragic death of the telegrapher—at least no one living. That connection remained to be made by supernatural means.

Following the disappearance of David Smith, a comely young woman had been given his job in the canal office, and she immediately attracted a host of suitors. Among them was a fellow telegrapher stationed in the Port Jervis office of the canal company, as well as the Ellenville man who had once argued with David Smith. In his book, Charles Hine called this latter fellow Flicker, but Hine decorously did not name the Port Jervis suitor or the lady telegrapher, and no attempt will be made to do so here, for it would serve no purpose to speculate on who the two may have been. Their story is what counts—and an eerier experience would be hard to find.

Though wild and willful, Flicker could be charming when it suited his purpose, and the lady telegrapher welcomed his company when he began stopping in at the canal office to chat with her. It was during one of these conversations that the tapping of the telegraph key summoned the girl, whose face turned pale as she deciphered the message coming over the wire.

The staccato dots and dashes spoke disjointedly of murder...of a man being thrown into a rockbound shaft. Shaken but still in control, the girl telegraphed back, asking the sender to identify himself. But none of the regular operators acknowledged her query. No one was on the line. Nor did the usually smooth-tongued Flicker have anything to say; in fact, he suddenly was in a hurry to leave and managed only a brief farewell.

During the next few days—days during which Flicker did not come to call on her—the young woman received several more communications from the unknown telegrapher. All of them warned her to beware of a male acquaintance, but the messages were so garbled she could not make out the name of the operator. However, the sender did say something about lying in such a crumpled-up position that he could not properly operate the telegraph key. . . .

When Flicker finally returned to the canal office, he was greeted with a detailed account of the ominous and anonymous messages the young woman had been receiving. Whatever Flicker might have answered was interrupted by still another message. Translating out loud as the key clicked erratically, the young woman looked over to where Flicker had been standing, for the brief message referred to someone being with her. But Flicker had fled, this time without even saying farewell.

Had Flicker stayed away, the story might have ended right there, as did the mysterious messages arriving in the Ellenville canal office. Relieved of this worry, other messages occupied the young woman, including some from the Port Jervis telegrapher, who was in love with her. Meanwhile, Flicker was becoming desperate. Well aware that the telegraphed warnings had been about him, he dared not return to the canal office, yet his desire for the girl was unquenchable. Eventually his unbalanced brain formulated a plan to kidnap the girl and take her to an old tunnel in the base of Shawangunk Mountain. The tunnel contained a freshwater spring and, after stocking the tunnel with foodstuffs, Flicker was confident he could keep his prisoner there indefinitely if need be. The only thing the maddened man did not take into consideration was the ghostly telegrapher.

On the very night Flicker had chosen to execute his plan, the telegraph key in the Port Jervis canal office began clicking frantically. Unsigned but unmistakable in its urgency, the message was received by the young man in love with the Ellenville operator. She was in danger, the anonymous sender said, and the young man must hurry if he was to save her.

It is more than thirty miles from Port Jervis to Ellenville, but by galloping his horse along the D&H Canal towpath, the young man arrived in time to thwart the kidnapping. Thus, the story ended happily for the two telegraphers, who eventually married, though not so happily for Flicker, who was committed to a mental institution. As for the mysterious messages...was it the ghost of David Smith who sent them? Charles Hine left it up to his readers to decide.

There are those who believe that Hine's story is made up more of whole cloth than factual fabric, but there is no question concerning the very real places where the eerie events allegedly took place. The old Ellenville canal office, though moved a short distance from its original site, stands at the intersection of Berme Road and Canal Street, while the lead mine where David Smith's bones were found is a short distance to the north. Walk along Berme Road until you get to the Ellenville Dump—a landfill area bordered by the volunteer firehouse on the north and the bare-rock flank of Shawangunk Mountain on the east. A jagged cleft in the rock marks one of the openings of the mine, which should be viewed only from the outside.

Documentary evidence of lead mining in Ellenville dates back to Revolutionary War times, and some digging was probably done by seventeenth-century Dutch settlers or even earlier inhabitants. However, it was not until the mid-1800s that a sensational report intensified interest in what was by then being called the Ulster Mine. "At a depth of 25 feet," the report stated, miners "broke into a large 'vug' or cave...found to open into a chamber...not less than 16 feet wide...and so high one could not reach the roof." On the walls was "a rich face of galena and yellow sulphuret of copper, intermingled with beautiful bunches of quartz crystals," while "the lead ore was more abundant near the roof," and on the floor were "scattered masses of both lead and copper ores, some of them weighing several hundred pounds each."

Unfortunately, the rest of the deposit did not match this one rich find. And though it produced the largest block of galena (a silvery lead sulfide) ever found in the United States prior to 1896, the Ulster Mine was operated only sporadically in the following decades. Today, the sole mineralogical activity going on there is accomplished by amateur "rockhounds," who scour the area outside the mine for clusters of tiny quartz crystals and specimens of pyrite-speckled stone to add to their collections.

Much older than the Ulster Mine—and certainly more mysterious— is the legendary Sun-Ray Tunnel (also called the Spanish Mine), less than half a mile to the north along Berme Road, where the thwarted kidnapper Flicker had planned to hide out with his hostage. (The site is private property, and permission to see it must first be obtained from the owners of the factory on whose land the tunnel is located.)

A century before the Dutch arrived in the 1600s, it is said that a party of Spaniards traveled through this area. One legend has them gold seekers, while another tradition is that they were remnants of Ponce de León's ill-fated expedition to discover the Fountain of Youth. Wandering far, they eventually arrived in the Rondout Valley, following an even-then ancient Indian trail to what is now Ellenville. Finding a gushing spring, the Spaniards attempted to locate its source by tunneling more than 500 feet into the base of Shawangunk Mountain—or so the story is told.

Whether the tunnel was excavated in the hope of finding magical water or mineralogical wealth may never be known, though the latter reason is more likely. For pyrite, which abounds in the region, has deluded more than one treasure seeker—which is why this brassy mineral is nicknamed "fool's gold."

Another tale says the tunnel was already there when the Spaniards came in the early 1500s—that the Indians showed it to them, or (in still another version) to the Dutch. Thus, the origin of the tunnel seems forever masked in the mists of time, with only two things positively known: the 6-foot-high, 5-foot-wide passageway is man-made, and it has been there for at least two and a half centuries.

Back in the early 1800s, it almost wasn't. During the building of the D&H Canal, some of the "canawlers" heard treasure tales about the Spanish Mine and decided to blast through the back wall of the tunnel by using hundreds of kegs of black powder. Not surprisingly, the authorities objected. That much black powder, they maintained, could well have blasted Ellenville off the map, if not half of Ulster County. So the project was abandoned, and the tunnel was all but forgotten until the turn of the century.

At that time, an engineer inspecting other excavations on the mountainside took a look at the Spanish Mines and rediscovered the spring of unusually pure water at the end of the tunnel. Realizing that all gold is not necessarily metallic, he bought the site, and in 1905 he formed the Ponce De Leon Spring Water Company. The company was sold a year later, renamed the Sun-Ray, and in 1907 construction began on a huge water-bottling plant. Rising high above the new building, and still a local landmark, was a 125-foot chimney bearing the name Sun-Ray in a wide band of bricks on top.

Meanwhile, a reservoir was formed by building a wall across the back of the tunnel, then electric lights and railroad tracks were installed along its length. The lights and tracks were not for transporting water (which was brought to the bottling plant via a pipe), but for tourists who rode in a narrow, hand-operated tram down the 500-foot tunnel to see the source of "the purest water in the world." It was also with visitors in mind that the mouth of the tunnel was embellished by a concrete arch and steps, while the surrounding grounds were turned into a garden with a winding walkway leading from the bottling plant to the tunnel.

Vestiges of this Victorian spa-like setting are still visible, though it has been many years since the last tourist tram was pushed along the tunnel's tracks. During those decades, different businesses briefly located there then moved on. And for fifteen years, starting in 1960, the bottling plant lay deserted, with only an occasional hiker or local school group to explore the deteriorating tunnel. Then, in 1975, the property was purchased by a toy-manufacturing company. The new owners quickly recognized the historic value of the tunnel, as well as the profit potential of the still-gushing spring. They began collecting information and artifacts relating to the tunnel, in the hope that a museum would someday be established in the old bottling plant. (At the time of this writing, a sampling of artifacts and photographs of the Sun-Ray Tunnel, along with other memorabilia of the area, may be seen at the Ellenville Library and Museum on Canal Street.) There also is a plan to begin bottling the water again, for it is indeed some of the purest to be found.

Whatever its future, the Sun-Ray Tunnel will remain an intriguing part of Ellenville's past history as well as its hauntings—a point to ponder if you happen to walk down Berme Road and hear what sounds like the staccato tap of an old-fashioned telegraph key....

37 WITCHES, WARLOCKS, AND WALPURGIS NIGHT

NOWADAYS, MANY PEOPLE have never even heard of Walpurgis Night. But there was a time when that other name for May Day eve evoked fear in the hearts of many a Hudson Valley family, who firmly believed that witches romped as wildly on Walpurgis Night as they did on Halloween. So, along with bright blossoms and May Pole dances, witchcraft belongs to springtime, too, as well as to all the other seasons, since this legacy from the distant past has never entirely died out in the Hudson region and probably never will.

Indeed, a quick check of the classifieds, or attendance at any of the psychic fairs periodically held in such places as New Paltz and Poughkeepsie, will show that a few witches still practice their craft hereabouts, and until recently Rockland County's Call Hollow Road reputedly hosted at least one coven. But these modern-day witches are far removed from the time when any antisocial activity, odd appearance, or herbal knowhow might be construed as evidence of "dallying with the devil."

There was, for instance, Elizabeth Dobbins, a widow who lived on the slope of Orange County's Sugar Loaf Mountain during the late 1700s. Advanced in age and cantankerous by nature, the pipe-smoking crone was looked upon as a witch by local inhabitants, who held a similar view of another old woman, for whom nearby

Warwick's Witch Hollow was named. As far as is known, neither lady was harmed by her accusers, for the Hudson Valley never did fall prey to the kind of frenzy that earned Salem, Massachusetts, its infamy. Even so, the region witnessed witch hunts and even witch trials, including one in Rockland County that is purported to be the last ever conducted in New York State.

Unlike New York's first witch trial, which occurred in 1665 and was a duly documented judicial proceeding involving a Long Island couple, the Rockland County case was a kangaroo court affair. Hence, stories vary as to the exact time it took place (some say 1816; others believe it happened earlier), as well as the given name of the accused woman (Naut or Jane or Hannah). But all agree her last name was Kannif and that her eccentric antics and herbal expertise caused her Clarkstown neighbors to suspect she was a witch.

Naut did nothing to dissuade the damning gossips—at least not until a mob showed up on her doorstep one day, having decided to dunk her in a nearby millpond for her devilish doings. Trial by water was one method for determining whether someone was a sorceress: if she floated, that meant she was a witch; if she sank beneath the surface and drowned, then she was innocent. Either way, the accused could not win.

Something happened at Naut's trial, however, to change the mob's mind, and she was given the Bible test instead. This involved setting a suspected witch on one pan of a huge balance scales, such as the kind used to weigh grain in a gristmill. A Bible was then placed in the other pan. If the Word proved weightier than the woman—and everyone knew witches were light enough to fly around on broomsticks—then the suspect was adjudged a sorceress. Innocence, it might be said, could be proved by a pratfall, which is what happened in the case of Naut Kannif, and she was set free.

The story doesn't end there, though. It is said that not long after Naut Kannif's ordeal, a child of one of the mob's leaders was crushed to death in the mill where the trial took place. Retribution or mere coincidence? The local folk couldn't help but wonder, and the gossip grew. But this time Naut wanted no part of such notoriety, and she reportedly instituted a legal suit against those who had tried her.

Nothing came of it, but neither was old Naut ever again bedeviled by a witch-hunting mob.

Trial by water was a favorite way of dealing with witches, for water has ever been symbolic of purity and cleansing, and the test was not always as cruel as it sounds. Victims who sank, and thus showed innocence, were often saved—sometimes under unusual circumstances, as is seen in the following tale from Rensselaer County, where a suspected witch was tossed into the Hoosick River, near the Vermont border, back in the winter of 1765.

It seems that when a hitherto healthy young man suddenly took sick and died, his widow was accused of doing him in. The woman was tried in a court of law and acquitted, but then she was charged with witchcraft, for there were those who insisted she had hexed her husband. Convicted, she was tossed through a hole in the frozen-over river. Watching through the translucent ice, the townspeople took this to be a sign that she really was innocent, whereupon a hole was chopped into the ice and the gasping widow rescued.

Farther along the same river, at Hoosick Falls, water was used in still another way to take care of a woman whose husband dreamed she was in league with the devil. Supposedly her witchiness was revealed when she suffered a hand injury at the same time that someone shot a silver bullet into the front paw of a black cat that had been hanging around the couple's home. The woman's husband immediately forced his wife to sail with him for England, and he returned alone, saying he was now safe from her sorcery, since witches won't willingly cross running water. He then took up residence with another woman—which might well cause some readers to question what his true motives were.

By the way, there were warlocks as well as witches at work in the Hudson Valley, among them a Woodstock wizard who failed the water test but was allowed to live on anyway. And let's not forget Westchester County's famed Sleepy Hollow, which Washington Irving said was so named for the somnolent spell cast over it by a male conjurer.

Tales abound about the association between black cats and witches, including one concerning a fiery-eyed feline that terrorized crewmen of a D&H Canal boat back in the nineteenth century. But by no means was that the only animal form witches were believed capable of assuming. Crows and ravens appear as witches in Hudson Valley folklore, and there was even an instance of some witch-possessed insects in the Taconics of Columbia County.

Spook Swamp, atop Brundige Mountain in Harriman State Park, supposedly was called that because of Auntie Emmits, who could change herself into a toad. Auntie Emmits, it should be noted, is not the Rockland County sorceress that Maxwell Anderson reputedly used as a model for the witch in his play *High Tor*. Anderson's inspiration is said to have been another alleged witch named Biddy Weed, who lived near Nyack.

Then there was Orange County's Mollie Oldfield, the notorious Witch of Minisink, who decided one day to be a horse. Legend says a neighborhood man was passing the old woman's cabin when his horse suddenly balked. No amount of coaxing could budge the animal, and the man—nervous about whose house he was near—began beating the beast. But Mollie's power was greater; the horse stayed put. Finally the man lost his temper entirely, and bashed the beast between the ears with a rock. The horse fell dead. The next day, Mollie Oldfield's lifeless body was found inside her cabin, her skull caved in like that of the horse.

Witches not only "possessed" the bodies of horses, but borrowed them for joy rides as well. Farmers who found their horses listless in the morning were apt to blame it on a witch's having ridden the animals during the night. A sure sign that this had happened was a presence of "witch stirrups"—matted knots of hair found in a horse's mane or tail.

Pigs, too, could be bewitched, and there is a delightful tale from the Ulster County community of Woodstock that tells of a whole litter made to dance on their noses. Dogs pretty much escaped unscathed, while cows seemed to be a favorite target of conjurers. Milk that soured or cream that would not churn into butter was said to be the doings of a witch. A hot horseshoe placed in the bottom of the churn might break the spell, but there was little that could be done for a witch-milked cow, which was the reason given when Bossie dried up for no apparent reason.

Hudson Valley folklore collector Anne Lutz came across a story of just how witches were thought to accomplish this feat. One Rockland County witch simply hung a piece of cloth above a bucket. Then after uttering an incantation, she squeezed the cloth, and milk flowed into the pail. Another story Miss Lutz has collected concerns a witch plucking hairs from the tail of a cow, then braiding the hairs into a string, which she then proceeded to milk.

Witches could also cast spells on inanimate objects, or so the legend goes of the *Martin Wynkoop*, a Hudson River sloop that was cursed from the time it was constructed at Rondout during the 1820s. A host of problems bedeviled the builders, who several times had to redo whole sections of the sloop, and there was an inordinate amount of accidents. But the worst was yet to come. After a troublesome launching, the *Martin Wynkoop* went on to rack up a record number of sailors' deaths and injuries, groundings on river sandbars, collisions with other craft, lost cargoes, and other misfortunes. For more than six decades, until it sank in 1889, the sloop brought nothing but bad luck to its owners, despite the fact that one of the region's leading witch doctors had twice tried to rid it of its curse—a curse supposedly placed on it by a disgruntled demoness who didn't like the way the first owner did business.

It was a fairly common practice in rural areas for a professional curse lifter to be called upon whenever sorcery was suspected. Usually these witch doctors were people possessing healing powers, such as the famous Dr. Jacob Brink of Lake Katrine, north of Kingston, who tried his hand at the *Martin Wynkoop*. He (or another of the Brink family, which numbered several witch doctors down through the generations) had better luck with a bewitched boat on the D&H Canal. It took Brink only a short time to decide which witch had caused the curse, but when he called on her, she wasn't home. So Brink simply stalked over to the clothesline, where a skirt belonging to the absentee was flapping in the breeze. Flailing the skirt with his trusty witch whip (likely a willow switch), Brink declared the woman would soon complain of a sore bottom, and the boat would be de-witched. Tradition holds he was correct on both counts.

As important as beasts and boats might be, it was bewitched people that understandably caused the most concern to early day residents of the Hudson Valley. All kinds of potions and poultices were part of the witch doctor's pharmacopoeia, including one vile brew concocted by boiling nails in urine or blood or both. But basically people relied on a variety of antiwitch devices, ranging in size from herbal amulets worn around the neck to iron-spike witch catchers placed in chimneys to prevent access by some evil enchantress.

The chimneys of the Polly Crispell Cottage in Hurley still contain such pointed deterrents, while Knox's Headquarters State Historic Site in Vails Gate hosts a flight of narrow, wedge-shaped "witch's steps." According to Ann L. Feeney of Knox's Headquarters, such odd staircases were constructed in some eighteenth-century houses so that occupants could flee to the attic without a witch being able to follow. Witch's feet, you see, were extremely long and inflexible, so they simply couldn't manage the steps.

The best idea, of course, was to keep a witch from ever entering a house, and dozens of ways were devised to accomplish this goal. The traditional horseshoe nailed over the doorway—ends pointed up, please, so the good luck doesn't run out—is the most familiar now, but in years gone by it was also common to see a broom placed diagonally across an open doorway, or twigs of ash and witch hazel above each lintel (on fireplace mantels, too, if the chimney contained no witch catchers).

Door panels sometimes bore crudely carved symbols or glass panes containing a bull's-eye, while latches in the form of a cross were considered especially effective. Needless to say, a cross was anathema to a witch, who also was supposedly stymied by any multiple of the number three. In some areas the number six was considered most powerful, which is why the hex signs used to protect barns often contained a half dozen of the principal motif (e.g., six petals, six circles) or a six-pointed star.

Perhaps the most intriguing of all these devices were "witchballs." Though rarely seen nowadays—and considered an antique collector's coup—these beautiful glass spheres were prevalent in Hudson Valley homes from the mid-1600s to 1900. They came in a variety of sizes, from 2 to 14 inches in diameter, but the majority averaged 4 to 6 inches, with a hole in them.

They were filled with such antiwitch herbs as agrimony, rue, dill, and maidenhair, and then suspended from a chain or set on a stand. Smaller witchballs were sometimes used as bottle stoppers, or placed atop cream pitchers to prevent witch-caused curdling, while other spheres might be filled with smoke, feathers, or even bits of brightly colored thread. The latter was inserted in the belief that bright colors attracted a witch's attention, and she would thus be distracted from her nefarious errand.

Witchballs should not be confused with the witch bottles some superstitious folk buried beneath their thresholds or hearthstones when building a house. Straight pins and other items witches were known to dislike were inserted in these bottles, which could also be used to break a spell, but only when buried upside down. Hence, if you happen to find such a bottle while digging in your garden, mayhap, 'twould be best to leave it in place; that is, if you're at all wary of witches.

Most people were wary of them at one time, for the preceding paragraphs show how filled our folklore is with references to witchcraft. Our language is, too. Consider, for instance, such terms as "witch grass," "witch milk," and "witch's thimble," not to mention "witches' broom," "witch chick," "witch moth," or that other name for dowsing—"water witching." All are still in use today, as is one term that is strictly Hudson Valley in origin: "baker's dozen." It dates back to the days of the Dutch, when Albany was still called Beverwyck and a baker ran a prosperous shop just off Broadway.

One evening a strange woman entered the shop and said she wanted a dozen cookies. The baker promptly filled her order, but the customer was not pleased. "There are only twelve cookies," she protested. "I ordered a dozen. Give me one more!"

"A dozen is twelve," the baker retorted, "and twelve you have."

The woman continued to insist a dozen meant thirteen, but the baker remained adamant, and she stormed out of the shop. She returned the next day, though, demanding the missing cookie. This time the proprietor's wife—possibly sensing the supernatural powers of the stranger—pleaded with the baker. Still he would not bend. "A dozen is twelve, not thirteen," was his only reply.

The customer came back a third time. Again her demand was denied, and she headed for the door. Before stepping over the threshold, however, she turned to glare at the baker, hissing a hideous curse on him and all he held dear.

From that day forward, bad luck beset the baker, and he was close to bankruptcy when the woman returned one last time. "Here is your cursed cookie!" the baker cried, handing over the best of his latest batch.

No sooner had the now-satisfied woman departed than the baker's good luck returned. But just in case, he continued counting a dozen as thirteen, perhaps mindful that thirteen is the number of witches required to hold a midnight sabbat.

Was the old woman taking those cookies to such a witch's convention? That question is left for the reader to ponder, along with a reminder that, in addition to Halloween, May Day eve is the most important sabbat date on a witch's calendar. So do watch out for a baker's dozen of witches on Walpurgis Night! (And that sign-off sentence contains exactly thirteen words...just in case....)

38 THE GREGARIOUS GHOST OF MONTGOMERY STREET (AND OTHER HAUNTS OF HISTORIC HUDSON VALLEY HOUSES)

A CHILL AUTUMN wind was wafting wisps of mist from the Hudson far below as workers in the old Montgomery Street mansion began decorating the formal first-floor parlor of what had been nineteenth-century shipping magnate David Crawford's home. Now headquarters of the Historical Society of Newburgh Bay and the Highlands, the house-museum was being readied for the holiday season, when candlelight tours would augment the regular daytime hours the public was welcome.

Despite the graying day, the atmosphere inside the handsomely appointed parlor was cheerful, with crimson holly berries and bows on evergreen boughs brightening the stolid dark wood of a bygone age. Even the black, Belgian marble fireplace had been polished to a soft sheen by a worker, who then proceeded to decorate the mantel. In doing this, she decided the alabaster urn that usually rested in front of the mantel's mirror might look better somewhere else—and so she moved it.

The urn remained as placed for several minutes. Then without warning the lid flew into the air, shot across the room, and landed on the floor several yards away, shattering into irreparable pieces.

During the shocked silence that ensued, the woman looked from one to another of her coworkers, as if to confirm there was no way—no natural way, that is—the lid could have sailed so far. No human hand knocking into the urn. No heavy truck traffic on the street outside that might rattle the building's foundation. No open window through which a sudden gust could have come.

Finally, one of the workers ventured, "Maybe David didn't want the urn moved."

The reference to David Crawford—dead for more than a century—was readily understood, since most of the regular staff had witnessed a wraithlike figure that occasionally appeared in the old mansion. Although unidentifiable, since it was seen more as a tall vaporous shaft than a distinct human shape, the apparition had triggered a tradition that the long-dead owner of Crawford House had never left the beloved home he built in 1830.

Oddly enough, these sightings never occurred on the second floor; not even in the upstairs room, where a telescope still stands by a window facing the river—a vantage point from which David Crawford was wont to watch his merchant sloops approaching and leaving the Newburgh docks. Instead, the specter has been reported only on the main floor, an exclusivity that may be explained in part by the fact that Crawford loved company, and it was in the formal parlors that he and his family entertained their many friends. It was also downstairs that on quiet evenings the gregarious shipowner would read Shakespeare aloud. And last, it was the place where, in 1859, a room was converted into a bedchamber for the dying man.

But if David Crawford does roam his former home, he does so circumspectly and in an unthreatening manner. As one witness reports: "You sort of sense his presence, as if he merely wants to be part of whatever is going on. He doesn't confront you either. Whenever I've caught a glimpse of him, it's usually out of the corner of my eye—just a grayish shape, almost like mist off the river, and not frightening in any way."

As for the urn lid being hurled across the room, one person who was present that day attributes it to a brief flare-up of Crawford's Irish temper, or perhaps the pique of a man who was nearing seventy and very sickly when he died. For there has never been any similar poltergeistic performance, even though Crawford House has undergone major renovation in recent years, including the installation of an unusual hand-painted floor cloth in the front hall. Like as not David approves the addition, since his vaporous presence purportedly pauses there from time to time, as if savoring the Greek-key pattern that complements the neo-Classical architecture of his home.

This well-preserved, white-pillared mansion on Newburgh's Montgomery Street is a dramatic contradiction to the traditional image of a haunted house being some gloom-draped, decaying dwelling off-limits to all but the most intrepid trespassers. Of course, the Hudson Valley has a lot of the latter kind, but it also boasts a bevy of beautifully maintained, open-to-the-public buildings that have interesting histories, and a haunt or two.

Albany being the capital of New York, as well as one of the Hudson Valley's first settled cities, it deserves to lead off the list— particularly so because a mysterious ghost reportedly roams the fifth floor of the rococo old capitol atop State Street hill.

Over the years, more than one member of the nighttime cleaning staff have requested a transfer after hearing footsteps following them down the deserted top-floor hallways, or a nearby but disembodied voice uttering unintelligible words. The mystery, therefore, is not where or what happens, but who the haunt might be.

Three possibilities have been suggested, including Samuel Abbott, a night watchman who expired in the 1911 fire that gutted part of the capitol, and a construction worker named Cormack McWilliams, who fell to his death from a scaffold in 1877. A different account says McWilliams was a foreman, who went alone one Sunday to inspect some work on the capitol, which was then being built. A floor gave way beneath him, and he was left to writhe in agony until death claimed him scant hours before his workmen arrived for the Monday morning shift.

The likeliest candidate, however, is Boston painter William Morris Hunt, who became the official artist of the capitol in 1878 and promptly executed several murals for the arched ceiling of the assembly chamber. Hunt did not live to see part of the chamber's ceiling fall, or the resultant repairwork that hid his paintings; it was hurtful enough for him to be fired from his job when New York Governor Lucius Robinson decided the taxpayers' money was being misspent on such "ornamentation" of the capitol. The blow was too much for the already ailing artist, and Hunt committed suicide a short while after returning to Boston. His heart remained in Albany, though, for he reportedly had said when first entering the capitol, "Here I am in my own world....I want to stay here." And if the spectral footsteps are his, it would seem his wish was granted.

Another Albany ghost whose identity is debatable is the haunt of Historic Cherry Hill, the South Pearl Street mansion built by Philip Van Rensselaer in 1787. Now an impressive house-museum whose operators would—understandably—rather talk about the building's architecture and artifacts than apparitions, Cherry Hill still draws visitors who want to see the place where hired man Jesse Strang murdered estate manager John Whipple one rainy May night in 1827.

Strang had fallen under the spell of Whipple's wife Elsie, who convinced the hired man to kill her spouse. A proven adultress as well as an active accomplice to the crime, Elsie nevertheless got off scot-free (she was, after all, a member of the powerful and intermarrying Van Rensselaer-Schuyler-Lansing clan) while Strang paid the ultimate price. In fact, his was the last public hanging ever held in Albany—a botched job that left Strang choking at the end of a rope for a full thirty minutes before he finally expired.

Thereafter, passers-by often spotted a spectral male presence on the second-floor porch that stretched around Cherry Hill mansion. And although the lengthy porch was later abbreviated, the supernatural sightings continued. Some people thought the ghost might be one of the Van Rensselaers, since five generations of that family had lived at Cherry Hill. But most maintained it emanated from the 1827 murder, and was either Strang or Whipple.

Noted folklorist Louis C. Jones, whose 1982 *Murder at Cherry Hill* is a thoroughgoing study of the tragedy, thinks the manifestation must be that of John Whipple, since victims of violent death return as haunts more often than do murderers. Yet while Jesse Strang was undeniably a murderer, he was also very much a victim. So the jury is still out on who it is that haunts Historic Cherry Hill.

No such identity crisis exists for the several specters associated with Lindenwald, the Columbia County home of President Martin Van Buren that is now a National Historic Site. The president himself is said to have been seen climbing the stairway to the second floor long after his death in 1862, while the downstairs kitchen is unquestionably the haunt of the Van Burens' cook, whose pancakes sometimes fill the air with their mouth-watering aroma, although she has been absent from her stove for a dozen decades.

At least two other servants haunt the estate: a maid murdered at the gatehouse entrance, and a butler who hanged himself in the orchard. Van Buren also has been seen meandering beneath the fruit trees on nights when the moon is full, but Aaron Burr purportedly is the orchard's most frequent ghostly visitor.

Prior to Van Buren's purchase in 1839, the property was owned by William Van Ness, the man who served as Burr's second in the pistol duel that resulted in the death of Alexander Hamilton. Following that tragic day in July 1804, and the public outrage that resulted, Burr is believed to have taken temporary refuge at Lindenwald, where he spent many soul-searching hours in solitary walks through the orchard.

Yet it is Van Cortlandt Manor, farther downriver at Croton-on-Hudson, that can claim the greatest ghostly population—seven in all, though one bedcover-snatching spook was evicted when the wing of the house he haunted was torn down.

Of the remaining six, three date back to the days of the Revolution, when the manor was taken over by the British. During their occupation, a delirious Hessian soldier supposedly was bound to a bed in the Prophet's Chamber, a small room in the rear of the house that in peacetime had been reserved for visiting clergymen. Although tied down for his own protection, the German-speaking mercenary could not have understood the motives of those tending him, and repeatedly returned after death to the scene of his final torture.

It was torture of another kind for a lady named Hannah, who secreted her silverware when the British arrived, then was unable to find it after the war. Poor Hannah spent the rest of her life looking for the lost utensils and continues the quest from her grave. Or so the story is told of a hand-wringing wraith sometimes seen searching the grounds around the house.

The last of the mansion's Revolutionary trio—a Redcoat who tampers with a large wooden linen press in the upstairs hall—is certainly the oddest. For the linen press was not even in the house during the British occupation, and the phantom Redcoat only showed up after the richly carved article was installed.

The three other Van Cortlandt Manor visitants are of more recent vintage, and all are women. Alas, two remain anonymous: a graceful ghost whose long gown has brushed the legs of guests ascending the staircase, and a laughing girl who reportedly arrives by horse-drawn carriage and gaily runs up the front steps of the mansion's marvelous wrap-around porch.

A definite identity, however, has been assigned the order-giving elderly lady a workman heard but did not see back in the 1940s. According to one account, that could only have been Anne Stevenson Van Cortlandt, one of the last of the family to live in the manor, and perhaps a bit peeved when it was sold to "outsiders."

Fortunately, Van Cortlandt Manor has come under the expert care of Historic Hudson Valley (formerly Sleepy Hollow Restorations), and its future is now secure. The same holds true for Montgomery Place, which was acquired by Historic Hudson Valley in 1986 and opened to the public in June 1988.

Thought by many to be the most beautiful of all the great estates lining the Hudson's east shore, this gracefully pillared, Federal-style mansion memorializes the love between Janet Livingston and General Richard Montgomery. The couple had been married barely two years when Richard died a hero at the 1775 Battle of Quebec. The childless widow never remarried, choosing instead to buy a 242-acre farm in northern Dutchess County and build the kind of home she and Richard would have shared had he lived.

For all her romantic loyalty, Janet Livingston Montgomery was also a practical woman, and when she decided to establish a commercial nursery on her property, she sought the services of her dead husband's Irish-born nephew William Jones, since it was the young Jones to whom she planned to leave her vast estate. But that was before the banshee cried—and therein lies Montgomery Place's single supernatural tradition.

According to Julia Delafield, whose family later owned Montgomery Place, it was during the winter of 1815 that thirty-five-year-old Jones came down with "some ailment which neither he nor his friends considered of an alarming character," and "It was not long before he was pronounced convalescent."

Then on Valentine's Day, Jones sent a message for his physician to come immediately; the proposed heir to Montgomery Place wished to put his affairs in order, for he was convinced he was at death's door. Vainly the doctor sought to placate his patient, pointing out that Jones was well on the road to recovery. Jones remained adamant, however, saying that on the previous night a banshee had cried three times outside his bedroom window. "Whenever a death occurs in my family," the Irishman went on, "the banshee gives warning in this way."

William Jones died the following day.

While it is not known whether Janet Livingston Montgomery believed in banshees, there is evidence that she did know something about these disembodied spirits said to haunt old Irish families. For one time when a female visitor expressed fear over sleeping in the room where William Jones died, the mistress of Montgomery Place told her, "You are a Yankee: the banshee will not come after you. Jones was an Irishman."

Nor has the cry of the banshee ever been heard again at that marvel of American architecture in Annandale.

More carping than crying is the ghost of Sara Delano Roosevelt, said to haunt the Hyde Park house that was the home of her famous son Franklin and is now a National Historic Site. Occasionally a caustic voice has been heard by the current custodians, and the fact that it emanates from an empty room is the basis for their conclusion that the long-dead doyenne of the Delano clan cannot resist registering her disapproval of something or someone.

About 20 miles southeast of Hyde Park, the Fishkill Historical Society maintains the Van Wyck Homestead Museum on Route 9. This Dutch-derived frame dwelling dates back to 1732 and served as headquarters for the Revolutionary War supply depot George Washington established at Fishkill. But while many a famous military figure visited the house during that time, and court-martials were held in a main-floor chamber (including the trial of Enoch Crosby, immortalized in James Fenimore Cooper's novel, *The Spy*), the only ghost said to haunt the Van Wyck Homestead is a nineteenth-century civilian named Sidney.

One of the last Van Wycks to live in the house, Sidney committed suicide in the barn, but his spirit didn't stay there. Instead, his presence has been felt in the museum's Brinkerhoff Room and in the kitchen—a somewhat sad and silent ghost whose unthreatening presence raises a few goosebumps on the flesh of those who encounter him.

For a more assertive spook, one can head across the river to Montgomery, where the sturdy nineteenth-century mansion known as Brick House has a backstairs ghost that is blamed for many of the weird goings-on that have happened since the Georgian-style building became a county-run museum in 1978. Curator Robert Eurich once said, "I don't believe in ghosts myself, but many visitors and even some staff members have had eerie experiences that convinced them Brick House is haunted."

A spinning wheel on the backstairs landing revolving by itself, a dog repeatedly refusing to climb the steps, ornaments tumbling from a tabletop, a burglar alarm ringing for no apparent reason, a phonograph unaccountably shutting off, and visitors who feel they are being watched—these are only some of the events that lend weight to tales former tenants told about footsteps frequently heard overhead or on the stairs leading to the attic. In fact, a bullet hole in the living room ceiling shows how unnerved one resident became over the continued sounds.

What puzzles purveyors of this piece of ghost lore is why the manifestations occur, since the house was not the scene of any known tragedy or violent death—the traditional reasons given for restless revenants. But as pointed out with Crawford House, haunts are not necessarily unhappy, and it well could be that Nathaniel Hill—the affable Irishman who built Brick House from ship's ballast in 1768, after making a mint in applejack brandy—is merely exhibiting a Gaelic penchant for pranks.

The story is decidedly different at Brick House's sister museum, called Hill-Hold, which also is owned and operated by Orange County. A stunning two-story stone structure set atop a prominence in the Hamptonburgh hamlet of Campbell Hall, Hill-Hold harbors a haunt that some people thinks hangs around just to display his dissatisfaction. He does so, they say, by cackling or making loud pinging sounds around midnight, by rattling knobs and slamming doors during the day, plus a general stamping around the house. And one time he even whispered in a visitor's ear that he didn't like the name Hill-Hold, which had been given *his* house.

This message meshed with someone else's report of seeing a sour-faced man in old-fashioned dress seated in the parlor, and Hill-Hold's haunt was tentatively identified as Cadwallader Bull. The son of Thomas Bull, who had built Hill-Hold in 1769, Cadwallader reportedly was forced to relinquish his home in the 1830s because of financial difficulties—reason enough for his disgruntled after-death antics.

Yet even the cranky Cadwallader couldn't be displeased with the way his homestead has been carefully maintained—or with the many other historic Hudson Valley houses that have been preserved for the enjoyment of present and future generations. That some of them may be haunted makes them all the more worthy of a visit, especially around Halloween!

39 THE MYSTERY OF ST. JOHN'S FIRST MIDNIGHT MASS

WINTER CAN BE HARSH in the Orange County community of Goshen, and the season of 1847–48 began no differently. However, since the heaviest snows usually came in January and February, the parishioners of St. John the Evangelist were hopeful the cold but clear weather would hold until after the special Midnight Mass scheduled for their first Christmas in the brand-new church.

The planned celebration was particularly meaningful to the parishioners because they had built the church almost entirely with volunteer labor and donated materials. Even the parcel of land on which St. John's stood had been the gift of an Irish immigrant who had risen from domestic servitude to a position of prosperity.

Many of those mid-nineteenth century parishioners had come from a similar background, and to them the church also symbolized a triumph over past religious, economic, and ethnic oppression, not only in their native land but also in America. For "Irish Need Not Apply" had too often been the sign that greeted them when they debarked from immigrant ships and sought jobs in New York City. Backbreaking work building the Erie Railroad was one of the few avenues open to those arriving in the early 1840s, and so they had followed the twin streamers of steel as the railbed was extended west across the country.

When the Erie tracks reached the Ireland-like hills and boglands of Orange County, some of those immigrants had signed off the railroad payroll and settled in and around Goshen. But even here the welcome was not always warm from the predominantly Protestant populace, nor was there any church where the Irish Catholics could worship.

The newcomers had persevered, though, aided in great part by the faith and enthusiasm of those Catholics already in the area. There was no church building, it was true, but a mission had been established as early as 1820, and seventeen years later the parish of St. John the Evangelist had been set up in Goshen. Each week a missionary priest was sent from St. Peter's in New York City, and services were held in various parishioners' homes until a church could be constructed.

It had taken six years from the time the ground was broken to complete St. John's. Six years of farmers finishing a long day's labor in their fields, then devoting a few hours more to building the church. Six years of endless cake sales, dances, and other benefits to raise funds for the new fane. Six years when it sometimes seemed they had taken on an impossible task. But there had been fun, too, during those six years, as when the whole congregation turned out with flags and music to welcome the cart carrying the new church's cornerstone from a nearby quarry. And always there had been faith—faith that God would see to it that their dream became a reality.

All these things were what gave added meaning to St. John's first Midnight Mass, which was to be a masterpiece of cooperative effort—from the carefully rehearsed choir, to the closet of new cassocks made by the best seamstresses in the parish, and of course an assurance from St. Peter's that a priest would arrive in Goshen on Christmas Eve. The only thing that did not cooperate was the weather.

On December 22, mares'-tail clouds began scudding across Goshen's blue skies, and by morning it had started to snow. The flakes fell faster and thicker with each hour that passed. The wind increased, too, piling up drifts higher than a tall man's head.

There was no dawn on Christmas Eve—or so it seemed in

Goshen, where the sky remained clogged by heavy gray snow clouds. Five miles to the east, drifting snow had filled a ravine through which the railroad tracks passed, and all service on the Erie had been halted.

Knowing there was no way the expected priest could arrive from the city by train, several parishioners set out in a horse-drawn sleigh, hoping they might meet the priest along the turnpike. There was a slight chance, they thought, that the priest had taken a route used by his predecessors in the days before the railroad was built: sailing up the Hudson to the west-shore city of Newburgh, then overland by wagon to Goshen. But the parishioners succeeded in covering only a couple of miles before they were forced to turn back due to the dense drifts. Nor did they encounter any other vehicles along the way.

Disappointed but undaunted, the parishioners decided they could at least hold a prayer service in their new church, even if they had no priest to celebrate Midnight Mass. Deep down, they still had hope that some way the priest would arrive in time, but by 11 P.M. on Christmas Eve, even the most stalwart among them acknowledged that this was a forlorn hope. Still, they struggled through the slackening snow to gather in St. John's, and at midnight the pews were filled as the choir started the services with "Adeste Fidelis."

At that moment, the door to the sacristy opened, and a robed figure made its way to the altar.

"The priest!"

"The priest got here after all!"

The excited murmur that rippled over the congregation gave the altar boys the few minutes they needed to scramble into their cassocks, and as soon as they joined the priest at the altar, St. John's first Midnight Mass began.

As the service progressed, the parishioners strained forward to see if they recognized the priest as being one who regularly came from St. Peter's in the city. In the flickering candlelight it was hard to tell, but most agreed the gentle-voiced man at the altar was a total stranger. Therefore, it was with great impatience that the parishioners politely waited outside the sacristy door after the Mass in order to give the priest time to change his vestments. For they had been deeply moved by this stranger who had braved a blizzard to meet the spiritual needs of a rural parish, and they wanted to thank him, as well as learn his identity.

Fifteen minutes elapsed, then twenty, and still the priest had not emerged from the sacristy. A tentative knock on the door produced no results. So after a half hour of anxious waiting, it was agreed that the head of the parish committee should find out what was the matter.

With a sharp knock of his knuckles, along with a call of "Hello in there," the appointed parishioner slowly pushed open the sacristy door and peered inside. Then with a baffled expression, he turned to face his fellow parishioners. "The...the room...it's empty!" he stammered. "See for yourselves."

The puzzled parishioners did just that, shuffling around the sacristy and even peering into the closet. The priestly vestments were there, but the one who had worn them was gone.

"Perhaps he was just shy," some suggested, "and left by the side door to the churchyard. Let's see if we can catch up with him and thank him."

But when that outer door was opened, the parishioners proceeded no farther. Sometime during the Mass the snow had stopped and bright moonlight now illuminated the churchyard. No trace of footsteps marred the smooth surface of the freshly fallen snow—no steps leading up to the sacristy's side door and none leading away from it.

The mystery of the vanishing priest deepened a few weeks later, when an inquiry sent to St. Peter's revealed that the New York City church had not sent any priest to Goshen on Christmas Eve, because of the inclement weather.

Who was the priest and where did he come from? Down through the decades since 1847 these questions have been asked countless times and all sorts of solutions have been offered by those seeking a scientific explanation. It is said, however, that few of the folk present at that memorable Mass in St. John's ever agonized over an explanation— for the faithful, none was really needed.

The original St. John's is no longer standing, but its location is recalled in the Goshen street by the same name. A second St. John the Evangelist, erected in 1884, was destroyed by fire in 1918. It was replaced by the Gothic structure that now graces Murray Avenue, a few blocks west of St. John's Place. As for the Church of St. Peter, also mentioned in the chapter, that is the one on Barclay Street in lower Manhattan; incorporated in 1785, it is believed to be the first Roman Catholic Church in New York City.

ACKNOWLEDGMENTS

As is evident in the Selected Bibliography, I owe a debt to other authors and historians whose works have supplied me with background material or guided me into fresh discoveries. But I feel the greatest debt I owe is to the largely unsung heroes of preservation: the librarians of the region. I have tried to include in the following list all the names of those librarians and other people who in some way have contributed to the compilation of this book, but if I inadvertently omitted any, it was not from lack of appreciation.

My thanks to: Arlene P. Booth, Lisa Browar, Carol F. Bullard, Margaret Clinton Burt, Jens J. Christoffersen, Sally Dewey, Madeleine J. Douet, Elaine Eatroff, Myrtle Smith Edwards, Gordon F. Ekholm, Robert Eurich, Ann Feeney, Eleanor Fitchen, Barbara Fite, Sidney Forman, Irma Franklin, Nancy D. Gold, Jacquetta M. Haley, Suzanne Cullen Harris, Marguerite Hartwell, William Heidgerd, Eloise K. Hoffman, Ronald Januzzi, Melvin Johnson, Elizabeth Burroughs Kelley, Don Kent, Bob Kimball, Thomas F. King, Kenneth Kral, Thomas Kyle, Anne Lutz, Paul Machlis, Wilkens H. MacMillen, Don Martin, Mary McTamaney, John Mead, and Florence Morrissey.

Also: James M. Ransom, Bruce Reisch, Barbara Ruch, John Scott, Pete Seeger, Mildred Parker Seese, Oliver E. Shipp, Nicholas Shoumatoff, Adelaide R. Smith, Mabel Parker Smith, Euretha Stapleton, Donald B.

Stewart, Leslie P. Symington, Wilfred B. Talman, Chuck Thomas, Uluss (Gus) Thompson, David Tipple, John P. Tramontano, Salvatore M. Trento, Kathleen Wade, Candace H. Wait, Gardner and Josephine Watts, Loretta M. Winkler, Yvonne H. Yare, and Tom Zabadal.

Many of the chapters in this book are based on previously published articles of mine, and I would like to acknowledge the periodicals in which they appeared: *Adventure*, *Boy's Life*, *Camperways*, *Fairfield County*, *Hudson Valley*, *On the Sound*, *Passages*, *South of the Mountains*, *Times Herald-Record*, *Westchester*, *Woodmen of the World*, and *Yankee*.

I am grateful, as well, to Susan Tomson, for our long conversations on the creative process; without her clarity and caring this book might never have been written. Nor could it have come about without the staunch support of my husband, Frank, who believed in me even when I didn't.

SELECTED
BIBLIOGRAPHY

Abbatt, William. *The Crisis of the Revolution*. New York: William Abbatt, 1899; reprinted Harrison, N.Y.: Harbor Hill Books, 1976.

Adams, Arthur G. *The Hudson: A Guidebook to the River*. Albany, N.Y.: State University of New York Press, 1981.

———. Roger Coco, Harriet Greenman, and Leon R. Greenman. *Guide to the Catskills*. New York: Walking News, 1975.

Akers, Dwight. *Outposts of History in Orange County*. Washingtonville, N.Y.: Blooming Grove Chapter D.A.R., 1937.

Allerton, James M. *Hawk's Nest, or the Last of the Cahoonshees*. Port Jervis, N.Y.: The Gazette, n.d.

American Guide Series. *Dutchess County*. Philadelphia: William Penn Assoc., 1937.

Anderson, George Baker. *Landmarks of Rensselaer County, New York*. Syracuse, N.Y.: D. Mason, 1897.

Anderson, Jane McDill. *Rocklandia*. N.p., Morgan & Morgan, 1977.

Anderson, Maxwell. *Dramatist in America*. Letters edited by Laurence G. Avery. Chapel Hill, N.C.: University of North Carolina Press, 1977.

Appalachian Mountain Club Publication Committee. *In the Hudson Highlands*. New York: Walking News, 1945.

Barrel, Donald M. *Along the Wawayanda Path*. Middletown, N.Y.: T. Emmett Henderson, 1975.

Beach, Lewis. *Cornwall*. Newburgh, N.Y.: E. M. Ruttenber, 1873.

Bedell, Cornelia F. *Now and Then and Long Ago in Rockland County, New York*. Privately printed, 1941.

Bicentennial History of Sloatsburg, New York, 1776–1976. Sloatsburg, N.Y.: Bicentennial Commission, 1976.

Bolton, Reginald Pelham. *Indian Life of Long Ago in the City of New York*. 1934; reprinted New York: Harmony Books, 1972.

Boyle, Robert H. *The Hudson River: A Natural and Unnatural History*. New York: W. W. Norton, 1969.

Brawer, Catherine Coleman, ed. *Many Trails: Indians of the Lower Hudson Valley*. Katonah, N.Y.: Katonah Gallery, 1983.

Bruce, Wallace. *The Hudson*. 1882; reprinted New York: Walking News, 1982.

Burroughs, John. *The Writings of John Burroughs*. Riverby edition. 23 vols. Boston and New York: Houghton Mifflin, 1904–23; reprinted New York: Russel and Russel, 1968.

Burroughs, Julian. *Hudson River Memories*. Edited by Elizabeth Burroughs Kelley. West Park, N.Y.: Riverby Books, 1987.

Butler, Joseph T. *Washington Irving's Sunnyside*. Tarrytown, N.Y.: Sleepy Hollow Restorations, 1968.

Carmer, Carl. *The Hudson*. New York: Henry Holt & Co., 1939.

Clyne, Patricia Edwards. *Caves for Kids in Historic New York*. Monroe, N.Y.: Library Research Assoc., 1980.

———. *Ghostly Animals of America*. New York: Dodd, Mead & Co., 1977.

———. *Patriots in Petticoats*. New York: Dodd, Mead & Co., 1976.

Cole, David, ed. *History of Rockland County, New York*. New York: J. B. Beers, 1884.

Crèvecoeur, Hector St. John de [Michel-Guillaume St. Jean de Crèvecoeur]. *Journey into Northern Pennsylvania and the State of New York*. Translated by Clarissa Spencer Bostelmann. Ann Arbor, Mich.: University of Michigan Press, 1964.

———. *Letters From an American Farmer and Sketches of Eighteenth-Century America*. New York: New American Library, 1963.

Cullen, James J., John E. Mylroie, and Arthur N. Palmer. *Karst*

Hydrogeology and Geomorphology of Eastern New York. Pittsfield, Mass.: Northeastern Regional Organization of the National Speleological Society, 1979.

Cullen, T.J.V. *St. John the Evangelist: A House For Worship in Goshen, N.Y.* Jeffersonville, N.Y.: Sullivan County Record, 1962.

De Lisser, R. Lionel. *Picturesque Catskills: Greene County.* Northampton, Mass.: Picturesque Publishing, 1894; reprinted Cornwallville, N.Y.: Hope Farm Press, 1971.

de Noyelles, Daniel. *Within These Gates.* Thiells, N.Y.: privately printed, 1982.

Delafield, Julia. *Biographies of Francis Lewis and Morgan Lewis.* New York: Anson D. F. Randolph, 1877.

Drumm, Judith. *Mammoths and Mastodons: Ice Age Elephants of New York.* Education Leaflet No. 13. Albany, N.Y.: University of the State of New York, 1963.

Dunn, Violet B., ed. *Saratoga County Heritage.* Saratoga, N.Y.: Saratoga County, 1974.

Dutchess County Planning Board. *Landmarks of Dutchess County, 1683–1867.* New York: New York State Council on the Arts, 1969.

Dyson, John S. *Our Historic Hudson.* Roosevelt, N.Y.: James B. Adler, 1968.

Eager, Samuel W. *An Outline History of Orange County.* Newburgh, N.Y.: S. T. Callahan, 1846–7.

Eichner, Frances, and Helen Ferris Tibbets, eds. *When Our Town Was Young.* North Salem, N.Y.: North Salem Board of Education, 1945.

Ellis, David M., James A. Frost, Harold C. Syrett, and Harry J. Carman. *A History of New York State.* Ithaca, N.Y.: Cornell University Press, 1957.

Ellis, Franklin. *History of Columbia County.* Philadelphia: Everts & Ensign, 1878.

Evers, Alf. *The Catskills from Wilderness to Woodstock.* New York: Doubleday, 1972.

———. *Woodstock: History of an American Town.* Woodstock, N.Y.: Overlook Press, 1987.

Fell, Barry. *America, B.C.* New York: Quadrangle/New York Times, 1976.

Figliomeni, Michelle P. *The Flickering Flame: Treachery and Loyalty in the Mid-Hudson During the American Revolution.* New York: Martin Pine, 1976.

Forest Trail at John Boyd Thacher State Park, The. Saratoga Springs, N.Y.: Saratoga-Capital District State Park & Recreation Commission, n.d.

Freeland, Daniel Niles. *Chronicles of Monroe in Olden Times.* New York: DeVinne Press, 1898.

French, J. H. *Gazetteer of the State of New York.* Syracuse, N.Y.: R. Pearsall Smith, 1860.

Funk, Robert E. *Recent Contributions to Hudson Valley Prehistory.* Memoir 22, New York State Museum. Albany, N.Y.: State Education Department, 1976.

Gekle, William. *A Hudson River Book.* Poughkeepsie, N.Y.: Wyvern House, 1978.

———. *The Lower Reaches of the Hudson River.* Poughkeepsie, N.Y.: Wyvern House, 1982.

Gilchrist, Ann. *Footsteps Across Cement: A History of the Township of Rosendale, New York.* Rosendale, N.Y.: privately printed, 1976.

Glunt, Ruth R. *Lighthouses and Legends of the Hudson.* Monroe, N.Y.: Library Research Assoc., 1975.

Green, Frank Bertangue. *The History of Rockland County.* New York: A. S. Barnes, 1886.

Hamptonburgh Presbyterian Church Historical Society. *150th Anniversary Town of Hamptonburgh 1830–1980.* Campbell Hall, N.Y.: First Presbyterian Church of Hamptonburgh, 1980.

Hasbrouck, Frank, ed. *The History of Dutchess County.* Poughkeepsie, N.Y.: S. A. Matthieu, 1909.

Hine, Charles Gilbert. *The Old Mine Road.* 1909; reprinted New Brunswick, N.J.: Rutgers University Press, 1963.

Hoeferlin, William. *Harriman Park Trail Guide.* New York: Walking News, 1973.

Hornby, Mrs. E. *Under Old Rooftrees.* Jersey City, N.J.: privately printed, 1918.

Howell, William Thompson. *The Hudson Highlands*. New York: Walking News, 1982.

Hufeland, Otto. *Westchester County During the American Revolution*. Tuckahoe, N.Y.: Westchester County Historical Society, 1926.

Hull, Richard W. *People of the Valleys*. Warwick, N.Y.: Historical Society of the Town of Warwick, 1975.

————. *Sugar Loaf, Its History, Mystery and Magic 1703–1980*. Sugar Loaf, N.Y.: privately printed, 1980.

Indian Ladder Trail at the John Boyd Thacher State Park, The. Saratoga Springs, N.Y.: Capital District State Park Commission, n.d.

Irving, Washington. *A Book of the Hudson*. New York: G. P. Putnam's, 1849.

————. *The History of New York*, by Diedrich Knickerbocker. 1809; revised by Irving in 1848 and published by G. P. Putnam's, New York.

————. *The Sketch Book of Geoffrey Crayon, Gent*. 1819; revised by Irving in 1848 and published by G. P. Putnam's, New York.

Jackson, S. Trevena. *Fanny Crosby's Story of Ninety-four Years*. New York: Fleming H. Revell, 1915.

Jagendorf, M. *Upstate, Downstate*. New York: Vanguard Press, 1949.

Johnson, P. Demarest. *Claudius, the Cowboy of Ramapo Valley*. Middletown, N.Y.: Slauson & Boyd, 1894; reprinted Middletown: Trumbull Publishing, 1972.

Johnston, Henry P. *The Storming of Stony Point on the Hudson*. New York: DeCapo Press, 1900; reprinted 1971.

Jones, Louis C. *Murder at Cherry Hill*. Albany, N.Y.: Historic Cherry Hill, 1982.

————. *Things That Go Bump in the Night*. New York: Hill and Wang, 1959.

Keller, Alan. *Life Along the Hudson*. Tarrytown, N.Y.: Sleepy Hollow Restorations, 1976.

Kelley, Elizabeth Burroughs. *A West Parker Remembers When*. West Park, N.Y.: Riverby Books, 1987.

————. *John Burroughs: Naturalist*. New York: Exposition Press, 1959.

————. *The History of West Park and Esopus.* Hannacroix, N.Y.: Hillcrest Press, 1978.

————. *With John Burroughs in Field and Wood.* South Brunswick and New York: A. S. Barnes, 1969.

Kligerman, Jack, ed. *The Birds of John Burroughs: Keeping a Sharp Lookout.* New York: Hawthorn Books, 1976.

Kraft, Herbert C., and John T. Kraft. *The Indians of Lenapehoking.* South Orange, N.J.: Seton Hall University Museum, 1985.

Lederer, Richard M., Jr. *The Place-Names of Westchester County, New York.* Harrison, N.Y.: Harbor Hill Books, 1978.

Leiby, Adrian C. *The Revolutionary War in the Hackensack Valley.* New Brunswick, N.J.: Rutgers University Press, 1962.

Leslie, Vernon. *Faces in Clay.* Middletown, N.Y.: T. Emmett Henderson, 1973.

Levy, S. J. *Chester, N.Y.: A History.* Chester, N.Y.: Chamber of Commerce, 1947.

Loeb, Harold. *The Way It Was.* New York: Criterion, 1959.

Lossing, Benson J. *The Hudson from the Wilderness to the Sea.* Troy, N.Y.: H. B. Nims, 1866; reprinted Somersworth, N.H.: New Hampshire Publishing, 1972.

Mabbott, Thomas Ollive, ed. *Collected Works of Edgar Allan Poe.* 3 vols. Cambridge, Mass.: Belknap Press of Harvard University; vol. 1, 1969; vols. 2, 3, 1978.

MacGahan, John A. *Twilight Park: The First Hundred Years.* South Yarmouth, Mass.: Allen D. Bragdon, 1988.

McMartin, Barbara, and Peter Kick. *Fifty Hikes in the Hudson Valley.* Woodstock, Vt.: Backcountry Publications, 1985.

Mailler, Marion M., and Janet Dempsey. *18th Century Homes in New Windsor and Its Vicinity.* Cornwall, N.Y.: Courier-Local Press, 1968.

Mitchell, Julia Post. *St. Jean de Crèvecoeur.* New York: Columbia University Press, 1916; reprinted New York: AMS Press, 1966.

Mulligan, Tim. *The Hudson River Valley.* New York: Random House, 1981.

Mylod, John. *Biography of a River.* New York: Hawthorn Books, 1969.

New York: A Guide to the Empire State. Complied by the Writer's Project. New York: Columbia University Press, 1962.

New York–New Jersey Trail Conference and the American Geographical Society. *New York Walk Book*. Garden City, N.Y.: Doubleday/Natural History Press, 1971.

Northshield, Jane, ed. *History of Croton-on-Hudson, New York*. Croton-on-Hudson, N.Y.: Croton-on-Hudson Historical Society, 1976.

O'Brien, Raymond J. *American Sublime: Landscape and Scenery of the Lower Hudson Valley*. New York: Columbia University Press, 1981.

Original Life and Adventures of Tom Quick. Deposit, N.Y.: Deposit Journal, 1894.

Palmer, Dave Richard. *The Rock and the River*. New York: Greenwood Publishing, 1969.

Pelletreau, William W. *History of Putnam County, New York*. Philadelphia: W. W. Preston, 1886; reprinted Brewster, N.Y.: Landmarks Preservation Committee, 1975.

Perry, Clay. *Underground Empire*. New York: Frederick Ungar, 1948.

Polhemus, Mary, ed. *Town of Esopus Story 3000 B.C.–1978 A.D.* Esopus, N.Y.: Town of Esopus Bicentennial Committee, 1979.

Polk, Julia Brandi, and Jean Schroeder Settin, eds. *A History of the Roeliff Jansen Area*. Publication No. 1 of the Roeliff Jansen Historical Society. Lakeville, Conn.: Lakeville Journal Press, 1975.

Quinlan, James Eldridge. *History of Sullivan County*. Liberty, N.Y.: G. M. Beebe and W. T. Morgans, 1873.

Ransom, James M. *Vanishing Ironworks of the Ramapos*. New Brunswick, N.J.: Rutgers University Press, 1966.

Rockwell, Charles. *The Catskill Mountains and the Region Around*. New York: Taintor Bros., 1867; reprinted Cornwallville, N.Y.: Hope Farm Press, 1973.

Ross, Claire L., and Edward R. Kozack. *Greene County, New York*. '76 *Bicentennial Overview: Beginnings and Background*. Catskill, N.Y.: Catskill Enterprise, 1976.

Ruffin, Bernard. *Fanny Crosby*. Philadelphia: United Church Press, 1976.

Ruttenber, E. M., and L. H. Clark. *History of Orange County, New York*. Philadelphia: Everts & Peck, 1881.

Salomon, Julian Harris. *Indians of the Lower Hudson Region: The*

Munsee. New City, N.Y.: Historical Society of Rockland County, 1982.

Sanderson, Dorothy Hurlbut. *The Delaware & Hudson Canalway: Carrying Coals to Rondout.* Ellenville, N.Y.: Rondout Valley Publishing, 1965.

Scharf, John Thomas. *History of Westchester County, New York.* Philadelphia: L. E. Preston, 1886.

Seese, Mildred Parker. *Old Orange Houses.* 2 vols. Middletown, N.Y.: Whitlock Press, 1941–43.

Sharts, Elizabeth. *Land O' Goshen.* Edited by Mildred Parker Seese. Goshen, N.Y.: The Bookmill, 1960.

Shivers, Alfred S. *The Life of Maxwell Anderson.* New York: Stein and Day, 1983.

Sickler, Vera Van Steenbergh. *History of the Town of Olive 1823–1973.* Olive, N.Y.: Sesquicentennial Committee, 1973.

Smith, Anita M. *Woodstock History and Hearsay.* Woodstock, N.Y.: privately printed, 1959.

Smith, Ernest D. *Valley Tales: Historical Stories of the Lebanon and Taconic Valleys.* 2 vols. Canaan, N.Y.: Echo Publishing, 1979.

Smith, James H. *History of Dutchess County.* Syracuse, N.Y.: D. Mason, 1882.

Smith, Mabel Parker. *Greene County, New York: A Short History.* Catskill, N.Y.: Greene County Board of Supervisors, 1963.

Smith, Philip H. *Legends of the Shawangunk (Shon-Gun) and Its Environs.* Syracuse, N.Y.: Syracuse University Press, 1965.

Smith, Richard. *A Tour of Four Great Rivers: The Hudson, Mohawk, Susquehanna and Delaware in 1769.* Edited by Francis W. Halsey. Port Washington, N.Y.: Ira J. Friedman, 1906; reprinted 1964.

Stephens, John Lloyd. *Incidents of Travel in Yucatan.* 2 vols. New York: Harper & Brothers, 1843; reprinted New York: Dover Publications, 1963.

Swanson, Susan Cochran. *Between the Lines: Stories of Westchester County During the American Revolution.* Pelham, N.Y.: Junior League, 1975.

Sylvester, Nathaniel Bartlett. *History of Rensselaer County, New York.* Philadelphia: Everts & Peck, 1880.

————. *History of Ulster County, New York.* Philadelphia: Everts & Peck, 1880.

Talman, Wilfred Blanch. *How Things Began . . . in Rockland County and Places Nearby.* New City, N.Y.: Historical Society of Rockland County, 1977.

Terwilliger, Katharine T. *Napanoch: Land Overflowed by Water.* Ellenville, N.Y.: Ellenville Public Library and Museum, 1982.

————. *Wawarsing: Where the Streams Wind. Historical Glimpses of the Town.* Ellenville, N.Y.: Rondout Valley Publishing, 1977.

Thomas, Dwight, and David K. Jackson. *The Poe Log: A Documentary Life of Edgar Allan Poe, 1809–1849.* G. K. Hall, 1987.

Thompson, Harold W. *Body, Boots & Britches: Folktales, Ballads and Speech From Country New York.* New York: J. B. Lippincott, 1939; reprinted as *New York State Folktales, Legends and Ballads,* New York: Dover Publications, 1962.

Trento, Salvatore Michael. *The Search for Lost America.* Chicago: Contemporary Books, 1978.

Vedder, J. Van Vechten. *History of Greene County 1651–1800.* 1927; reprinted Cornwallville, N.Y.: Hope Farm Press, 1985.

Vogel, Robert M. *Roebling's Delaware & Hudson Canal Aqueducts.* Washington, D.C.: Smithsonian Institution Press, 1971.

von Behr, H. A. *Ghosts in Residence.* Utica, N.Y.: North Country Books, 1986.

Von Hagen, Victor Wolfgang. *Maya Explorer: John Lloyd Stephens and the Lost Cities of Central America and Yucatán.* Norman, Okla.: University of Oklahoma Press, 1947.

Waite, Marjorie Peabody. *Yaddo Yesterday and Today.* Albany, N.Y.: Argus Press, 1933.

Wakefield, Manville B. *Coal Boats to Tidewater: The Story of the Delaware and Hudson Canal.* Grahamsville, N.Y.: Wakefair Press, 1965.

————. *To the Mountains by Rail.* Grahamsville, N.Y.: Wakefair Press, 1965.

Welles, E. R., III, and J. P. Evans. *The Forgotten Legend of Sleepy Hollow.* Manset, Maine: Learning Inc., 1973.

Wilstach, Paul. *Hudson River Landings.* Indianapolis, Ind.: Bobbs-Merrill, 1933.

Wyckoff, Jerome. *Rock Scenery of the Hudson Highlands and Palisades.* Glens Falls, N.Y.: Adirondack Mountain Club, 1971.

Zimm, Louise Hasbrouck, A. Elwood Corning, Joseph W. Emsley, and Willitt C. Jewell, eds. *Southeastern New York.* 3 vols. New York: Lewis Historical Publishing, 1946.

INDEX

Where towns are indexed, county names are in parentheses.